Body Parts of Empire

Body Parts of Empire

Visual Abjection, Filipino Images, and the American Archive

Nerissa S. Balce

University of Michigan Press ANN ARBOR

Published in the United States of America by the
University of Michigan Press
Manufactured in the United States of America
♾ Printed on acid-free paper

2019   2018   2017   2016   4   3   2   1

A CIP catalog record for this book is available from the British Library.

Library of Congress Cataloging-in-Publication Data

Names: Balce, Nerissa, author.
Title: Body parts of empire : visual abjection, Filipino images, and the
    American archive / Nerissa Balce.
Description: Ann Arbor : University of Michigan Press, [2016] |
    Includes bibliographical references and index.
Identifiers: LCCN 2016030542| ISBN 9780472119783 (hardback : acid-
    free paper) | ISBN 9780472121755 (e-book)
Subjects: LCSH: Philippines—History—Philippine American War,
    1899–1902—Social aspects. | Philippines—History—Philippine
    American War, 1899–1902—Sources. | Philippines—Colonization—
    Social aspects—History. | Imperialism—Social aspects—United
    States—History. | Visual communication—Political aspects—United
    States—History. | Human body—Political aspects—United States—
    History. | Racism—Political aspects—United States—History. | Sex—
    Political aspects—United States—History. | Philippines—Relations—
    United States. | United States—Relations—Philippines. | BISAC:
    LITERARY CRITICISM / American / General.
Classification: LCC DS682 .A155 2016 | DDC 959.9/031—dc23
LC record available at https://lccn.loc.gov/2016030542

Para kay Tatay at Nanay.
For my parents, Norberto Veloso Balce and Nymia Suterio Balce.

Contents

Acknowledgments

This book took time to complete due to my migrant academic life. It was difficult to take apart what one Filipino poet described as "the wall of language" that constructs the official narrative of the Philippine-American War after 1898. This book is an attempt to piece together a different story about American empire building by analyzing race and gender in U.S. fin de siècle popular culture. The assistance and support of many *barangays*, or communities, in the Philippines and the United States, enabled the completion of this book.

I would like to thank Aaron McCollough and Allison Peters of the University of Michigan Press for their kindness, professionalism, and support. I would also like to thank the staff of the National Archives, the National Library of Congress, the Newberry Archives in Chicago, the University of California's Bancroft Archives in Berkeley, and the New York Public Library. Special mention must be given to two friends who helped my archival research with their friendship and encouragement: Jody Blanco and Anna More. *Salamat* to Anna's kind parents, Livy and John More, who welcomed me into their beautiful home in Washington, DC, while I conducted research in the National Archives. And sincere thanks to my cousin in-law, Michael Colmenar, who drove from Philadelphia to DC on weekends to make sure I was eating and not spending too much time in the archival stacks.

In graduate school at the University of California, Berkeley, I was extremely fortunate to be mentored by Oscar V. Campomanes, now at Ateneo de Manila and the University of Santo Tomas, Manila. His pioneering work on the U.S. empire, postcolonial studies, and the Filipino immigrant condition influenced my own research. Oscar is a generous teacher and a kind professor who always took the time to answer questions on literary theory and historiography over cups of coffee or a Filipino dinner he prepared. He advised many Filipino and Asian American graduate students, and it is not an exaggeration to say that there is a generation of cultural studies scholars who were influenced by his work.

This book began as a dissertation and took shape with the guidance and support of various scholars in ethnic studies and cultural studies who were at UC Berkeley at the time: José David Saldívar, Abdul JanMohamed, Tiya Miles, Michel Laguerre, Julio Ramos, Patricia Penn Hilden, and Elaine Kim. At the University of Oregon, I would like to thank my kind postdoctoral mentor, Shari Huhndorf, and my wonderful peers Cynthia Tolentino, Steven Morozumi, and Lynn Fujiwara. My *utang na loob*, a debt I will always carry, goes to many brilliant scholars in the fields of Filipino American studies, Philippine studies, Asian American studies, and gender studies. These scholars' generous acts of kindness have positively impacted my academic life: my fabulous mentors, Martin F. Manalansan IV and Rick Bonus; and my academic *barangay/* community: Sarita Echavez See, Theodore Gonzalves, Jose B. Capino, John Labella, Robert Diaz, Kale Fajardo, Cathy Schlund-Vials, Anita Mannur, Antonio Tiongson, David Kim, Viet Nguyen, Jonathan Okamura, Candace Fujikane, Pia Arboleda, Rick Baldoz, Elynia Mabanglo, Benito Vergara Jr., Jane Po, Marcelo Estrada, Kim Alidio, Francisco Benitez, Kathy Yep, Wesley Uenten, Mike Chang, Carole Castro, Joe Ponce, Denise Cruz, Karin Aguilar-San Juan, Roland Sintos Coloma, Chi-hui Yang, Maria Cecilia Regalado Hwang, Ruby Lazatin, Allan Bernardo, Dylan Rodriguez, and the Latin Americanist Adam Lifshey. Sincere thanks to two Asian American literary critics for their early support and generosity of spirit: Lisa Lowe and David Palumbo-Liu. And special mention must be given to Allan Punzalan Isaac, who not only read my book proposal and suggested brilliant edits and the book title, but has seen me through challenging times in my academic career and is one of my favorite cocktails-and-dinner companions.

I would like to thank my peers who were my writing partners in Berkeley and early critics: Caroline Streeter, Isabelle Thuy Pelaud, Mia Ong-Brown, Jill Esbenshade, Eithne Luibheid, and Susan Lee. A special thank-you to a wonderful group of Pinoy academics, the scholars I marched with in many antiwar rallies in the Bay Area after the September 11 attacks, the original members of the Critical Filipino Studies Collective: Lucy Burns, Peter Chua, Vernadette Vicuña Gonzalez, Rowena Tomaneng, Robyn Rodriguez, Gladys Nubla, and Joanne Rondilla. Two members of the original collective became my beloved colleagues in Massachusetts: Richard Chu and Jeffrey Santa Ana. Both Richard and Jeff deserve special thanks for the countless dinners we shared during those long New England winters. Jeff and I, by sheer luck, are colleagues again in New York and continue our tradition of dinner-and-movie nights, either in Brooklyn or in Long Island. Richard's and Jeff's continuing love, good humor, and support helped me adjust to the colder climes of the East Coast.

In (western) Massachusetts, I will always be grateful for the camaraderie, warmth, and compassion of my former colleagues in the Five Colleges: Amy Martin, Daniel Weinbaum, Greg Mullins, Asha Nadkarni, Dayo Gore, Arianne Miller, Jessica Delgado, Daniel Rivers, Vahram Elagoz, James Heintz, Stephanie Luce, William Moebius, David Lenson, Edwin Gentzler, Laszlo Dienes, Guillermo Irizarry, Alice Nash, Priscilla Page, Floyd Cheung, Amina Begum, Kavita Datla, Jennifer Guglielmo, Lisa Armstrong, Vijay Prashad, and Sabina Murray.

In Long Island, New York, I am delighted to have a community of scholars at the State University of New York at Stony Brook who sustain my spirit, my teaching, and my life as a scholar. *Maraming salamat* to my beloved writing partners E. K. Tan and Melissa Forbis; *salamat din* to my wonderful colleagues, my mentor Shirley Jennifer Lim, Lisa Diedrich, Victoria Hesford, Iona Man-Cheong, Elizabeth Newman, Abena Ansare, Tiffany Joseph, E. Ann Kaplan, Joseph Pierce, Adrián Pérez-Melgosa, Daniela Flesler, Agnes He, Andrew Nicholson, Liliana Davalos, Angelique Corthals, Georges Fouron, and Katherine Sugg. I am grateful for the generous support of the FAHSS (Faculty of Arts, Humanities and Social Sciences) fellowships and the College of Arts and Sciences. In New York City, much love and *pasasalamat* to Filipino and American writers and scholars with whom I have broken bread and shared many delightful meals: to Gina Apostol, Sunita Mukhi, and Lara Stapleton, *aking mga kapatid*/my sisters; and to Ken Byrne, Edilberto Soriano, Sarah Gambito, Ricco Siasoco, R. A. Villanueva, Nita Noveno, Hossannah Asuncion, and Joseph Legaspi. Over the years, and across many academic institutions, our dear friends Paula Chakravartty and Gianpaolo Baiocchi have always welcomed us into their home to enjoy delicious food, wine, chocolates, and the hilarious company of their lovely daughters, my *mahal* Aisha, and Safina.

Returning to Manila, I became part of a new community, the Artery Manila collective, composed of brilliant and kind Filipino literature, art, and cultural studies scholars: Ferdinand Lopez, Gary Devilles, Delan Robillos, Jae Robillos, Lito Zulueta, Rebecca Añonuevo, and Jack Wigley. The final chapter and revisions of this book were written during writers' residencies at the beautiful seaside Silliman University, in Dumaguete, Negros Oriental, with the support of Irma and Alex Pal, Margie Udarbe, Ian Rosales Casocot, Warlito Caturay Jr., Alana Leilani T. Cabrera-Narciso, Parts Partosa, Cesar Ruiz Aquino, Bron Teves, Annabelle-Lee Adriano, Simon and Tata Stack, and Myrna and Lorna Peña-Reyes. Special mention and thanks go to dear friends, in Manila and elsewhere, who have kept ties over many years, despite the oceans that separate us: Francine Marquez, Ricky Torre, Luna Sicat, Joi Barrios, Rosario Cruz Lucero, Isagani Cruz, Nicanor Tiongson, Mauro Feria Tumbocon Jr., Jerry Torres, Roland Tolentino, Shirley Lua, Dinah Roma, Bennet Dychangco, Maria Bautista, Jo Tan, Alma Obligacion, Sharon Fuentebella, Ala Domingo, and Camille Sevilla.

To my siblings and family in Vancouver, much love and gratitude always: Natasha Balce-Hillier, Jamie Hillier, Max Hillier, Nestor Balce, Monchette Ledesma-Balce, Diego Balce, and Nicolas Balce. In California, blessings and love to the generous Suriaga family for keeping my humor and health intact during grad school. Thank you for the countless Filipino picnics, beach outings, and family holidays: Ederlyn Suriaga, Anne and Dennis Suriaga, Deanne, Daniel, Monica, Efrenny, and Prudencio Suriaga, Dan and Lynn Suriaga, and Marta, David, and Ethan. In Manila, blessings and appreciation to Mrs. Mercedes Cortes and Celeste Cortes; my late aunt Marilyn Suterio; my uncles and aunts, Salvador and Tita Balce, Don and Aidyn Suterio; and to my cousins: Baba Balce, Tong Balce, Pamela Balce, Victoria and Arlem Bolado, Miguel and Zinnia Suterio, Veronica Pimentel, Alan and Brita Geronilla, Lanelle Abueva-Fernando, and Amihan Abueva.

Last, I would like to thank my first and most critical reader, the writer Fidelito Cortes, for his love and support for many years. With the snow in our hair and the roots we have grown, I feel blessed. *Buhay ay langit, sa piling mo.*

Today I tried to give a talk about
Philippine history to a bunch of
Americans and ran into a wall
of language . . .
It was formidable and tall, bricked with
impregnable verbs, impossible idioms.
On it rested the ruins of foreign accents
used as scaling machines. At its feet
the foiled battering rams of gutturals
and sibilants. Caught on its barbed wire
of nuance, truth. But history heeds more
than language, and I brought blood and gore
of my forebears, marrow of their crushing,
spit of their muzzled insurrection.
Let Americans play deaf behind walls.
I will not give comfort to their ghosts.
    —Fidelito C. Cortes, "English as a Second Language"
    (With permission from the author)

Introduction

Nothing but Objects: America's Shadow Archive

Empire requires and produces, in a word, objecthood, and along
with it a discourse of objectivity. All these it then mobilizes around
an ideal object, an objective or goal, which motivates the imperial
quest. . . . God and money, the ultimate "Big Objects" and the many
little objects of desire, coalesce to form the object choice of empire.
And when the empire declines and falls, as It inevitably must, it
leaves behind nothing but objects—relics and ruins, inscriptions.
   —W. J. T. Mitchell[1]

Immigrants are the survivors of empires, its witnesses, the inhabitants of its borders.
   —Lisa Lowe[2]

The violence and romance of empire haunts the representation of the Filipino
in the American imaginary. In *Born of the People* (1953), a memoir in English written by the controversial Filipino peasant leader Luis Taruc, the black
American actor-activist Paul Robeson wrote a remarkable introduction about
the continuing anti-imperialist struggle of Filipino farmworkers in Hawai'i.
Robeson recalls a conversation he had with some Filipino labor organizers and
farmworkers who were working there.

> When I was in Hawai'i a few years ago it was my privilege to sing for and
> with the sugar and pineapple workers, to clasp their hands in firm friend-
> ship, to share for a short time their way of life . . . many [were] workers from

the Philippines. . . . They talked of their land, of the Hukbalahap, of the fight to survive against Japanese fascism and later against the vicious forces of American imperialism. . . . My mind often went back to 1898, the year of my birth, the same year that President McKinley felt the divine call to export "freedom and liberty" to the people of the Philippines. The real story of that time has been recorded, one of the most shameful periods of United States history, comparable to the British in India and South Africa, the Belgians in Congo, or for that matter, the United States in almost any section of Latin America, beginning with Mexico and Panama.[3]

There is a mordant tone to Robeson's description of President William McKinley's "divine" mission in the Philippines, framing the American expansion in the Philippines within the imperialist continuum that began centuries back with Western nations in Africa and in Latin America (Taruc 7). His historicist reverie is triggered by his encounter with actual American colonial subjects—the Filipino farmworkers who were at the time living and working in the plantations of Hawai'i. In the early decades of the twentieth century, Filipinos were indeed "U.S. colonials," a legal category used for Filipinos following the U.S. military occupation and control of the Philippine Islands that began in 1898. In Robeson's introduction of a Filipino memoir, published a decade after World War II, he reconfigures what was then a common depiction of Filipinos as "Little Brown Brothers"[4] by locating the critical origins of U.S.-Philippine relations within American imperial history in the Pacific, and not in World War II, as was commonly and mistakenly done back then.

What is remarkable about this literary moment recorded in a Filipino peasant leader's memoir are the different overlapping historical registers embodied in Robeson and Taruc. There is Paul Robeson's birth year 1898, his identity as a descendant of African slaves, his historic place in the civil rights struggles, and his anti-imperialist politics. And there is Luis Taruc: a charismatic yet enigmatic revolutionary figure, and a socialist and anti-imperialist peasant leader of the Hukbalahap, who was central in the guerrilla war against the Japanese in World War II and in the armed uprising against a newly independent Philippine government (1946) backed by an American-led counterinsurgency.[5] Taruc refused to denounce, and possibly even perpetuated, the rumor that he was the reincarnation of the Filipino revolutionary-mystic Felipe Salvador, who was killed by the U.S. military in 1912, when the U.S. colonial government had finally crushed the remaining Philippine resistance. The rumors Taruc fueled about his spiritual connection to the anti-imperialist mystic Salvador, whose name in Spanish felicitously means "savior," led to Taruc's rift with members of the Philippine Communist Party, who did not share Taruc's atavistic tendencies. (Taruc later supported the late dictator Ferdinand Marcos's right-wing politics after his conditional pardon and release from prison in 1968, after spending fourteen years in jail.) Implicated in the very bodies of Robeson and Taruc are layers of anti-imperialist histories and transnational narratives connected through time, place, people, and artifacts. Similarly, this study begins with the significance of 1898 and the ensuing Philippine-American War, which established the United States as a true imperial power. This study will ask us to look "awry at 1898," in order to "permeate and distort" dominant U.S. histories, ask new questions, analyze forgotten archives, and trace other genealogies.[6]

ABJECT RELIQUARY

Among the many wonders of the early twenty-first century are what used to be rare images from a forgotten war in the Philippines that can now be bought online. On eBay, the Internet planetary supermarket, collectors of war memorabilia and amateur history buffs can buy artifacts on the Philippine-American War for their own personal collections. One wintry Saturday evening, an electronic bidding war on eBay caught my attention. The item up for auction was the personal photo album of a ninety-nine-year-old man living in the Pacific Northwest whose father was an officer of an Oregon regiment sent to fight in what was then known as the "Philippine Insurrection." The "Spanish-American-Philippine war album," as the collection of images was advertised, contained 136 photographs taken during the insurrection and was described thus:

> A superlative and museum quality large photographic record of 136 original images of the Philippine theatre of the Spanish-American War of 1898 from the original U.S. officer's family. . . . Children and those offended by great violence and brutality, are advised to look no further!

At the end of the cyber auction, this album sold for $4,160, a seeming bargain since photographs from that period can fetch $150 apiece. While similar photographs have found their way to eBay in the past few years, what drew my attention to this auction were some photographs I had seen before in the U.S. National Archives in Maryland.

In 2008, the historian Paul Kramer published an essay in the *New Yorker* on the practice of "the water cure," a form of torture practiced by the U.S. Army against suspected Filipino insurgents more than a century ago, which has been described as the precursor to the infamous modern practice of waterboarding.[7] In the article, a black-and-white photograph shows an American soldier holding down a Filipino man on the ground. A Filipino native assists in the torture by pouring water down the man's throat. One hundred years ago, the U.S. military denied using the water cure, despite photographs like this that showed the contrary, just as authorities today are denying that waterboarding is a form of torture despite its undeniable similarity to the water cure. Kramer used a relic of empire, a century-old photograph, to illustrate the savagery of the act and to refute the official denials.

Images of violence and war are relatively straightforward to process; they are hard to look at but easier to analyze—the roles of the protagonists are usually clear and well defined; the actions and outcomes are recognizable, if not predictable; the context is often well known or at least open to conjecture. Philippine images, and others like it, have allowed keen observers like Paul Robeson to denounce the American colonization of the Philippines as "one of the most shameful periods of United States history" and locate it squarely within the cruel continuum of Western imperialism, which the United States itself at one time fought. But what about other images, other imperial relics and artifacts, where the violence is subtle or implied, or where the violence is of another form?

Certainly, in the continental United States during the turn of the twentieth century, nothing could be farther from a Pacific war and the disquietude of colonization than the New York vaudeville stage. Yet preserved in the digital collection of the New York Public Library are the songs of American musical stage composers that paid heed to, if not celebrated, this imperial moment of the United States. These archival remnants from the age of vaudeville show that empire, race, and sex were already very much on the minds of those who created, performed, and watched theater. Vaudeville theaters had opened their gates to larger audiences, including women and children, and minstrel shows were all the rage.[8] Yet vaudeville was popular not only because of the numbers who watched it but also because its songs were able to reach even more people. Music lovers who fancied a song they heard in a performance, or who learned about the songs from these people or from newspapers, could buy the sheet music through catalogs or in department stores in the cities and, in their homes at leisure, would sing or play these tunes on their musical instruments (Harris 7).

In 1899, Charles "Chas" Harris, a successful musical composer for vaudeville and minstrel shows, wrote and published the song "Ma Filipino Babe." By his own account, the sheet music for "Ma Filipino Babe" sold more than one hundred thousand copies (Harris 7). The illustration on the music sheet of "Ma Filipino Babe" is a young, brown, smiling maiden, waving a pure white kerchief from a red dais set against a tropical background of sea, islands, and palm trees. The Filipina wears a version of the long, traditional dresses worn by women at the time, that is, an American artist's version of the *baro't saya* with the *tapis*—a white lace-fringed frock clinched around the waist by a heavier, dark-colored skirt and topped with a sheer veil worn around the shoulders. The flowers in her hair, her red smiling lips, and her arms held out with kerchief in one hand and the other lifting a skirt hem suggest hospitality, openness, and winsome youth, all hopeful signs to any would-be colonizer. The song begins with a description of American soldiers on a ship looking lovingly at "the Islands, where they'd / spent happy days, Making love to ev'ry pretty girl they met." The risqué lyrics touch on the taboo of miscegenation and continue with more abject images. The protagonist of the song is a "colored sailor" who keeps a photograph of his beloved, a young Filipina. He shows her photograph to his white fellow sailors, and they laugh when they see her dark face. The black soldier sings, undeterred, "I love ma Filipino baby / . . . Though her face is black as jet; For her / lips are sweet as honey, and her heart is pure I know. She's ma / pretty black faced Filipina baby." The romance between a black soldier and a Filipina is set against the background of American imperial expansion. The song's hilarity (to its white audiences) is based on the abject racial humor that the black soldier believes that his Filipina maiden is attractive "though her face is black as jet." But even as the white sailors laugh after seeing the Filipina's photograph, the black soldier ends the song by adamantly repeating, "She's ma pretty black faced Filipina baby."

Another song, composed by James Dewey, is almost identically titled, "My Filipino Babe." The similarities between the songs suggest not just a rivalry between the music composers but the more important place of the newly acquired Philippine colony in the popular imagination. The idea of the "Filipino babe," the erotic body of the Filipina, went the rounds of the vaudeville circuit. The sheet music features a photograph of Josephine Gassman, a white American vaudeville performer known for her acts that featured a "Pickaninnie chorus," composed of young black child actors dressed in clothes and hair that followed white stereotypes of black slave children from the rural South.[9] Gassman was a "coon singer," a white female performer who would go on stage in blackface and sing and dance with "her Pickaninnies."[10] On the cover, Gassman smiles as she poses with one hand on a flowered hat on her head, and a leafy plant in the other hand. The performance is advertised as "A Coon simplicity," or a minstrel show. The song tells the story of a black American soldier who will wed his "Filipino babe," a woman named "Manila Lou" whom he describes as a "chocolate color'd dazzler, she's a dream." The black soldier mentions that the other army men have sexual relations with their "Mexicano wenches," but he chooses to marry his Manila Lou. He imagines it will be a "swell weddin'" and that "lots of coons and wenches 'round Manila, will envy Lou and I." As a min-

Fig. 1. Imperial tunes: The sheet music for "Ma Filipino Babe," by Chas Harris (1899), which sold more than a hundred thousand copies.

Fig. 2. Cover of sheet music for "My Filipino Baby," by James Dewey (1899). New York Public Library digital collection.

strel performance, white singers, including Josephine Gassman, performed the parts of black Americans and Filipinos by wearing blackface. The conflation between black and Filipino images, seen as logical and entertaining by white audiences, would, unsurprisingly, harden opposition of black communities to the Philippine-American War, as it would serve to cement, for these communities, the connection between the brutal conduct of the war by Americans against Filipinos and the upsurge of lynchings committed by whites on black Americans.

What are the meanings behind these images taken from the moment of American empire building at the turn of the twentieth century? As imperial inscriptions and relics of the Philippine-American War, what do these images tell us about the story of the U.S. empire and its first and only formal colony in the Asia-Pacific, the Philippines? How are we to read these archival bodies from the era of 1898? What do these images tell us about American imperialism, modernity, the sexualization of war, Orientalist fantasies? Do they encapsulate all these meanings? What are the limits and possibilities of thinking about these "vestiges of war"[11] and relics of empire and their connection to the history and cultures of Filipino America?

Body Parts of Empire: Visual Abjection, Filipino Images, and the American Archive is a study of American imperial abjection from the turn of the twentieth century. The visual abject in this case is every image, photograph, narrative, or cultural relic connected to a forgotten American imperial war in the Pacific—the Philippine-American War—which launched the United States as an imperial power in Asia. A central argument of this book is that the colonization of the Philippine Islands by the United States, witnessed by the rise of visual and print technologies, created abject peoples whom American "imperialism rejects but cannot do without."[12] These abject peoples are most notably nonwhites, bodies that the U.S. nation, then and now, "seeks to expunge" even as "the expelled abject haunts the subject as its inner constitutive boundary" (McClintock 71). In other words, abjection is the process for analyzing the sensory conditions for perceiving the American empire through the actual bodies subjected to its violence and benevolence. As figures in an archive, abject bodies are icons and indices of the U.S. nation's institutionalized acts of forgetting, repressing, and revising the violent occupation of its first colony in Asia. American imperial abjection will be discussed through a reconsideration of forgotten popular objects—war photographs, newspaper accounts, letters, and essays by African American soldiers, travel writing by white women, and obscure American romance novels and other cultural artifacts—produced during the period of the Philippine-American War of 1899. Rather than a cultural history of these imperial ephemera, the study will focus on the logics and visual forms of American imperial abjection as it scans different colonial figures of the American empire: white American soldiers, black Americans soldiers, the dead bodies of Filipino *insurrectos*, or "rebels," Filipino women and schoolchildren, and white American and European women who lived in the Philippines during the war.

Abjection, in this study, is the process we trace in American popular culture that creates bodies that violently disturb U.S. national identity. The abject is reproduced by the nexus of racialization and sexualization in the history of the American empire, where abject bodies occupy the ragged edges of modernity that American imperialism cannot do without. In the late nineteenth century, sites of American abjection were Indian reservations and Native boarding schools, plantations in the South, factories in the industrial North, immigrant ghettos in the urban centers, orphanages and asylums, the segregated military camps, saloons and brothels, and the United States' newest acquisitions of island colonies and territories. The production of abjection is the creation of images and discourses from these sites that are racially repugnant and sexually erotic yet formative to American imperial identity. Public culture—which includes popular cultural forms and administrative and legislative discourses— reproduces and stages the paradox of abjection as a foundational aspect of American empire-building. By visualizing abject bodies, white American imperial identities are reframed, romanticized, and memorialized: these abject bodies of savagery and sexuality then become negative markers of the American imperial self-image, but only after they have served as catalysts of empire and then discarded.

Body Parts of Empire interrupts and engages with three distinct yet interrelated fields: Asian American studies, Asian studies, and postcolonial feminist studies, spooling through a discussion of U.S. modernity during the period of American imperial expansion into the Pacific after 1898. My book attempts a genealogy of *the Filipino native as an idea* and will seek to establish how the tropes of Filipino savagery and docility borrow from earlier racialized and gendered discourses of "red savagery" and "black docility."[13] The abject figure of the Filipino native, after all, reconfigured and recast the histories of continental imperialism, slavery, and the "New Empire of the 1890s."[14] The very idea of the Filipino native is the visual form of American imperial abjection. Extending Sarita See's decolonial paradigm,[15] my study will focus on cultural texts on the Philippine-American War of 1899 and how these texts facilitated the circulation of racial and gendered ideas about the Filipino native even before the arrival of thousands of Filipino farmworkers in the United States in the 1920s. This textual traffic had serious repercussions on the lives of the early Filipino immigrant laborers due to the negative portrayals of Filipinos as primitive savages or docile natives.[16]

My work hopes to "disfigure" what others have perceived as the theoretical impasse of postcolonial studies in the early twenty-first century and to splinter the field's Anglocentric, Eurocentric, and disciplinary limitations.[17] This study takes the term *Filipino American* as "a function of U. S. colonialism and its aftermath in the Philippines."[18] Because Filipino Americans constitute the largest undocumented Asian immigrant group in the United States,[19] the history and culture of Filipino Americans cannot be understood as just another variant of the Asian American immigrant narrative, but as one that is uniquely scarred by colonization and codependence. This study therefore grapples with the possibilities of what Allan Punzalan Isaac calls narratives of the "postcolonial ethnic."[20] As if recalling Lisa Lowe's epigraph, Isaac reminds us that the Filipino "archipelago and its inhabitants' global dispersal" (xxiv) return us to repressed memories of the American empire from the late nineteenth century onward.

As of this writing, the term *American empire* has lost much of its charm. Besieged by its worst economic crisis since the Great Depression, mired in one long and very expensive war (Afghanistan—twelve years and counting) and recently ending another (Iraq—ten years), the United States is finding little will and fewer resources to sustain its empire. Yet just a hundred years ago, "U.S. empire" was an attractive concept and a giddy reality to most Americans, who embraced overseas expansion as eagerly as they did Manifest Destiny and hungrily consumed what information they could get about their new possessions from newspapers and popular culture. If postcolonial studies began with the critical assessment of "the legacy of the 'great men' who invented English literature" (Agnani et al. 635), this book takes on a humbler set of authors and popular or nonliterary texts that created and popularized the romance of an American empire in the Pacific. In brief, the abject texts I will analyze are popular and noncanonical texts that created the idea of empire more than a century ago. I chose to focus on visual texts and popular prose on the U.S. empire and the Philippine colony to highlight the complicity of what were then modern technologies in the service of American empire-building. Such cultural texts were not only inventions of American imperial modernity but also its visual and literary forms. This book therefore seeks to contribute to the larger study of the archives of 1898.[21]

We begin with the assumption that American imperialism is a visual and textual language, and that the U.S. colonial archive is not merely a source of knowledge but an object of analysis. This "archive-centered approach"[22] to studying race and American culture from the turn of the twentieth century contributes to larger discussions on the braided ideologies of American imperialism, modernity, heterosexualization, race, and domesticity. By "archive" I refer to the massive political and cultural archive of 1898, the year of the emergence of the American empire in the Pacific (Campomanes). An archive might be "a fantasy of knowledge," where "imperial fictions" are collected and united in the service of the state and empire.[23] In this sense the literal or physical archive, such the U.S. National Archive in Maryland, is a site for understanding colonial or official knowledges. To complement and to render these unstable, we juxtapose the "official" narratives of the colonial period with a discussion of an abject or shadow archive—borrowing from Allan Sekula's notion of a "shadow archive"[24] as a cultural repository of images and ideas that are outside or in opposition to the nation's official historical narratives—that is, obscure or forgotten cultural texts that highlight the centrality of race and sex in the occupation and colonization of the Philippine Islands that are inscribed in American popular culture after 1898. When the materiality of the American empire is combined with a shadow archive, we have at our disposal a broad range of cultural texts that interpret, produce, popularize, contradict, or oppose the logics of American imperial modernity.

While some scholars have described the turn of the twentieth-century United States as the triumph of modernity marked by the rise of "industrial production, the bureaucratization of modern life, the rise of consumerism and commodity capitalism's economic hegemony,"[25] I turn to Paul Gilroy's formulation of the relationship of Western imperial modernity and its complicity with Western colonialism's racial violence, or the "unforgiving historical light of the brutal encounter" between Westerners and "the conquered, slaughtered, and enslaved."[26] While Gilroy's notion of modernity refers to Europe in the late eighteenth century and after, this study will extend his ideas to American imperial modernity after 1898 and the emergence of the United States as an empire in the Asia-Pacific. According to Gilroy, "the social and political subordination of blacks and other non-European peoples" does not feature in academic debates about the consequences of Western modernity, and this observation holds true for the descendants of Filipino colonial subjects. Instead there is an "innocent modernity" (Gilroy 44) that is disarticulated from darker historical narratives. The deliberate removal of any traces of the very people subjected to the brute force of modernity is complicated by the physical traces of the past, the ordinary objects left behind by Western colonial rule and, in this case, American colonial rule. These objects bear colonial images, or what Sekula refers to as "the bodies in the Archive."[27] My periodization and analysis of U.S. imperial abjection begin with these "bodies"—naked savages, corpses, clothed native elites, uniformed American soldiers—and bodies of writing that document the benevolence and violence of American imperial expansion in the Philippines, a racial project that was not a singular isolated event but had roots in the conquest of the frontier, the appropriation of Native lands, and the legacies of the institution of slavery. Imperial abjection, then, is a theory of empire that highlights this violence and situates it in a continuum of genocide, land grab, and slavery, in texts that may or may not represent imperial violence overtly, but which can be revealed by racial and gender discourses. Accordingly, I work with Laura Wexler's notion of the relationship between empire and domestic ideology, and the visibility of imperial violence in sentimental, seemingly tranquil or "domestic images."[28] While Wexler describes imperial domestic images as "mothers, babies, and family groupings" and "configurations of familiar and intimate arrangements intended for the eyes of outsiders" (21), *Filipino imperial domestic images* include American soldiers lounging in a military campsite after battle, soldiers posing calmly beside Filipino corpses, white schoolteachers photographed with their Filipino students, descriptions of American soldiers' wives enjoying tea under coconut trees, and songs about black soldiers in love with foreign brown maidens. These Philippine images confirm that "the *heimlich* (private)" can be imperial propaganda (Wexler 21), which was distributed to American publics through modern and increasingly mass-produced visual technologies of the time, such as photographs, travel books, newspapers and magazines, sheet music, and popular romance novels. These American artifacts represented U.S. imperial aggression as "a peace that keeps the peace" (21). This study of imperial abjection will focus on the forgotten archives of the U.S. empire by returning to the instabilities and incommensurabilities of American imperialism as a heterogeneous and contradictory language on conquest, race, and sex, a discourse that is "internally complex and unstable."[29]

Before the 1990s, most studies of Filipino American history and culture centered on the great Filipino immigrant saga that started in the 1920s with the arrival of farmworkers in the fields of Hawai'i, California, Oregon, and other agricultural areas.[30] However, the work of pioneers such as E. San Juan Jr.,[31] Oscar V. Campomanes, and many other excellent scholars, who will be discussed in the succeeding chapters, eventually shifted the narrative coordinates of Filipino America from the agricultural fields of the West Coast and Hawai'i to the battlefields of Manila, where seventy thousand U.S. troops arrived in 1898.[32] These new Filipino American studies began examining the "Americanization" of Filipinos through war and colonial rule rather than migration and found that these earlier events better explained the peculiar traumas and deficiencies suffered by Filipino Americans, which relocation alone could not have caused and which had no parallels in other Asian American immigrant communities. Sarita See observes that "Filipino America is strangely and structurally invisible, and its position at the crossroads of race and empire has everything to do with that invisibility" (xvi). The common perception of Filipino Americans as "forgotten Asian Americans"[33] despite their early presence in the United States, their singular history of U.S. colonization, their growing numbers as the third largest Asian immigrant community in the nation,[34] and their ranking as the Asian community with the highest number of undocumented immigrants,[35] must therefore be understood in the context of U.S.-Philippine colonial relations. Filipino invisibility is underwritten by race and empire.

While the history of the Philippine-American War and the rise of photography are the impetus for my preliminary analysis, this book is not a history of the war or of American photography. Rather it is an examination of American culture and the creation of an American discourse of imperial abjection in the U.S. empire's ephemera, such as American popular culture and artifacts from the turn of the twentieth century. The objects and artifacts of the U.S. empire will be read in relation to what W. J. T. Mitchell, in the opening epigraph, has described as "empire and objecthood" (149), focusing on the materiality of empire and the legacies of Filipino "objecthood," with Filipinos as objects of "scientific" study, as objects of colonial rule, as subject peoples with no sovereign status, and as objects of racial discourse.

The project considers the central role played by the Philippine colony in the American imperial imaginary at the turn of the twentieth century, and the work of culture, both in the United States and in the Philippines, in the production of racial difference and American modernity. Culture during the Philippine-American War was pivotal to "race-making" and "war-making" (Kramer 89) and the creation of American imperial ideologies that justified the violence of the war. The Philippine colony is a *fissure*, an "imaginary signification," something invented that, "paradoxically, becomes necessary because 'that something' plays a key role, both in the world the West constitutes for itself and in the West's apologetic concerns and exclusionary and brutal practices towards others."[36] Narratives about the Philippine colony were foundational fictions in the violent creation and propagation of the American empire.

INTERRUPTING ASIAN AMERICAN STUDIES, ASIAN STUDIES, AND POSTCOLONIAL FEMINIST STUDIES

By "interrupting" three fields that have produced knowledges about the Philippines and its global diaspora, I take on the observations of postcolonial and American studies scholars, notably Brian T. Edwards, who cites Timothy Brennan "for a reinvigoration of postcolonial studies and [for pushing] practitioners . . . to practice clarity, and to make visible the unpayment and other systemic acts of violence by the state that cultural production has rendered invisible."[37] Edwards highlights the need to expose the complicity of culture in historical violence. He proposes "*interruption* as a critical tactic for literary studies" and as a pedagogical tactic in American studies (73). Through interruption we short-circuit dominant accounts of various fields by reading and analyzing "suppressed or forgotten archives" and mapping "narrative interruptions" with non-Western and non-English texts (73).

I locate my analyses of the American archive of imperial modernity in these fields of study precisely because of the liminal status of the Philippines, Filipino history, and culture in these disciplines. The book challenges the American imperial notion, codified for more than a century in American literary culture and political thought, that "the Philippines and Filipinos do not matter to the United States." Or, as the late Filipino poet Alfredo Navarro Salanga once wrote, "They don't think much / about us / in America. / That's where Manila's / just as small as Guam is: / dots / on a map."[38] Or if Filipino subjects matter, as in the case of recent U.S. scholarship in gender and migration studies, Philippine experiences and narratives can only be studied in terms of contemporary formations such as global migration. The North American diaspora of Filipinos, however, began with the colonization of the Philippines by the United States, and this suppressed history entwines Filipinos with other colonial histories. As francophone scholar Françoise Vergès once observed regarding the significance of obscure or micropolitical colonial histories,

> In the last decade, re-visions of the colonial and imperial project have shown that the study of a micropolitical colonial phenomenon can shed light on the complex mechanisms of the colonial relation. On the one hand, such a study insists on the singularity of each colonial experience; on the other, it allows analogies, comparisons, contrasts with other colonial experiences.[39]

Since the late 1990s, Filipino American studies scholars have explored the question of American imperialism in Filipino American culture. In his book *American Tropics*, Allan Punzalan Isaac maps a genealogy of a set of "cultural and reading practices" that articulate America as "fantastic metaphor and physical metonymy."[40] He argues that the American tropics are tropes that represent the "enfolded borders and disavowed subjectivities" (17) we find in U.S. legal, cinematic and literary texts. The American tropics are both "discursive practice and place" and a "set of controlling metaphors or tropes of imperial tutelage and entertainment that separate the primitive from the civilized, chaos from order, property from the proper" (2). My work extends Isaac's and Campomanes's claims on the disavowed subjectivities of the American empire by suggesting that the production of America as "fantastic metaphor" coincided with the creation of figures of imperial abjection, the bodies that served as the "borders" or negative boundaries of the American empire.

After the centennial of the Spanish-American War in 1998, American studies and gender studies scholars have focused on the cultures of the U.S. empire.[41] In Shelley Streeby's work *American Sensations: Class, Empire, and the Production of Popular Culture*, she observes that the mid-nineteenth century witnessed the formation of ideologies of white masculinity, femininity, and the racialization of Mexican males and females in "story papers" and pamphlet literature.[42] The emergence of "sensational mass culture" produced gendered and racialized notions of ideal and abject bodies. During the 1840s and 1850s, for example, the U.S. Army volunteer was viewed as "the virtuous citizen-soldier who defended the nation out of love for his native land" (Streeby 82). This manly ideal was limited to white Anglo-Saxon men but included some working-class males, Irish immigrants, and a few Mexican men who "were thought to be white" by virtue of their "political or business relationships with U.S. men" (82). A corollary to the idealization of white masculinity was the romanticization of white women and the debasement of white immigrant women from poorer European nations and Mexican women. Streeby notes that "the U.S.-Mexico War (of 1848) dramatically and violently transformed the lives of the women who lived where battles were fought and where military forces were present" (83). Thus Streeby observes that more than a century ago, international relations between the United States and Mexico were represented as heteronormative "erotic relations" through the marriage of "feminine" Mexico and the masculine United States (37). The rhetoric of heterosexual relations was deployed not only by proexpansion leaders but also anti-imperialists who "were more interested in showing why a marriage between nations was impossible, ill advised or unnatural" (84). Both sides, however, mobilized "emergent conceptions of heterosexuality in order to legitimate their positions on international relations" (84).

In Asian and postcolonial studies, colonial relations between the European metropole and its non-Western colonies were narrated in terms of modernity and its intimate connection to the project of European Enlightenment. As Dipesh Chakrabarty put it, the place of Europe in the creation of ideas and artifacts of what he calls "political modernity" is unavoidable and indispensable.[43] Modernity meant "modern institutions of the state, bureaucracy, and capitalist enterprise," as defined by European categories and concepts. Yet the project of modernity that was introduced in the Age of Enlightenment was also a racial project based on the notion that phenotype defined one's civilized status or lack of it (Chakrabarty 9). Western imperial tutelage via military occupation, discipline, and punishment were necessary for the nonwhite's inclusion in the ranks of the modern. New scholarship on formerly colonized countries, such as the work of John D. Blanco on the nineteenth-century Philippines,[44] confirms Chakrabarty's famous phrase: that European thought is both "indispensable and inadequate" in analyzing modernity (Blanco 6). Saree Makdisi adds that for European colonizers, Asia was seen as "a space that needed to be raised and improved until it became identical to modern Europe as a sphere that needed to be propelled up the stream of time to the shores of modernity."[45] Western modernity is the unattainable goal of the nonindustrialized developing world. To be subjected to modernity meant "entering into the flow of the river of evolutionary time, which had already been charted by Europe" (Makdisi 269), and to reject modernity was to move backward in evolution. My own project borrows but also departs from these cultural and historical studies of European modernity by focusing on the United States' imperial moment.

Newly published studies have since engaged with a critical assessment of empire and Filipino American studies. The work of scholars already mentioned, along with that of others who will be cited, suggests the growing interest of a new generation of scholars eager to historicize and theorize the afterlife of the American empire in the cultures of Filipino America. As Isaac, paraphrasing Homi Bhabha, put it, "Colonies, like repressed memories, have a return effect on the metropole; they leave a ghostly, and sometimes bloody, trail that haunts the center" (xxiv–xxv). In other words, the legibility or the recognition of Filipino American communities comes with the return of repressed U.S. national memories regarding the violent occupation and colonial rule of the Philippines by the United States, or the "uncanny effect" of Filipino bodies in the American metropole (xxiv).

This study proposes a new approach to reading the culture of a specific Asian American community directly affected by U.S. imperialism and neocolonialism, that is, Filipino Americans. We return to the imperial archive for early representations of the Filipino native in order to reconstruct the language of the American empire more than a century after colonial contact. My own hopeful contribution would be to argue for a historical materialist optic for reading the cultures of Filipino America as part of the cultures of the "post-1965 Asian immigrants" who settled in the United States following the 1965 Immigration Act, which saw a surge of immigrants from Asia.[46] The literatures and cultural forms of the post-1965 immigrant communities, according to Lisa Lowe, emerged out of colonial and geopolitical wars in Asia and the histories of Western imperialism (103). Rather than notions of ethnic identity, intergenerational conflict, and authenticity, categories that defined the beginnings of Asian American literary studies, the cultures of Filipino America affirm Lowe's historical materialist concept of "hybridity." Hybridity defines Asian American culture as "material traces," as "cultural objects and practices" produced by histories of colonialism, U.S. neocolonialism, domination, and survival (67). As Lowe observes, the new immigrant communities that arrived after the 1965 Immigration Act were "from South Korea, the Philippines, South Vietnam, and Cambodia, countries deeply affected by U.S. colonialism, war and neocolonialism" (16). A historical materialist optic is a politicized strategy of reading the contradictions, the disjunctions, and the historical specificities of Filipino American community and cultural formations. The narratives of Filipino America chronicle the psychic and physical violence of an Asian immigrant life reeling from the legacies of American imperialism.

Imperial abjection offers a theory of reading empire, race, and gender by analyzing American imperial discourse as a tropological process rendering "the unfamiliar into the familiar."[47] By "tropological" I refer to the production of figures of speech in American fin de siècle culture that drew on earlier racial and gendered grammars from the histories of U.S. wars. By understanding American imperialism on a tropological level, we consider the formation of a set of abject metaphors related to literary and popular texts—that is, the face (colonial photographs), skin (newspapers), bile (women's travel writing), blood and bones (race romances and ethnographic images)—that highlight the centrality of race and gender in the language of U.S. empire. The icon of the Filipino native body replicates both the racial horror and the sexual fascination that were part of the visual economy of late nineteenth-century U.S. culture. At the moment of the emergence of new visual technologies, forms of popular culture produced the negative images or the constitutive boundaries of American imperial whiteness: by seeing figures of race, sex, and empire, American imperial nationhood was crystallized by abjection. Abjection, then, is a theory of empire, race, and sex that we can trace in artifacts and objects from the Philippine-American War, and the chapters that follow are titled as abject body parts that serve as imperial metaphors of the particular genre or subject discussed in the chapter.

The first chapter, "The Abject Archive of the Philippine-American War," is a brief discussion of the cultural history of the Philippine-American War as a forgotten war. The war's cultural archive will be read as an abject archive. The second chapter, "Face," focuses on photography as a medium that catalyzed and reinforced the idea of an American empire in the Pacific. In this chapter, colonial photographs from the National Archive's Bureau of Insular Affairs collection that show figures in life and death, war and occupation, are examined and credentialed as icons of abjection. White American soldiers posing in parade dress or standing beside a Gatling gun or posing with Filipino corpses after battle are images from the Philippine war that articulate colonial necropolitics, that is, the violence of American imperial modernity and sovereignty. But no less abject are photographs of domesticity, taken in the same period, such as Filipino women in traditional dress, that instead of ameliorating the violence served to accentuate it because of their surreal docility and domesticity.

In the third chapter, entitled "Skin," I examine editorials and articles on the Philippines that were published in African American periodicals and the mainstream press at the turn of the twentieth century. The abject skin, in this chapter, is the imagined black body of Filipinos and its contrasting meaning for white and black soldiers who were sent to fight the war, as well as its impact on African American readers who read about the war while suffering lynchings on U.S. soil.

Chapter 4, "The Bile of Race," will analyze travel accounts by white female travelers, who represented Filipino natives as primitive, filthy, violent, exotic, and uncivilized, employing a colonial vocabulary drawn from earlier European travel writing on the tropics. The bile of colonial travel writing will be contrasted against moments of "anticonquest," or anecdotes and scenes of colonial ambivalence, anti-imperialism, and unintentional critique of the violence of imperialism and military occupation. The chapter focuses on the anti-imperialist essay of Helen Calista Wilson, a member of the Boston Anti-Imperialist League.

In the conclusion, "Blood and Bones," I analyze two novels set during the Philippine-American War as narratives of the romance of counterinsurgency: *Daniel Everton, Volunteer-Regular: A Romance of the Philippines* by Israel Putnam (1902) and *The Woman with a Stone Heart: A Romance of the Philippine War* by Oscar William Coursey (1914). Here abject blood refers to native or Filipino blood, unfit to mix with white, and the taboo of miscegenation that entangles the plot of both race romances set in a time of an imperial war. Since the Philippine-American War is not just the setting of the novels but also the moment of the creation of the American military science of counterinsurgency, the chapter will examine the discourse of counterinsurgency as the imperial context and structural logic of the romance narratives. The "bones" of this chapter discuss the afterlives of the photographs of Dean C. Worcester, a colonial administrator and a pioneer of counterinsurgency studies. His photographic representations from a forgotten war are remnants, the bones of empire, the visible reminders of an event now in the shadows of national memory.

Postcolonial critic Françoise Vergès reminds descendants of colonial subjects of the necessity and the difficulty of remembering empire. Despite the challenges, the frustrations, and the limits of returning to and reexamining the bitter colonial histories of islands like the Philippines, there is still the ethical responsibility of scholars writing after the end of empire:

> I do not underestimate the difficulty of retrieving the history of present times, when memory and history are deeply entangled. I play with what a French historian has called "human flesh," and I recognize that the stakes are still high. There is always the temptation to offer an anachronistic or embellished representation of the events. On which testimonies, which documents, which archives, do I rest my argument? How do I choose among archival sources? . . . There is a high risk of producing a text that ends up being a plea, an apology, or an accusation rather than an explanation. It is a risk that I have consciously taken. (Vergès xi)

Chapter 1

The Abject Archive of the Philippine-American War

In his classic work *The American Adam* (1955), R. W. B. Lewis writes that American writers created the white imperial masculine figure that conquered the frontier.[1] "The white Adamic"—a literary theme Lewis traces in diverse American authors from Emerson and Melville to Ellison and Salinger—is in fact an articulation of American imperial masculinity informed by whiteness and heterosexualization. White male settlers were sent out to the frontier to work on the "restoration of Adamic perfection, knowledge, and dominion, a return to Eden" (Dinerstein 575). More than a half a century after Lewis's work, critic Rey Chow argued that critical theory in the early twenty-first century must highlight the deconstruction of the Western logos that includes Western imperialism and colonialism.[2] This deconstruction must necessarily historicize the ascendance of the United States as "successor to and advancer of Europe and European *intentions* and *tendencies* over the course of modern history" (Chow 14). With Lewis and Chow in mind, this study begins with the imperial figure of the white Adam and the dark, abject figures in contrast to his white body as the visual primers for understanding the American empire at the dawn of the twentieth century.

"Abjection," from the Latin word *abjicere*, which means "to expel, to cast out or away,"[3] will be offered as the foundational logic of American imperialism. Following the work of postcolonial, ethnic, and queer studies scholars,[4] I use the term *abjection* beyond its psychoanalytic origins, but as a *discourse* and *theory* for understanding how race (racial ideas) and gender (erotic and/ or heterosexual fantasies) frame the narratives of the history of the Philippine-American War, the Philippine colony, and, by extension, the global Filipino diaspora.[5] By considering a colonial order, such as the American military rule in the Philippines after 1898, as a symbolic structure based on an exclusionary logic, abjection is a theory for studying the visual forms of the U.S. empire and by extension the Philippine-American War. Abjection is the production of the horror of the racial Other, often "the scapegoat," "the feminine," and "the savage," who are representations of both domination and desire.[6] And at the turn of the twentieth century, the Philippine colony was America's Congo, the dark heart of the American empire, with a guerrilla war that cost close to $50 million (around $1.3 billion in 2013) in its first year alone.[7] The cost of the war, its growing unpopularity among black and white Americans, the military censorship regarding the actual number of deaths of American soldiers and Filipino civilians, and U.S. congressional debates regarding torture and atrocities committed by American soldiers in the Philippines highlight the abject status of the Philippine-American War in the American popular memory.

Abjection in colonial discourse is the imperial trope of debasement (Spurr 74–82), created by a constellation of ideas and images such as filth, waste, dung, defilement, sin, misery, dirt, disease, moral and intellectual degradation, fear, and loathing. In the history of Western empires, the discourse of the abjection of the savage has often served as a pretext for conquest and colonization, often couched in religious terms. In nineteenth-century America, this racialized and gendered discourse was elevated into truth through scientific explanations about evolution, race, and culture, with popular culture as the primary site of abjection.[8] If abjection, according to Julia Kristeva, is what is "radically separate, loathsome," and a "primer" of a culture (2), the figure of the Filipino native and all images connected to a forgotten American war in the Philippines serve as primers for reading and understanding American imperialism and U.S. popular culture at the turn of the twentieth century.

At the center of this project is a discourse of a "politicized abjection," a term I borrow loosely from queer theorist Alberto Sandoval-Sánchez, as a framework for understanding the *mierda y sangre*, the "shit and blood" of the American colonization of the Philippines and its aftermath (544). Abjection politicizes what are the dark legacies, the detritus, the filth and fantasies of the U.S. empire. This project then engages with the work of scholars in Filipino studies that historicize the origins of Filipino America, or the migration of Filipinos to North America, as a phenomenon related to empire and diaspora.[9] While Karen Shimakawa and Darieck Scott engage with abjection as a theory for understanding Asian American and African American expressive cultures respectively, I engage with "the paradox of abjection" as a formative aspect for understanding the role of race and gender in the American visual economy of the late nineteenth century (McClintock 72). Abjection is the foundation and structural logic of the American imperial archive. The discourse of abjection pivots on the construction and production of certain groups who are "expelled and obliged to inhabit the impossible edges of modernity," such as a colony, yet the abject peoples who work or live in the colony "are those whom industrial imperialism rejects but cannot do without" (McClintock 72). Thus after 1898, the Philippine colony was an *abject zone* policed by and through violence and benevolence; American soldiers, military wives, colonial officials, and white travelers were state-sanctioned *agents of abjection*; and African American soldiers, a forgotten white anti-imperialist female writer (Helen Wilson), and all Filipino natives were *abjected groups* or abject peoples. In the late 1890s, in order for the U.S. nation to maintain and popularize its imperial ambitions, abjected groups— the dissenters, critics, and subjects of American imperial violence—were constructed "through the force of expulsion" (McClintock 71). At the same time, with the emergence of new technologies of visual culture, American popular culture served as *the* cultural site of imperial abjection. From 1898 to 1910—the first decade of American colonial rule of the Islands—images of imperial abjection appeared in American popular culture, borrowing from earlier American grammars of otherness, particularly nineteenth-century notions of "black inferiority," "red savagery," and white imperial identities. Thus Filipino images became visible at the moment when imperial violence was made "invisible" or nonexistent in American culture, through cultural texts that denied, repressed, or displaced the violence of the Philippine-American War.

THE PHILIPPINE WAR OF 1899, OBJECTHOOD, AND ABJECTHOOD

We examine the Philippine-American War of 1899 by considering how narratives of American modernity after 1898, or after the Spanish-American War, are intertwined with ideologies of abjection. More than a century ago, discourses of scientific and technological advancement, together with popular culture, made the case for romanticizing imperial modernity. Narratives of progress drummed out or "expelled" news of violent racial and class conflicts that were fissuring the postbellum landscape. The latter half of the nineteenth century witnessed the terrible aftereffects of the Civil War, crippling labor strikes, economic depressions in newly industrialized cities, immigrant unrest and marginalization as millions arrived from Asia and Europe, and the continued genocide of Native Americans and their forced removal from their lands. It could be argued—and it has been, repeatedly and almost universally—that these events were the growing pains of a fledgling yet *necessarily* expanding nation. But this growth, which *unnecessarily* annihilated much of what was believed to have stood in the way of its manifest destiny, was also achieved while upholding an American exceptionalism of democracy and inalienable human rights for all.

As Native American scholar Shari Huhndorf writes, "The history of America, a nation born from the genocide of Native peoples and built on slave labor, undermined the values of liberty and equality the nation claimed to hold dear."[10] To rewrite these unpleasant racial histories of genocide and slavery, Huhndorf argues that popular culture became a crucial site for narrating the nation's history by refashioning modernity. Thus, for example, the late nineteenth-century international expositions or world's fairs became popular ideological spectacles that celebrated American modernity by burying the brutal histories of Native genocide, conquest, and African American slavery under some very exotic and diverting ethnographic displays, and by directing the gaze forward to a shared future made possible by a civilizing and liberating technology. "Slaughter and domination" were therefore subtly transformed into popular entertainment, such as through the live exhibits of Native peoples in the world's fairs (Huhndorf 47). The political work of the world's fairs promoted American modernity by producing romantic and glorious images of scientific progress without the bloodier aspects of conquest, opening American eyes to the world and limitless opportunities abroad, especially as the country's expansion had stretched from coast to coast with nowhere to go and needed to cross either ocean in order to satisfy its infinite destiny. In the world's fairs, the abject subjects of American imperial modernity were on display to reaffirm American national identity as a "synthesis of progress and white supremacy" (Rydell 4).

In 1898, the United States entered into a war with Spain that was the first to be fought entirely outside U.S. soil, thus opening a new chapter in the country's official narrative of modernity and progress. It was also the first American war to be fought using telegraph communications and newer cartographic and surveying technologies developed by the U.S. Army's freshly created Military Information Division.[11] Years before the outbreak of the Spanish-American War, the Military Information Division had already been gathering substantial resources for U.S. military intelligence that could be used in an overseas war, including "a data set of three hundred thousand cards, a collection of six thousand maps, a military monograph series, and a photographic unit" (McCoy 27). It was the first American war where motion pictures played an important documentary and propaganda role. New film companies such as the Edison Manufacturing Company and the American Mutoscope and Biograph Company filmed actual war footages on the battlefields and later reenacted battle scenes from the war,[12] making it one of the first spectator wars, and short and one-sided enough to be entertaining for its American audience. The Spanish-American War lasted only sixteen weeks, resulting in "345 combat-related deaths among U.S. forces" and 2,565 deaths from disease, and around fourteen thousand Spaniards dead from combat and disease.[13] Quickly won at the expense of relatively light battlefield casualties, the Spanish-American War brought popular goodwill, a national belief in "higher manhood," and a growing sense of the United States as an emerging world power that had easily defeated an imperial power, albeit one in decline. Many Americans celebrated the event as a "splendid little war," as John Hay, American ambassador to England and later secretary of state, did in a letter to Colonel Theodore Roosevelt (Hoganson 6).

There was, by contrast, much less fanfare for the Philippine-American War, which followed on the heels of the Spanish-American War. The Philippine-American War of 1899 is a forgotten war, often downgraded to an "insurrection" by U.S. historians, if discussed at all. In fact, many historians have considered the Philippine-American War of 1899 as a "mere footnote" to the Spanish-American War[14]—a curious assessment given that the mere footnote lasted at least ten times longer than the original event. To this day, the specific loss of human life is unknown. Paul Kramer writes that "over 4,000 U.S. troops and an estimated 50,000 Filipino troops" died during the Philippine war.[15] The war witnessed the spread of unknown diseases brought by American soldiers through "hikes" and interisland transport, the destruction of villages by U.S. troops, the burning of crops and the killing of livestock, and the policy of "reconcentration," or the creation of garrisoned towns that brought on malnutrition, overcrowding, and mass diseases (Kramer 157). Accordingly, "the estimate of 250,000 Filipino war deaths" seems conservative (Kramer). Historian Luzviminda Francisco offers a more staggering number that echoes some of the editorials of Mark Twain: a million Filipino deaths, or one-sixth of the Filipino population.[16]

The Philippine War is "categorically displaced" by the Spanish-American War for two reasons: one, to reproduce the fiction of the "splendid little war" and to uphold the legitimacy of U.S. claims over its island possessions after 1898; two, to narrate the international crisis of 1898 as merely a small concern between two empires, "one in its emergence (the United States), the other in its decline (Spain)" (Campomanes, "Casualty Figures" 136–37). This fiction has the advantage of being simple and straightforward and therefore easily acceptable as truth: good (the United States) over evil (Spain) in a noble effort to succor the weak and oppressed (Cuba, Puerto Rico, the Philippines) who were fighting for their freedom. This narrative also provides a convenient cover for anything ugly that might happen afterward, as it did in the case of the Philippines specially, where the Filipinos—supposed beneficiaries of American intervention but who were defeating the Spaniards anyway without help—resisted when the Americans stayed and took over as colonizers. So it is entirely possible the Philippine-American War might have also ended up as another splendid little war and become a celebrated chapter, not just a footnote, in U.S. history had the Filipino people not resisted too vigorously and the war had not dragged on too long and cost as much as it did, $600 million, plus $8 billion in veterans' pensions (Campomanes, "Casualty Figures" 138), in addition to the military casualties. Not to mention the one million civilian deaths.

For a nation that had had previous experience of a genocide, one million deaths are still a breathtaking number. Even Twain couldn't help but marvel at the immensity of this achievement:

> One million. We have had as many as 60,000 men out there at a time—but not in the field. Half were in the field, possibly, but not more; of the other half, many were in hospital, the rest were distributed everywhere on garrison duty. *Thirty thousand killed a million.* They must have killed all; a 6,000,000 population can by no possibility furnish more than 1,000,000 fighting men. *Thirty thousand killed a million.* In eighteen months.[17]

It is no wonder that the Philippine-American War slid into the back pages of U.S. history books as a footnote to a splendid little (indeed, much tinier) Spanish-American War. A nation founded on the noble principles of democracy, equality, and justice would certainly wish to "expel, to cast out or away" this not so gallant episode in its history when it came to the Philippines as seeming ally and "liberator" and stayed as conqueror, colonizer, and committer of genocide. It is therefore not hard to understand why the Philippine-American War disappeared from the face of U.S. history. But given all that had happened, it is still astonishing how such an eventful war could be made to vanish. While it was being fought, the war was followed avidly in the United States. Newspapers reported regularly on the progress of the war, frequently on their front pages. A vigorous and vocal anti-imperialist movement, led by prominent Americans such as Twain and the industrialist Andrew Carnegie, even sprang up in opposition to the war and the annexation of the Philippines.[18] The war became a constant companion for many Americans at the start of the twentieth century.

In February 1901, Twain described the military occupation of the Philippines in imperial modernity's terms: "What we wanted, in the interest of Progress and Civilization, was the Archipelago, unencumbered by patriots struggling for independence; and War was what we needed" (Twain 35). His criticism of the conduct of the war would increase, as news of American military atrocities would reach the U.S. despite the military censorship later instituted by the military command in the Islands, perhaps the first indication that the war would not figure prominently in official history. Twain provides a summary of what the war had wrought, taking care to scathingly expose the real meanings of favorite colonial euphemisms such as "pacification" and "Benevolent Assimilation":

> We are as indisputably in possession of a wide-spreading archipelago as if it were our property; we have pacified some thousands of the islanders and buried them; destroyed their fields, burned their villages, and turned their widows and orphans out of doors; furnished heartbreak by exile to some dozens of disagreeable patriots; subjugated the remaining ten millions by Benevolent Assimilation which is the pious new name of the musket. (Zwick 57–58)

Here, Twain narrates the historical events of the Philippine-American War: the violent military encounters between the U.S. forces and the Filipino army of the newly created Philippine Republic; the destruction of Filipino towns and villages; the civilian deaths; the exile and banishment of captured Filipino revolutionaries who served in General Aguinaldo's revolutionary cabinet; and the hypocrisy behind McKinley's policy of "Benevolent Assimilation." Twain mentions Filipinos as abject figures: as corpses, grieving widows, orphans, broken patriots, and civilians living under the terror of the American musket.

Even now, when many myths of American exceptionalism have been exploded and America's behavior shown to be no better than other imperial nations' in human history, the Philippine-American War remains an abject or forgotten war. In American academe and in popular memory, there continues to be what historian Matthew Frye Jacobson describes as an "exquisitely structured silence," a "nontreatment of the Philippine-American War," which I take to mean that not only is the war not mentioned, there is also no accounting for this absence.[19] In Ken Burns' 2014 documentary film *The Roosevelts: An Intimate Portrait*, the director briefly mentions Theodore Roosevelt's presidency during the "war in the Philippines." The documentary even shows a photograph of the infamous "water cure," the torture committed by U.S. soldiers against suspected Filipino rebels who were fighting against the American occupation of the Philippine Islands. But the documentary quickly moves on to more charming narratives about the Roosevelts. It is a small crack in the wall of American "imperial amnesia," regarding the brutal military campaign in the Philippines, but the crack is quickly covered up with the charming family stories of the remarkable Roosevelts.

Even in late-nineteenth century American studies scholarship, the Philippine war still receives minor attention. For example, while critical Americanists defined the contours of what they called the "cultures of United States imperialism" in their eponymous anthology, only one essay discussed the Philippine war, as against multiple essays on Mexico, Cuba, and Africa.[20] And while John Carlos Rowe attempts to engage with American imperialism and American literature,[21] there is no discussion of American writings on the Philippine war or on Filipinos, despite the various books and a wealth of archival sources on the war from the turn of the twentieth century. The scope and scale of the Philippine War and the institutionalized acts of forgetting the war by subsuming it under the events of the Spanish-American War suggest the complex braiding of modernity and American imperial abjection.

To interrupt the discourse of imperial modernity and historical amnesia, I consider how objects from the period of the Philippine-American War articulate abjection. W. J. T. Mitchell writes that objects left by empires are both imperial "relics" and "inscriptions."[22] Because American cultural texts from the turn of the twentieth century are artifacts informed by the "rhetoric of empire and colonization" (Mitchell 147), this study highlights the discursive instabilities and incommensurabilities of objects left behind by the U.S. empire, which had been subjected to a willful forgetfulness by official history, subsumed into the larger classification of American modernity, and survive as art, popular culture, or nonart, often without any overt indication of their colonial or imperial provenance. As Mitchell notes: "What would it mean to think of empire in terms of a broad range of objects and object types?" (146). We might also ask what occurs when colonial and, later, contemporary technologies enable and assist the "worlding" with their circulation across frontiers and continents, across temporal and national boundaries, flowing from the printed work or daguerreotype to the computer screen. All such categories have, in fact, origins in Western colonialism. As Mitchell writes:

This division between art objects and mere, unredeemed objecthood, between art and non-art, has a deep connection, I want to argue, with the rhetoric of empire and colonization. . . . The very notion of art as a distinctive category of objects (and the category of objecthood more generally) is forged with the colonial encounter. . . . My claim is that *both art and objecthood are imperial (and imperious) categories*, and that aesthetics as a quasi science of artistic judgement is a separation of the redeemed from the damned, the purified and the corrupt and degraded object. As an imperial practice, aesthetics enlists all the rhetorics of religion, morality, and progressive modernity to pass judgment on the "bad objects" that inevitably come into view in a colonial encounter. (147; emphasis mine)

Here, he offers a genealogical reading of "high art," tracing its provenance to Western imperial encounters. He views aesthetics as an imperial science, a colonial optic for deciding the value and non-value of objects forged by the colonial encounter. Mitchell thus extends Edward Said's claims of the relationship between imperialism and culture,[23] by recognizing that "culture" is based on colonial categories of high art versus non-art, which are decided by an aesthetics that is skewed overwhelmingly towards the occupying power that has the better of that colonial encounter. Further, the colonial encounter seals and defines who are the creators and the consumers of art, and who are merely objects of artistic depiction. Objecthood and its echoes to non-beinghood for the colonial subject[24] recall Sarita See's observation that, historically, "Filipinos cannot 'have' culture" but are instead 'culture.'" To quote See:

Filipinos instead "are" culture, displayed as dehumanized objects in past World's Fairs and present-day natural history museums in the United States. Of course, this drastically uneven allocation of culture—who gets to have culture and who gets to be culture—is an intrinsic part of the workings of Western modernity and racism. (See xxxiv)

Thus, objecthood is a category reserved for the colonial native or those subjected to the violence of Western modernity and colonial racism. The imperial division between art and non-art is heightened further when we consider art as "synecdoches" of empires (Mitchell 154). According to Mitchell, art is a synecdoche for all "the crafts, skills, and technologies" of empire (154). In artifacts considered as "art," we witness values at work in decisions over aesthetics. Those deemed as non-art reveal what the empire rejects and deems as either primitive or banal or both.

This notion of high art versus lowbrow art, and literature versus popular culture, returns us to the idea of the imperial archive. My study considers these divisions by emphasizing a serious engagement with the literary *and* the popular, the visual *and* the printed text, and the multitude of *objects and narratives that produce the idea of the Filipino*. Objecthood, then, takes on another layer of meaning when we consider the "Filipino race" as a "subject race."[25] Extending Said's ideas, the figure of the Filipino native will be read as *both* subject and object of American imperial abjection.

Writing on postcolonial Africa, Achille Mbembe wrote that Western scholars represented Africa and Africans under two signs: bestiality and intimacy.[26] In European historical accounts, Africa and its people were depicted as beastly, "strange and monstrous," a mixture of "half-created" and "incomplete strange signs" that ultimately painted the region as "a bottomless abyss where everything is noise, yawning gap, and primordial chaos" (Mbembe 3). Africa and Africans as "signs of intimacy" meant the representation of the region and its people as familiar or legible subjects to Europeans, since the region was an object of study for generations of white historians and writers, let alone explorers and colonizers (Mbembe 2). Mbeme's observations on Africa as a postcolony shine a comparative light on the Philippine postcolony, where Filipinos, as resistant and dark-skinned colonial subjects, were represented as bestial and intimate figures in the American popular imagination a century ago, joining black and Native Americans as antagonists and familiars in a United States newly transitioned from republic to empire.

READING STRATEGIES: HETEROTOPICALITY AND ANAMNESIA

If discourse is a "mechanism and modality" of power,[27] American imperial abjection then is both an *instrument* (power as mechanism) and *form* (power as modality) of U.S. imperial violence. As mechanism, American imperial abjection is a network of texts and documents, both literary and non-literary (i.e. popular forms of culture, artifacts, photographic images, government documents, letters and reports, etc.) that articulate U.S. imperial power. American imperial abjection, recalling Lisa Lowe's work on Orientalisms, is a "network of texts, documents, practices, disciplines and institutions," which, together, produce certain objects and forms of colonial knowledge.[28] American imperial abjection thus functions through *heterotopicality*, a term Lowe derives from Foucault's "heterotopia." American imperial abjection's heterotopicality refers to articulations and rearticulations of U.S. imperial power that emerge from a variety of positions, texts and discourses (Lowe 15). Heterotopicality as a reading strategy also recalls Mitchell's suggestion of imagining empire through a multiplicity of texts, genres and convergent histories of conquest. At the turn of the twentieth century, American visual and literary cultures represented the Philippine colony through a network of texts, documents and practices that produced and invented the Philippine colony and abject ideas about the Filipino race.

A second approach for reading abjection is through *anamnesia*.[29] An anamnesiac reading is a "postcolonial practice" of remembering through an analysis of the "science of imperialism" or the imperial archive (Behdad 7). As acts of remembering, postcolonial critiques are not aimed at demonizing or accusing the imperial power of crimes committed in the past, although memories of historical atrocities or violence might be invoked or noted. Rather than accusation, the critiques are discussions of the cultural forms and mechanics of *empire-building* through an analysis of culture. As Behdad explains, "Postcolonial critiques in this sense are the belated return of the repressed, disrupting that structure of colonial amnesia that denied his or her story" (Behdad 6). "Belatedness" underscores the temporal reality of the contemporary reader who engages with the colonial past through textual analysis. This temporary lag enables what Behdad calls "historical hindsight," which becomes the "enabling conditions for oppositional theory" (Behdad 3). For indeed, postcolonial readings require a critical engagement with imperial "amnesiac practices" that "glorify the violent history of colonialism as a utopian time of benignity and exultation" (Behdad 8). Hindsight then renders visible the discursive tools of imperial violence. An "anamnesiac reading" is a postcolonial tactic that "unmasks what the (cultural) object holds back and exposes the violence it represses in its consciousness" (Behdad 8).

The artifacts of the American imperial archive celebrate and incriminate the American civilizing mission that came with the brutal imposition of U.S. military rule on the Philippine Republic. Using a heterotopical and anamnesiac approach, I return to the discourse of Filipino savagery and docility, to disturb and complicate the American narratives of 1898 and after. Since its "independence with strings" in 1946, the Philippines has not figured in contemporary discussions in postcolonial studies, a field began by radical historians who studied the British colonial history of India. The recent theoretical interventions by scholars in Filipino studies, American and ethnic studies discussed here challenge the American mind-set of the "irrelevance" of the Philippines by highlighting the former colony's intimate connection with American national identity and the creation of a U.S. Empire.

As a genealogy of Filipino images, the study returns to Behdad and Foucault's admonition that genealogy is "not merely an erudite knowledge of the past but . . . a kind of research activity that 'allows us to establish a historical knowledge of struggles and to make use of this knowledge tactically *today*'" (9). This study attempts to challenge what Reynaldo Ileto describes as the "politics of memory"[30] by reviving abject or forgotten American cultural texts "hidden away in the dark shadows of empire" (Ileto 233) so as to understand the legacies of imperialism for contemporary Filipinos in the Philippines and in the diaspora.

ABJECT SAVAGERY AND DOCILITY

For this study, the discourse of American imperial abjection can be traced through two major themes: the theme of abject savagery that we trace in discourses of imperial modernity and the pacification of black skin or the primitive savage; second, the theme of docility that we map in discourses by white American school teachers, travelers and soldiers. The Filipino native is an icon of the intimacies of American imperial modernity,[31] inhabiting two possible worlds enabled by Empire—the original savage world of the Philippine jungles, and the civilized world that requires the Filipino's submission and docility. The wildness of the Frontier (i.e., the jungles of the Philippine Islands) and the domestic civilized white world are not antithetical spaces of the American nineteenth century imaginary but in fact complement each other in the discourse of American imperialism.

If imperial power exists as modality, the many forms of American imperial abjection are embodied in two interrelated figures regarding Filipinos: the Filipino savage and the docile native. Savagery and docility have been attributed to the United States' colonial others. Hayden White writes that the figure of the Savage is a Western tradition with origins from seventeenth and eighteenth century European texts (150), with the idea of the Noble Savage or "the Wild Man" emerging out of the age of European colonial exploration. "Wildness" or its Latinate form, "savagery," was associated with a "set of culturally, self-authenticating devices which includes, among many others, the ideas of 'madness' and 'heresy' as well" (151). For many Greek thinkers, *barbaros,* the root of the word "barbarian," was used to refer to someone who did not speak Greek (165). The racial and racist inflection of "barbarian" recalls Gail Bederman's modern cultural history of how the image of the civilized man in the American imagination at the turn of the twentieth century was always a racial project. Within the term "savage" exists the racial logic of whiteness. White describes how race plays a part in the representation of the Savage:

> It was the oppressed, the exploited, alienated or repressed part of humanity that kept on reappearing in the imagination of Western Man—as the Wild Man, as the monster, and as the devil—to haunt or entice him thereafter. Sometimes this oppressed or repressed humanity appeared as a threat and a nightmare, at other times as a goal and a dream . . . but always as a criticism of whatever security and peace of mind one group of men in society had purchased at the cost of the suffering of another. (180)

We can conclude then that U.S. imperial peace and security are purchased at the cost of the physical suffering and the psychic suffering (via misrepresentation) of the Savage in late nineteenth century U.S. culture. We see the imperial work of American culture in the creation of racialized and gendered representations of the Filipino. As Julian Go reminds us in his study of elite Filipino and Puerto Rican political culture, "Culture was colonial power's very target and terrain, an object that colonialism was to manage, work upon and recreate."[32] This study, however, departs from Go's analysis by emphasizing and focusing on American *popular* (and not elite) culture and artifacts from the late nineteenth century to the early twentieth. Such forgotten and understudied American archives render unstable the imperial politics imbricated, as part of the science of American imperialism, in non-elite, even lowbrow American culture.

For Latin Americanist Walter Mignolo, imperial violence is "ritualized" or romanticized in European modern cultures, with the ritualization of imperial violence serving as an expression of abjection. As Mignolo observes, we come across narratives of modernity in cultural texts that narrate the life of "the civilizing hero" who "invests his victims (the colonized, the slave, the woman, the ecological destruction of the earth, etc.) with the character of being participants in a process of redemptive sacrifice."[33] By extension, the American texts that circulated during and after the Philippine-American War represented the violence and the romance of Empire-building through stories of the American soldier and the schoolteacher as the civilizing hero. Visual artifacts, popular literature and journalistic narratives that were disseminated during the turn of the twentieth century represented forms and inscriptions of this violence. In these three different types of text, Filipino natives were willing participants, hostile primitives or noble victims, or any combination of the three.

Another framework for theorizing imperial abjection is Paul Gilroy's critique of Western modernity and its relationship to racial terror and violence. For Gilroy, the institution of slavery in the eighteenth century was integral to Western civilization and its definitions of civilization and modernity, what he describes as "the unforgiving historical light of the brutal encounters between Europeans and those they conquered, slaughtered, and enslaved."[34] This study extends Gilroy's discussion of the violence of European modernity to late nineteenth century United States and its colonization of the Philippines after 1898. The discourse of American modernity, and its claim to newness and "innocence," requires the expulsion of the darker histories of American slavery, the conquest of Native lands and the Southwest. If, according to Gilroy, African slavery is "the ethical and intellectual heritage" of European modernity (Gilroy 49), then *military conquest and war are the ethical and intellectual heritage of*

American modernity. The late nineteenth century marks the rise of an American modernity that celebrates technology's imperial and erotic power that captured the American popular imagination. I shall consider how American military conquest and war are represented, reproduced and popularized through figures of abjection and are transformed into "intellectual heritage." Not all the texts are obvious representations of imperial violence, such as photographs of an American schoolteacher with her Filipino wards or a description of American military wives having tea under coconut trees. But tactics of reading imperial abjection will use modes of historical contextualization, comparisons and analogies for understanding American modernity and imperial violence.

My methodology for studying the images of Filipinos borrows from Edward Said's study of Orientalism (*Orientalism* 20). Said employed what he called a *strategic formation*, which he describes as "a way of analyzing the relationship between texts and the way in which groups of texts, types of texts, even textual genres, acquire mass, density and referential power among themselves and thereafter in the culture at large" (Said 20). Employing Said's ideas, I argue that racial ideas about an ethnic group or non-Anglo people have their origins in cultural texts that were disseminated for mass consumption, thereby acquiring what Said describes as "density and referential power" in the colonial culture or society.

The discourse of American imperial abjection is partly rooted in the racialized and gendered imagery used in stereotypes of American domestic Others: Native Americans and African Americans. In the case of the image of Native Americans, the tropes of savagery and docility were created by European travelers and European writers who were invested in the differences between the civilized and barbarous races. Puritan settlers, when they first encountered Native peoples, believed that Native Americans were both "demons of the continent" and "children of nature" who could lead the Pilgrims to a purer, simpler, more austere and natural way of life.

The discourse of the docile and noble savage can be traced in the sympathetic (such as they are) portrayals of turn-of-the-century Anglo writers who wrote popular texts regarding Native peoples for a general audience.[35] The writers were "lawyers, judges, journalists, educators, assimilationists, professional anthropologists . . . essayists and poets" (Smith 5). The tradition of Europeans and white Americans writing to define and articulate the meaning of Indianness had been a Western imperial tradition dating to the turn of the sixteenth century (Smith 5). Yet, while the place of the Indian in the American imaginary is a long-standing one, their actual physical presence in the American continent had been reduced by genocide, displacement and land grab into near nothing. Most of the white American writers from the late nineteenth century therefore concluded only two choices for the Native Americans: "assimilate or disappear" (Smith 6). This period was coincidentally the moment of American expansion into the Caribbean and the Pacific, along with the emergence of social Darwinist philosophies championed by scholars who believed in Indian inferiority. Thus, these seemingly "benevolent" and benign narratives written by Anglo writers must be taken in context with the events of the 1890s. National anxieties about the end of the Frontier, the acquisition of land for the growing industries of the North, and the failure of Reconstruction to bring racial equality and harmony bring more questions to popular white narratives that focused on the "humanity" of Native communities. While the writers labored to "humanize" American Indian peoples by emphasizing the significance of Indian cultures and how tribal cultures offered a refuge from the empty and crass life of Anglo American modernization (Smith 214), there was still the matter of the violence of the Conquest. In the end, the abject history of the Conquest of the West or the violence of the Frontier remains as the dark and larger backdrop of these narratives of Indian docility and nobility. The very taming of the Indian savage and the disappearance of the dangers they posed in the American West finally made these narratives palatable and popular.

The savage and docile images of the Indian were not the only templates for the visual and textual representation of the Filipino. There were also the racist representations from minstrel shows. The image of African Americans as pickaninnies and as grass-skirted savages can be traced as an antecedent of the racial representation of Filipino colonials. The mobility of racist discourses at the century's turn can be seen in editorials and editorial cartoons of the era that showed Filipinos with black faces and bodies, thick lips, wearing grass skits and hoop earrings. As Eric Lott reminds us, minstrel shows were profoundly popular and influential in the American imagination in the nineteenth century.[36] Minstrel troupes entertained presidents, and high-brow quarterlies wrote critically about them (Lott 4). Intellectuals such as Mark Twain, Walt Whitman, and Bayard Taylor were attracted to blackface performances even as African Americans such as Frederick Douglass were repelled by them. The discourse of minstrel shows articulated the varying emotions embodied in Jacksonian racial politics between white and black Americans. Given that envy, repulsion, "sympathetic identification as well as fear" inscribe the minstrel shows, these performances were then theaters of abjection. Minstrel shows were expressions of "racist curiosity" (Lott 15) and minstrel figures are in fact abject manifestations of white Americans' "fear and fascination" with blackness. Black inferiority was naturalized and made palatable by presenting the docile Negro or the "good Negro figure" who was feminized and inferior by definition (Lott 33). Examples of the docile Negro include the "gentle, childlike, self-sacrificing, essentially *aesthetic* slave" created as Jim in Mark Twain's *Huckleberry Finn* (1884) (Lott 34). Another docile Negro figure can be read in Harriet Beecher Stowe's *Uncle Tom's Cabin* (1852), with the character of Tom as the feminized, sentimentalized slave.

Turning to journalism, in editorial cartoons and newspaper articles, we can see similarities between the stereotypical images of African Americans and Filipino colonial subjects. The blackening of Filipino bodies, the representation of Filipinos as "darkies" similar to the feminized "good Negro," suggests not only the inferiority of Filipinos to white Americans, but also the need for disciplining the Filipino natives into a docility similar to that of black slaves. In the case of Filipinos, discipline would come through schoolbooks and Krags, or through education and military rule.

The theme of abject savagery would be immortalized by a historian's speech in a fair. It was in the 1893 World's Columbian Exposition in Chicago that American fairgoers commemorated the imperial conquest of America, the winning of the West, as preparation for the nation's imperial future. On July 12, 1893, historian Frederick Jackson Turner read his famous speech, "The Significance of the Frontier in American History." His nostalgia for the loss of the savage frontier after "four centuries from the discovery of America" and "a century under the constitution"[37] dramatized the need to continue America's imperial destiny, since conquest was part of "American nature";[38] and this declaration attained "the status of myth" (Huhndorf 53). For Turner, expansion is the birthright of white Americans, which they inherited from the famous fifteenth-century explorer who gave his name to the exposition where Turner spoke. Purged from this narration is the violence unleashed by the arrival of Columbus in the New World—war, disease, land occupation, and the destruction of Native cultures. The exclusion of these abject historical realities was fundamental for Turner's thesis because in their place, in place of unbridled white imperial aggression, was what would be known as rugged frontier individualism: "coarseness and strength," "acuteness and inquisitiveness," "restless nervous energy," "dominant individualism," and "buoyancy and exuberance which comes with freedom" (Turner 37)—all of which reified and mythified the heroism of America's westward expansion and disavowed the darker side of frontier history, erasing the slaughter and near destruction of Native America.

Turner's imperial modernity rested on notions of rebirth, transformation, discovery, settlement, and conquest while repressing the true history of Native America. This benign modernity, without genocide and military occupation, required the ethnic transformation of the Old World roots of immigrants into new Americans, and excluded "the histories of Native peoples as well as nonwhite peoples" (Huhndorf 55). At the center of this tale is the white European "frontiersman," compelled by the spirit of "opportunity, freshness, confidence, and scorn of older society, impatient of its restraints and its ideas" (Turner 37). As Native American critic Shari Huhndorf argues:

> It was the frontier experience that transformed and unified these immigrants into the modern nation, in part by severing their ties to their homelands. . . . For Turner it was in part the European immigrants' complex relationships with Native Americans that rendered them *true* Americans. Often, Native peoples are simply absent from his imaginary landscape, which appears empty and unpopulated, the proverbial "virgin land." . . . At other times, however, Indians embody a savagery to be conquered along with the wilderness. (55)

The nineteenth-century American imperial ethos required the severance of white immigrants from their ethnic past and the romanticization of a sanitized version of the history of Native American genocide, retold as the discovery of a pure, untouched, and unpeopled Edenic continent.

A second theme that propagated American imperial abjection is the cult of domesticity and the creation of colonial docility. The discourse of nineteenth-century domesticity was crucial for the representation of white, heterosexual, imperial identities in the American imaginary. Domesticity as a narrative of American imperial modernity reshaped white male imperial aggression into civilization, calm, and order—the portrayal of "war as peace" (Wexler 34). This sentiment situated the horrors of empire outside the frame of domestic images, repressing and suppressing the image of American soldiers as "arsonists, rapists, looters and lynchers" (Wexler 35). A U.S. culture of war needed to present soldiers in the kindest, gentlest light, and domesticity served this purpose. Photographic images popularized the middle-class white home and the gentleman soldier as an imperial antidote to the class, gender, and racial anxieties threatening white manhood. Abjection is a reading strategy for engaging with imperial heterosexualization as a foundational logic of empire-building. Following the work of postcolonial feminist scholars mentioned here and in the next chapters, this study is a feminist reading of the American imperial archive as a productive site for examining imperial ideologies such as domesticity and its entanglements with race, "heterosexual arrangements and identities." Abjection offers a theoretical inversion of the American colonial archive by reading the heterosexualization and the eroticization of conquest in tandem with war and military occupation. Race and sex went hand in glove with customary

American ways of narrating "conquest and the continuing domination of foreign lands."[39]

Scenes of empire and abjection can be traced even before the Philippine-American War. Between 1873 and 1896, a series of economic depressions in the United States resulted in "tens of thousands of bankruptcies" that threatened the way of life of the white middle class.[40] Amid these economic threats, the suffragist movement for women's equal rights and the growing white immigrant men's efforts to control urban politics challenged nineteenth-century Anglo-Saxon men's identities (Bederman 13). By the 1880s, the American middle class "worked to remake manhood" by linking male power to whiteness (Bederman 20–21). By associating "powerful manhood with white supremacy," imperial modernity linked imperial aggression with whiteness and manhood. We witness this in the popular anthropology magazine *National Geographic*, which began publication in 1889 and created iconic images of the civilized white male explorer among primitive tribes (Bederman 22). But alongside the romantic depiction of white imperial manhood were the gendered discourses of white imperial womanhood and the savage. As Amy Kaplan notes, the nineteenth-century ideology of separate spheres, or the distinct realms of the male and female, configured "the home as a bounded and rigidly ordered interior space as opposed to the boundless and undifferentiated space of an infinitely expanding frontier."[41] Domesticity, then, was intimately linked with Manifest Destiny: "The home contains within itself those wild or foreign elements that must be tamed; domesticity monitors the borders between civilized and the savage as it regulates the traces of savagery within its purview" (Kaplan 25–26). What domesticity created was a spatial fiction of divided spheres: male and female, domestic and foreign, civilized and savage. Yet as a discourse, domesticity was often mobile and unstable, just as the American imperial borders were in constant flux and expansion through violent confrontations with Mexicans, Native Americans, and later Filipinos in the late nineteenth century.

The themes of abject savagery and docility became popular with ordinary Americans with the emergence of box cameras and the rise of newspapers. The reproduction of images enabled new forms of identity for late nineteenth-century white Americans, as it did the creation of the criminal and, later, colonial Other.[42] As scholars have noted, the "Age of Mechanical Reproduction" was also the age of modern scientific racism.[43] By the 1850s, the technological developments in "negative/positive photography" and the collodion/albumen printing process resulted in the proliferation of photographic practices. New cultural forms such as "the photographic calling card, or carte-de-visite, the popular celebrity image, the cabinet card, the stereograph card collection, and the family photograph" began a national romance around the figure of the middle-class white identities and the debasement or the abjection of nonwhites (Smith 51). These images started circulating freely among American households, like the newspapers that sprouted in almost every new town and city throughout the frontier.

EVE'S DARK CHILDREN: THE EROTICS OF ABJECTION

José Eduardo Limón discusses the "erotics of culture" or "the play of eroticism and desire in the relationship between Greater Mexico and the United States,"[44] and the erotics of imperial abjection is a theory for understanding empire, race, and sex as it relates to American empire-building in the Philippines and by extension other American territories in the Asia-Pacific. Abjection is the play of racialization and sexualization in the American imperial archive that incorporated the ideas, images, and vocabularies of the conquest of the New World, the frontier, and the legacies of slavery for narrating the Philippine colony and its people. By the *erotics of imperial abjection* I refer to eros or desire,[45] considering the relationship between heterosexual eroticization and racialization in the wake of the Philippine-American War. While Donald H. Mengay was the first to use the phrase "erotics of empire" to mean the discourse of Orientalism and queer desire in British imperial texts such as the writings of T. E. Lawrence,[46] the erotics of imperial abjection is the nexus of heterosexualization and race in narratives about the American conquest of the Philippines. The erotics of abjection is heterocolonial desire that romanticizes the violence of war and the U.S. occupation of the Philippine Islands after 1898. While Behdad describes "orientalist desire" as discourse that seeks to "capture the colonial Other through official or dominant discourses," the erotics of abjection is its analogue (20). Orientalist desire implies "observation and representation without any personal participation in the social reality of the Orient" (Behdad 20–21). The distant colonial writer-observer, removed from the social realities of the "natives," echoes the sexualized relationship of science and imperialism, beginning in the age of exploration onward to the age of the American empire in the 1900s. As Sarita See notes in her reading of a sixteenth-century woodcut that showed a male cartographer drawing a live female model's vagina, "The sixteenth century hidden pudenda plays a crucial function in the epistemology of colonial scientific discovery" (51). She describes the gendered, "gynophobic" gaze that links the white female body, specifically the woman's vagina, with the ideological production of the natural world and the "racial logic of colonial possession" (50). This sixteenth-century colonial notion of the "feminine sublime" (50), or the horror of, and fascination and confrontation with, the female body, informs the late nineteenth-century erotics of American imperial abjection. In American texts, we encounter the colonial sublime in the racialized and sexualized figure of the brown Filipino native. The icon of the Filipino native body registers both the *racial horror* and the *sexual fascination* that were part of the visual economy of late nineteenth-century U.S. culture.

Abject images of naked black and brown natives were a common visual trope in older European colonial cultures. Anne McClintock describes an "erotics of ravishment" in the writings of European male travelers that feminized and eroticized the "uncertain continents" of Africa, the Americas, and Asia (22). McClintock offers the term "porno-tropics," highlighting the relationship between pornographic fantasies of the tropics and the brutal, often violent facts of conquest. This European porno-tropic tradition constructed nonwhite women as "the epitome of sexual aberration and excess" (22). In travel writing by European male travelers, we witness what McClintock terms the "metaphysics of gender violence," with the unknown world as feminine object to be owned and possessed by a male explorer (23). Lee Wallace, on the other hand, argues that European imperial expansion of the Pacific was a queer "sexual event" and that the iconic figure of the Pacific archive is in fact the male body as the sign and site of "sodomitical pleasures."[47] Sexual initiation was a "compulsory aspect of the Grand Tour" of the colonies for British male aristocrats (Wallace 10), while Pacific cultures represented the possibilities of homosexual initiation and errancy. In a related work, Jonathan Goldberg writes that the representation of sodomy in the New World would become a justification for violent pogroms conducted by the Spanish against forty Quarequa Indians accused of "most abominable and unnatural lechery."[48]

In European literature, the hyperheterosexualization of the black female body can be mapped in the canonical writings of nineteenth-century French writers such as Balzac, Zola, Baudelaire, and others. The figures of the mulatta, the prostitute, and the slave woman in nineteenth-century French novels and essays were icons of the "Black Venus."[49] The lubricous images of black women as sexual and dangerous bodies are constructions of "feminized darkness" and representations of French imperial power (Sharpley-Whiting 11). Drawings and photographs of breast-baring brown women from indigenous cultures, on the other hand, have long been part of American porno-tropic tradition. Island women, particularly from the cultures and peoples of the Pacific, were part of an American Pacific fetish for centuries before the arrival of Admiral George Dewey to Manila in 1898. As far back as 1791, when American geographical knowledge of the Pacific was still rudimentary, there was already economic, political, and cultural interest in the region.[50] White American writers have long imagined the "South Seas" or the Pacific as a place inhabited by dark-skinned, cannibalistic savages or as a space for an interior voyage of the self facilitated by the backwardness of the primitive cultures encountered by the white traveler. Paul Lyons observes what he calls an "American Pacific Orientalism" tradition in the writings of hundreds of whale ship captains who sold their pamphlets to the American public in the 1790s, and traces this tradition to more established writers, such as Edgar Allan Poe in his South Seas novel *Narrative of Arthur Gordon Pym*.[51] During the first decades of the nineteenth century, American traders, explorers, and politicians wrote about the Pacific and its peoples, using racialized and gendered grammars of inferiority. The Pacific by then had been charted by cartographers who drew images of naked native women on maps as metonymic representations of an exotic paradise. By the late nineteenth century, anonymous photographers brought their Kodak Brownie cameras and took photographs of Pacific Islander women for their personal collections, for publication, and for scientific study, while generations of American children had grown up with adventure stories about the West and the Pacific seacoast (Leon 20–24).

The European heterosexual porno-tropic tradition, along with images from the conquest of Native American lands and the institution of slavery, would provide templates for the sexual images of the Philippine conquest. Among the earliest articulations of a heterosexual porno-tropic tradition in the Americas were representations of Native women, in particular the narratives of Sacagawea, Pocahontas, and La Malinche. In popular accounts of the lives of these indigenous women, they are reduced to heroines or antiheroines based on how they aided the white colonial enterprise. Sacagawea is enshrined as a mythic icon of American expansion as she guided the Lewis and Clark expedition while carrying her infant son on her back; yet her myth centers on her beauty *and* her superhuman abilities as a scout—how she enabled the project of American imperial expansion in the Pacific Northwest.[52] In the case of Pocahontas, American history books immortalize her as a beautiful Indian princess who saved the life of John Smith and became the savior of the fledgling Jamestown colony. Though she did not marry him and married another white man, she is the most celebrated indigenous female figure of miscegenation, a pioneer of what Robert Tilton has described as "the quiet genocide of the native population."[53] The narrative of La Malinche (or Doña Marina) narrative is more complex. In Mexican historical accounts, she aided Hernán Cortés in his conquest of the Aztec empire "as translator, informer, mistress and sexual pawn."[54] Her acts are mythologized as acts of female treachery, the original race traitor of Mexican history. The mestizo population of Mexico descends symbolically from her treacherous deeds, "the first mixing of Indian and European blood."[55]

In British and Dutch colonies at the turn of the nineteenth century, white women were held in high esteem in a metropolitan bourgeois discourse concerned with the endangerment of white middle-class morality and white motherhood. This privileging of white women occurred in tandem with the debasement of native women's bodies as sexual servants or concubines of European men. Native women's bodies served as sexual medicine for the "colonial soul."[56] In travel handbooks for incoming plantation employees bound for Tonkin, Sumatra, and Malaya, European men were urged to have native mistresses "for quick acclimatization, as insulation from the ill-health that sexual abstention, isolation, and boredom were thought to bring."

In the American imperial imaginary, savage bodies were also docile bodies needing discipline and tutelage. Violence and benevolence went hand in glove in the American imperial project, as it engaged in the pedagogy and practice of imperial sites of discipline, such as at the Hampton Institute and the various Indian boarding schools of the early twentieth century. Discipline was a "tender violence" (Wexler) that inaugurated the visual abject body as a modern subject, often at the cost of pain, physical and mental suffering, or even death.[57] Given the Western porno-tropic traditions, the many representations of nonwhite bodies underscore the necessity to theorize imperial abjection as both gendered violence and racial conquest. In the American imperial imagination, Adam's whiteness is set against the darkness of Eve, a fallen figure and an impure, abject body. The white Adam who claims the body of Eve is a synecdoche for American imperial power that lusts for colonized land. The indigenous natives are Eve's children. Even before the military occupation of the Philippines by the United States, Asia and the rest of the non-European world served as abject zones of Western empires, sites for "pornographic fantasies long before conquest was under way, with lurid descriptions of sexual license, promiscuity, gynecological aberrations, and general perversion marking the Otherness of the colonized for metropolitan consumption."[58] Thus we cannot sever the ties between imperial fabulists and military soldiers, or the relationship between colonial erotica, travel writing, scientific racism, and military science. The production of abjection is the creation of images and discourses that are racially repugnant and sexually erotic yet formative to American imperial identity. American public culture—which includes popular cultural forms and administrative and legislative discourses—reproduces and stages the paradox of abjection as a foundational aspect of American empire-building. The "capillaries of empire" (McCoy 43–45), what one historian describes as the lifeblood of U.S.

imperial power, are not just about the science of war and counterinsurgency. The rigorous taxonomies of botanical science and later military surveillance created by Western social scientists borrowed their logic from the gynophobic gaze and the sexual vocabulary of Western travelers and fabulists of the tropics. Through abjection, the racial and gendered fictions of conquest that created Filipino objecthood are unraveled, highlighting the role of late nineteenth- and early twentieth-century popular culture in American empire-building.

Chapter 2

Face

Necropolitics and the
U.S. Imperial Photography Complex

In 1900, a writer named Charles Ray chronicled the American public's fascination with the "Philippine campaign"[1] in an essay, "Following a War with the Camera." He described the war in the Philippine Islands as an "insurrection"—merely a military campaign against a ragtag band of Filipino dissenters, or *insurrectos*. This rhetorical strategy was an example of abjection at work, which uses more neutral terms such as "campaign" and "insurrection" to describe a war between an invading imperial power and a fledgling republic struggling to keep sovereignty. Muting or excising the violence of the Philippine-American War was a common practice of American writers at the time. History books in the Philippines published by the colonial government early on in the occupation emphasized the centuries of cruelty under Spanish rule and the positive introduction of modernity by the United States.[2] In the United States, Americans were being persuaded to forget the war's brutality by academics and writers who rewrote the war as a civilizing implement that opened the Islands to American education and culture.[3] These acts of revising history aside, what visibly remains of the period are photographic images taken by unnamed photographers.

An artifact of imperial modernity that Charles Ray discussed in detail is the stereoscopic card, or stereograph as it was commonly known: a mounted photograph viewed through a device called a stereoscope, which gave it a three-dimensional effect. Stereographs were popular diversions for middle-class white Americans to view and experience, among others, the Philippine campaigns and to gaze at the United States' new "marvelous possessions." Americans could order stereo cards or "stereo views" through catalogs, view them at home at their leisure, and acquire a 3-D perspective of their colony (Ray 477).

While "war sketches" or artist's depictions of war scenes were popular visual mediums, the lifelike depth of stereo cards allowed one to see, not mere artist's drawings, but "facsimiles of real scenes." This facsimile of reality through a photographic image was also accompanied by a caption, so that viewing an image included a specific interpretation of an event. The meaning of an image, after all, is dependent on its context, which includes information from the caption, as well as on the nature of the publication as a "channel of transmission."[4] For example, Ray's essay was accompanied by different photographs from the Underwood and Underwood Company, with captions lauding the benevolent and civilizing mission of the United States. Ray described the "United States bluejackets" as valiant soldiers who were fighting bravely despite being thousands of miles away from home. Another caption narrated the ethical treatment of Filipino insurgents cared for by American doctors in makeshift U.S. military hospitals (Ray 480). The photographer and the war correspondent, according to Ray, were heroic men who braved the dangers of war to fulfill their duty, "which is to get the very latest incidents" for the war-hungry American public (Ray 481). In all, the photographs and captions functioned similarly to Ray's euphemistic use of "campaign" and "insurrection," in which abjection provides an extenuating cover to the violence of the U.S. war of occupation in the Philippines. By identifying and analyzing abjection in these imperial images, one can therefore uncover the bloodier and more baneful aspects of American colonial expansion that were excised from the U.S. nation's myths.

FACES OF DEATH AND THE IMPERIAL SELF

Historically, the creation of photographic images of dead soldiers after battles is an American documentary tradition dating from the Civil War.[5] The corpse is the ultimate icon of abjection. While it is "the most sickening of wastes,"[6] the corpse of a soldier slain on the battlefield was nonetheless a meaningful image to the national imagination. For much of Civil War photography, the images of dead white soldiers taken after battle were more than just scenes of death but were scenes of American nationhood. As Alan Trachtenberg reminds us, Civil War images "participate by proposing the visual terms on which victory and healing—the remembrance of sacrifice—might be conceived" (23). I would add that the visual terms of victory and healing rested on *race and gender*, specifically through the sanctified bodies of white male American soldiers. Civil War photographs transformed the savagery of war, in particular the nation's memories of the deaths of hundreds of thousands of mostly white American soldiers, into martyrdom and the sacred. By elevating the carnage of war—such as through the iconic Civil War photograph entitled *The Harvest of War*—into a "sacral emblem" of sacrifice, violent war photographs ironically preserved the peace of mind and equanimity of the white, American, middle-class viewer (Trachtenberg 10).

It was during the "Indian wars" of the late nineteenth century that American stereo views and postcards featured images of "new" dead photographic subjects—Native Americans. The face of death was now a brown face, the savage enemy's face. Since the early explorations of the New World, Westerners have recorded images of native peoples for purposes that ranged from the "anthropological to (the) romantic" (Wexler 194–95). But it is historical violence that defines the image of Native Americans in the American imagination. The history of the genocide of Native peoples committed by the U.S. Army haunts the empathic portraits made by distinguished American photographers such as Gertrude Käisber, Edward Curtis, and William Henry Jackson. The context of Native American portraiture, after all, is death. As contemporary Native artist Jimmie Durham put it, "All photographs of American Indians are photographs of dead people, in that their use assumes ownership of the subject, which is seen as static, completely 'understandable.'"[7]

By "seeing Indians" as dead enemies, American victory was understandable and Native deaths acceptable, at least for some Americans of the nineteenth century. As Susan Sontag reminds us, "To photograph people is to violate them, by seeing them as they never see themselves.... It turns people into objects that can be symbolically possessed" (14). In the case of photographs of dead Native Americans, stereo views and postcards allowed a collector to celebrate American victory over the "savages" and to own a keepsake of an important historical moment. Such photographs were trophies of American military progress and Anglo-Saxon superiority. Through captions that frame the photograph's interpretation, American war images from the "Indian wars" minimized the human pain and suffering of the savage enemy. In this case, the enemy's body, dead or alive, is not a human body, but a collection of body parts—naked of sympathy or empathy, unrecognizable and unlamented.

The popular late nineteenth-century phrase "The only good Indian is a dead Indian" was an expression of imperial abjection that found its way to commercial postcards and stereograph images of dead Native Americans. Jokes about Native genocide were an ordinary part of fin de siècle American popular culture. The popularity of the saying was attested to by Theodore Roosevelt in 1886, when he said: "I don't go so far as to think that the only good Indians are dead Indians, but I believe nine out of ten are." Fifteen years after making this statement in a speech in New York, Roosevelt was president of the United States, proving that the coinage of the racist phrase had reached the highest office.[8] The phrase regarding "dead Indians" as "good Indians" requires the refashioning of the slaughter of Native peoples into humorous entertainment, as well as into more serious discourses of "racial and social progress" (Huhndorf 47). And by the late nineteenth century, after the U.S. Army's genocidal military campaigns and conquest of Native American lands, the once-feared Indians were now "good" abject subjects—either dead or confined in reservations.

Thus, photography's protean form enables the medium to be used *for and against* war and empire. Inscribed in its very form is what Susie Linfield describes as the "dialectic" of photography, or its paradox: while a photographic image renders violence visible, it also "embraces its opposite, though sometimes unknowingly."[9] In brief, while the history of photography has shown that, more than any modern medium, it has recorded and possibly celebrated the violence of war and empire, photographs also have the opposite effect—either muting the horror and instilling apathy, or shocking the viewer and organizing protest (Linfield 33).

A central argument of the chapter, and indeed the rest of this book, is the belief that images are "like living organisms," and images from the past "have lives and desires of their own"[10] that do not always correspond to the original creator's possibly racist or imperialist intent. As the Cherokee artist Jimmie Durham expounds:

> Even the system is not completely closed. Geronimo (Apache), as an Indian "photographic subject," blew out the windows. On his own, he reinvested the concept of photographs of American Indians. At least he did so as far as he could, concerning pictures of himself, which are so ubiquitous that he must have sought "photo opportunities" as eagerly as the photographers. Yet even when he was "posed" by the man behind the camera, he seems to have destroyed the pose and created his own stance. In every image, he looks through the camera at the viewer, seriously, intently, with a specific message. Geronimo uses the photograph to "get at" those people who imagine themselves as the "audience" of his struggles. He seems to be trying to see us. He is demanding to be seen on his own terms. (Holt 104)

Durham believes in the limitless meanings of a historical photograph—that is, the photographic system is "not completely closed"—as he shows in describing the portraits of the Apache leader Geronimo after his arrest by Major General Henry Ware Lawton in 1886.[11] Durham views Geronimo's many portraits as artifacts of agency rather than merely portraits of Native American defeat or death. He invests dignity and humanity in the portraits of an incarcerated Native American leader, suggesting that our contemporary acts of reading historical images are enabled by the paradox of photography. Thus, he argues for, not just "seeing the Indian" as an object, but seeing him as a historical agent, an actual, living individual who might have posed intentionally and created "his own stance."

Photographs thus provoke and disturb us into thinking of imperial abjection as both absence *and* presence. Philippine-American War photographs register multiple forms of absence: the invisibility or the abject status of the Philippine-American War in the American popular imagination as well as in its official history, and the absence of a reliable accounting of the deaths during the war. In other words, there is no mourning or melancholia for this forgotten American war. The Filipino colonial photographs are also literal representations of abject icons of death: that is, the images of Filipino cadavers after battle (abject bodies), and the American soldiers who were perpetrators and witnesses to the horror of a colonial war (agents of abjection). But while most war photographs are traditionally read as "spaces of death,"[12] other observers, like Durham, have described colonial images as spaces of presence, as artifacts of subject-making even under the most dehumanizing, brutal, and impossible conditions. The critical act of reading photographs of war demands that we account for the actual lives recorded in a visual image and reflect on what W. J. T. Mitchell describes as the paradox of a photographic image: "that it is alive—but also dead; powerful—but also weak; meaningful—but also meaningless" (11).

An example of a Philippine photograph that records and reveals the violence of empire can be found in the booklet of war photographs by F. Tennyson Neely entitled *Fighting in the Philippines* (1899). The book shows a photograph of dead Filipinos in a trench, surrounded by American soldiers looking on (figure 3).[13] The caption states, "After the battle of Santa Ana, February 5, 1899." More than a dozen American soldiers surround the trench littered with corpses, a heap of undistinguishable human bodies in soiled clothes and straw hats. Some of the white American soldiers stare into the camera, while the others look at the dead, all framed by a tropical backdrop of banana trees. The Anti-Imperialist League republished this same photograph for another purpose—as the frontispiece of a book *Liberty Poems: Inspired by the Crisis of 1898–1900* (1900), a collection of antiwar poems penned by members and supporters of the League.[14] The different political uses for the same photograph suggest the paradoxical power of the photographic image, and how photographs can celebrate as well as expose the violence of colonialism and war. While this photograph circulated in different publications and with different political messages at the turn of the twentieth century, the passing of time has rendered the photograph as abject, and its use as a polemic against power and war as having greater resonance and agreement. As Mitchell reminds us, "We need to account for not just the power of images but their powerlessness, their impotence, their abjection" (Mitchell

Fig. 3. Artifacts of war and empire: A photograph of dead Filipinos in a trench as American soldiers look on. The photograph was published in two politically different publications, *Fighting in the Philippines* (1899), an illustrated book of war photographs, and in an anthology of poems against the Philippine-American War, entitled *Liberty Poems. Inspired by the Crisis of 1898–1900* (1900). The photograph was auctioned on eBay a few years ago. From the National Archives collection.

10). The task then is to return to the imperial archive and study imperial images as representations of abjection.

THE EMPIRE'S PHILIPPINE ARCHIVE

Numerous photographs of elite native families, revolutionary leaders, ordinary citizens in towns, the countryside, cities, and other places were taken at the turn of the twentieth century by American soldiers, anthropologists, colonial officials, tourists, and others. Jonathan Best writes that throughout their colonial adventures, it was a common practice for American soldiers and visitors to Manila to collect inexpensive postcards and to take pictures of Philippine scenes with their Brownie cameras.[15] At the time, the Kodak Company offered inexpensive roll film that produced small photographic prints for souvenir albums (Best 9). Best writes that at one point after the arrival of U.S. forces in

1898, there were "276 photographers in the Philippines," suggesting that photography was very much in demand and part of late nineteenth-century Filipino life.[16]

Soon after the victory of Admiral George Dewey over the Spanish fleet in Manila Bay and the mock battle staged by Spain and the United States to cover up the negotiated transfer of the Philippines from one to the other, stereo photographers arrived to document scenes of Philippine life.[17] Before long, they were taking photographs of another war. The resulting stereo views of the Philippine-American War were quickly put on sale by companies such as Underwood and Underwood, Keystone, Kilburn, and H. C. White (Waldsmith 157). Gruesome images of dead Filipinos after battle with the U.S. Army became easily available to curious viewers (Waldsmith 157). Such war scenes were not only popular entertainment but educational. Public schools around the country bought "boxed sets," series of stereo views "sold in special containers as a unit" (Waldsmith 173). By 1901, Underwood and Underwood was producing and selling almost twenty-five thousand stereographs per day: "Thousands of sets were sold to schools and public libraries and larger churches for Sunday school lessons" (Waldsmith 174). In 1924, the Keystone Company produced sets of one thousand stereo views with accompanying handbooks.[18] These visual aids were seen by millions of American children in schools and in churches.

The American camera thus brought brown and black bodies into popular culture, when Asian, Pacific, and Caribbean images were introduced to the public as by-products of the Spanish-American War. Magazines such as *Leslie's Weekly* and *Harper's Weekly* ran advertisements that offered "war pictures" for framing or an album of a photographic history of "America's war with Spain," which included Philippine scenes.

The image of the Filipino thus entered the American "visual terrain"[19] mapped by race, nation, and abjection. For this chapter, we look at two sources of Philippine photographs: the National Archive's photographic collection (from the records of the Bureau of Insular Affairs and the War Department) and the Library of Congress's commercial stereograph collection. The National Archive's Records of the Bureau of Insular Affairs, General Photographs of the Philippine Islands 1898–1935 have alphabetical designations that correspond to a colonial taxonomy. The catalog begins with "agriculture," moves on to "education," "forestry," "mines and mining," "prisons and penal colonies," and Filipino immigrants in Hawai'i. The inclusion of Filipino migrant workers in Hawai'i with colonial photographs is a piece of a diasporic puzzle highlighting what other critical Filipino studies scholars have argued: empire and diaspora define the experience of Filipino communities who live and settle in North America.

Most Philippine colonial images do not cite the name of the photographer, and, in some cases, the names were blocked out, particularly for the more graphic views after a battle. There is also very little information about the human subjects who posed for the camera. Rather than viewing these images as an "authorless archive" (Morris 26), which is often the case for most photographs of colonial Southeast Asia, we consider the American colonial state as the author and the distributor of these Philippine images. More than a hundred years ago, the photographs were used for army surveillance but were later circulated in magazines, newspapers, journals, books, and other forms of mass culture, and then became popular texts that would heighten support for American imperial expansion by "erasing the violence of colonial encounters in the very act of portraying them" (Wexler 7). These photographic images are images of not only physical or actual death, but also social death and the psychic violence of abjection. The paradox of visibility will remain a central theme of much of this book—that by the very act of representing the Filipino colonial subject in American popular texts, the violent circumstances of her or his visibility are erased. These Philippine colonial photographs—whether they are stereographs sold for commercial profit or albums kept by an institution such as the Bureau of Insular Affairs or the War Department—then transform images of war into units of data that produce "sequential regularity" (Trachtenberg 5) and produce the enunciability of empire as a "way of life" for early twentieth-century Americans.[20]

From the time of the Spanish-American War onward, the star of the American empire burned bright. In magazines and journals of the time, advertisements for "war views" and pictorial books were published alongside ads for breakfast cocoa and cough drops (figures 4 and 5). The popularity of war photographs, stereoscope viewers, and illustrated journals can be read as the public's support for American expansion. It can also be read as the fascination for what were then new imperial "technologies of vision."[21] The violence of a war of conquest was viewed at a safe distance in the comfort of Victorian homes, what the late scholar Jim Zwick has called the "war from the parlor."[22] Turn-of-the-century Americans saw violent photographs of the war, such as that of Filipino corpses in trenches taken after battles, that were published in newspapers of the time, but the captions on the photographs emphasized the military victory of the U.S. Army and not the violence (Best 213). These visual technologies that focused on victory over violence underscore the importance of abjection in the creation of an American imperial ideology. An American empire in the Pacific was not only instituted through violence, but was also created through photographic images that excised the violence of war or framed violence as American victory. An army of unknown American photographers, scholars, journalists, artists, and writers formed the lifeblood of the American empire and produced what Lanny Thompson calls an "imperial archipelago,"[23] which

Fig. 4. Imperial visual culture. At the turn of the twentieth century, advertisements for the Kodak Brownie camera and "lantern slides of the war," a precursor of the photographic slide, were published in magazines. Circa 1898.

compiled knowledge, such as visual imagery of the Philippine colony, for military and ideological purposes. Photographic images served the U.S. empire's need for "serviceable information" that enabled military strength, produced consent at home, and silenced dissent in the Philippines and in the United States (McCoy 45).

For example, W. M. Goldthwaite's book *The United States of the World* (1902)

Fig. 5. Imperial visual culture. An advertisement for "war pictures" included photographs of Admiral George Dewey fighting in the mock battle of Manila Bay. Circa 1898.

begins with a poem that romanticizes war and the colonization of the Philippines as the imperial destiny of the United States: "Not Westward now alone, but to the sun—/ Full Eastward—must our Star of Empire run."[24] The verse summarizes westward imperial expansion as a natural process. The global reach of the U.S. nation must not be limited to the conquest of the continent, with the occupation of the Southwest and Native American lands, but "full Eastward" (actually, westward) to lands of the East, and to immortality or "to the sun." Goldthwaite's book contains several colorized photographs of war battles between the American military forces and the Philippine revolutionary army. The photographs illustrate the verse's romantic and naturalized description of empire-building, where imperial war is reduced to a visual spectacle that glosses over the messy reality of carnage, corpses, wounded Filipino civilians, grieving widows, and orphans.

To create consent and support for the forced occupation of the Philippine Islands, photography took on the ideological work of representing the pleasures of empire-building through *necropolitics*, a rhetoric of imperial abjection.[25] As Achille Mbembe observes, necropolitics is the supreme exercise of the power to kill, to allow to live, or to expose to death certain persons (11). Necropolitics is a logic of American imperial abjection that visualizes American imperialism as both an aggressive violence *and* a "tender violence" that includes gentle forms of social death such as everyday life under military rule and colonial discipline through education. In the late nineteenth century, American discourses on domesticity were coded with the necessity of violence for the abject subjects of American modernity (Wexler 52–53), and we trace these discourses of tender violence and racial sentiment in Philippine colonial photographs. Filipino colonial photographs produce and disseminate the "sensory conditions"[26] that rendered American imperial modernity visible and legible. Photography takes part in war by documenting those who are the agents of abjection, or icons and symbols of U.S. imperial power (the colonizer), and those who are the abject groups, or persons who must be subjected to the terror of U.S. colonial rule (the colonized Filipino native).

In this framework, the "colony," and earlier in history the "frontier," is "the location par excellence" of necropolitics (Mbembe 24) and abjection. American visual culture of the late nineteenth century romanticized the idea of the Philippine colony as the new American frontier in the Pacific. A colony is "the zone where the violence of the state of exception is deemed to operate in the service of 'civilization'" (Mbembe 24). This is exactly the logic of American necropolitics after 1899: to civilize the Filipino savages through violence and colonial rule. By creating the legal fiction of American sovereignty over the islands (Kramer 88) and by turning Filipino "rebels" into criminals, the colonial camera enabled this state of exception by projecting savagery and criminality onto the Filipino body.

As artifacts of American imperial abjection, photographs contributed to the success of U.S. empire-building in two ways. First, they reproduced American imperial abjection by their very *form*. Through the "aestheticizing tendency" of photography, Filipino suffering (the war) and Filipino otherness (racialization and eroticization) are reduced to visual spectacle, to mere images, thus minimizing the carnage of war and the trauma of occupation and racism, while offering reliable witness and justification to the triumph of American progress. When these photographs show proof of a winnable war to a young and brash nation ready to become a world power, such as the United States after the

Spanish-American War, they build consent among the public for the imperial enterprise.

Second, photographs reproduced imperial abjection through their inherently objective, dehumanizing documentary *function*. By reducing complex Filipino histories and realities into war documentation and colonial surveillance, photography transformed Filipino subjects into raw data—the disembodied bearers of anthropological information. This science of the "natural world" would be incorporated into the science of counterinsurgency in the succeeding decades of U.S. military rule in the Philippines. The relationship of photography to counterinsurgency will be discussed in the final chapter of this study.

Philippine colonial photographs from the turn of the twentieth century thus make up the *American imperial photography complex*, the archive that helped shape the reception of events and ideas associated with U.S. imperial expansion.[27] In the succeeding discussion, I trace the various articulations of abjection through three visual themes: white American imperial masculinity, death, and docility.

WHITE IMPERIAL MASCULINITY

In the mid-nineteenth century, European photographs operated through a double system of representation that functioned both "*honorifically* and *repressively*."[28] The honorific function of photography dates back to the origins of portraiture in seventeenth-century Europe, when portraits of the upper classes provided the "ceremonial presentation of the bourgeois self" (Sekula 345) and served as moral exemplars to the citizenry. The repressive function of photography, on the other hand, emerged from the requirements of sciences such as medicine, anatomy, and criminology to understand disease and human deviation. Bodies represented in the imperial archive are therefore mostly those of the nation's heroes, leaders, and upper classes and of the nation's marginalized deviant Others: "the poor," "the criminal, the nonwhite, the female, and all other embodiments of the unworthy" (Sekula 347).

Photographs of American soldiers in the Philippine-American War exemplify the honorific function of photography by reconstructing idealized images of white imperial masculinity and heterosexualization. Soldiers' photographs reproduce what Radhika Mohanram describes as a white imperial masculinity that compels "the social, cultural, and juridical injunctions of capitalism and colonialism."[29] Through their manliness and whiteness, American agents of abjection and empire cut honorable masculine figures. In figure 6, a photograph of General Arthur MacArthur, father of General Douglas MacArthur, presents

Fig. 6. White imperial masculinity: Portrait of General Arthur MacArthur in the Philippines. From the National Archives collection of the Bureau of Insular Affairs.

an imperial Adamic figure as the commander of the American army in the Philippines. His immaculate officer's uniform heightens his imperial whiteness, contrasted against the dark background of tropical foliage. The caption at the back of the photo says, "appears to be taken in the Philippines," again proving that the circumstances behind these early photographs are seldom known with certainty, even by sources close to the very famous figure in the photograph. General MacArthur has the stern yet serene pose of a leader in charge of superior forces, confident of victory. Yet he was at the same time one of the early advocates of surveillance and counterintelligence, even before the guerrilla phase of the Philippine-American War (McCoy 27), which would indicate that he understood the difficulty of jungle warfare even against an inferior foe.

In figure 7, MacArthur poses with his staff. The formal portrait of General MacArthur and his staff presents empire-building as a masculine task undertaken by the true sons of empire. Thirty-three men pose with MacArthur in front of two large American flags that serve as the backdrop. MacArthur sits with his higher-ranking officers as they hold their scabbard and swords with gloved hands, their hats on their laps. This photograph of white imperial manhood recalls similar photographs of the conquest of the American West, primarily because the officers and soldiers sent to the Philippine Islands in 1899 were the same men who fought and subjugated the American Indians during the "Indian wars."[30] In this image, the histories and ideologies connected to "Indian fighting" are continued: the Philippines was the new "West" or frontier that had to be conquered and won. The confident poses repeat the honorific representation by European portraiture and photography of capable soldiers of a Western colonial power who are peacefully civilizing savages yet are really pursuing the same brutal campaigns that have been used by white nations against the darker races. In this photograph, the officers personify superior Adamic figures, the noble sons doing the work of U.S. empire-building in the Philippine colony. The heterosexualization and racialization of conquest thus defined the American military images from the period, when imperialism was seen as an expression of American manhood, the unavoidable and logical future of a vigorous, young nation that cannot be held back by the past or "legislative traditions" (Hoganson 158). The gendered idealization of an emergent American world power was much utilized by U.S. imperialists, who argued that the nation was a virile young man who "should not be confined to the domestic sphere."

The photograph of General MacArthur and his staff is especially interesting because of two of the officers pictured therein. (All the officers were identified at the back of the original photograph.) The first officer of interest is Lt. James H. Blount (third row, far left), who would later serve as a judge in the Philip-

Fig. 7. White imperial masculinity: Sons of empire. Caption: "General [Arthur] MacArthur and staff Manila 1900." MacArthur is in the front row, fourth from right. In the photograph are two officers of note. First, Lt. James H. Blount, third row, standing in the far left, would later serve as a judge in the Philippines and published a critical account of the war, *The American Occupation of the Philippines* (1914). Second, Capt. John R. M. Taylor, back row, standing third from left, was commissioned by the Bureau of Insular Affairs in 1902 to write a history of the Philippine "insurrection" based on captured documents from the Katipunan. Taylor's multivolume manuscript displeased the War Department and was banned from publication for more than fifty years. Taylor's study was never published in the United States, but a version was published in the Philippines in 1971.

pines and would publish a critical account of the war in his book *The American Occupation of the Philippines* (1912).[31] Blount's book revealed, among other things, censorship by the military, particularly by General Elwell Otis, and the racism of colonial administrator Dean C. Worcester, whose "Kodak" images of Philippine "savages" will be discussed in the final chapter. James H. Blount would also later support independence for the Philippines.

The second officer of note is Capt. John Roger Meigs Taylor (top row, third from right), who was assigned to write an official history of the Philippine "insurrection" as a way to silence those who were critical of American military atrocities committed against Filipinos. For four years, Taylor and his staff examined more than two hundred thousand documents in Spanish and Tagalog, captured from the Filipino revolutionary government and shipped to Washington, DC, in 1902.[32] By 1906, Taylor had completed his five-volume manuscript, *The Philippine Insurrection Against the United States: A Compilation of Documents with Notes and Introductions*, which discussed only around fifteen hundred documents out of the "three tons of materials" he and his staff had looked at (Farrell 393). The galley proofs of his book were sent to then secretary of war and president-elect William Howard Taft. Influenced by a lengthy negative review of the manuscript by a rival historian (and former assistant of both Worcester and Taft) named James LeRoy,[33] Taft decided that Capt. Taylor's manuscript was too controversial, since it revealed some embarrassing facts. Among other things, it exposed that some former Filipino revolutionary leaders were now collaborators working for the American colonial government in 1906, and that Philippine independence had significant support from many sectors, including Democratic anti-imperialists (Farrell 58). As a result, the War Department would suppress the publication of Taylor's manuscript for half a century; Taylor in fact never saw his manuscript published and retired in obscurity. It wasn't until 1957 that the galley proofs were given to the Philippine government, and the book was later published in the Philippines in 1971, with an introduction by Filipino nationalist historian Renato Constantino.[34] Given the brutal nature of the U.S. military campaign, it is perhaps not surprising that at least two of the thirty-four officers in the photograph later criticized their country's conduct. Yet, taken at face value, this photograph—and countless other similarly posed photographs—seemingly shows nothing other than a united front of single-minded warriors. No one viewing the photograph would even think that any of these men would ever question their country's integrity. The concept of abjection encourages us to be aware of, and examine and understand, the fissures that can exist behind such apparently unambiguous images.

The stereo image in figure 8, copyrighted in 1899, seems to be of an armed encounter where the circumstances are not very clear but whose outcome the caption ("For the Stars and Stripes!—Death in the ranks of the Kansans") forcefully summarizes, emphasizing how the "dead" soldier, in the bottom right of the stereo views, had given up his life for the American nation. In truth, most of the encounters between American and Filipino fighters were one-sided, as the latter tended to be ill-equipped and poorly trained. This seems to have been corroborated by the photograph, which (despite the melodrama of the caption) shows that the disciplined American troops continued to fire back, in full standing formation without breaking rank, with an officer behind them directing, while one of their numbers ministered to their fallen comrade. Such

Fig. 8. White imperial masculinity: death as sacrifice. Original caption: "For the Stars and Stripes!—Death in the ranks of the Kansans." Copyright 1899. From the Library of Congress online collection.

Fig. 9. Imperial domestic image. Caption: "Filipino Women Seeking Help from American Soldiers." No date. From the Library of Congress online collection.

Fig. 10. Imperial domestic image from a stereograph. Caption: "A welcome to Uncle Sam's protection—three Filipinos entering American lines, Pasay, P.I. [Philippine Islands]." Copyright 1899. From the Library of Congress online collection.

supreme confidence under fire could only have been mustered by troops completely assured of their superior firepower.

Figures 9 and 10 are stereo images of American soldiers interacting with Filipino civilians. The photographs can be classified as "imperial domestic images" used as propaganda (Wexler 21), with soldiers engaged not in combat as in the previous photograph, but in nonaggressive, even humanitarian, activity. In figure 9, the caption on the stereo card points out the benevolence of American soldiers ("Filipino Women Seeking Help from American Soldiers," no year). Four soldiers surround two Filipinas, one holding an infant in her arms. In the far background, more soldiers are looking on. One Filipina on the left clasps her hands with a distraught look on her face, as she seems to be addressing the soldier in the foreground. The woman with the baby also seems worriedly focused on this soldier. Another soldier stands directly behind the women, with a strange smile on his face. It may well be, as the caption claims, that the women were seeking help from the soldiers. The photograph clearly shows that the configuration of power—white military masculinity set against brown feminine frailty—is completely skewed; only the soldiers are in any position to provide assistance, yet it appears from their expressions and body language that they are not feeling much solicitude toward the women. The soldier in front still has his rifle, even though he is resting on it. Two soldiers at the back have their arms crossed, which does not suggest empathy. Yes, it may very well be that the caption states the truth, yet absent any other information about the photograph, it would not be wrong to imagine a different scenario taking place here, such as that of an interrogation being conducted by the soldiers on the civilian women. At any rate, regardless of what the actual situation was, the one undeniable "domestic" scene being depicted in this photograph is that of a country at war with the United States, with the faces and bodies of the Filipino civilians suggesting the wretched conditions of war and occupation.

In figure 10, the caption reads: "A welcome to Uncle Sam's protection—three Filipinos entering American lines, Pasay, P.I. [Philippine Islands]." This caption is more believable than the one in the previous photograph if one compares the proximity between the American soldiers and Filipino civilians in both images. In figure 9 the Filipinos are standing more than an arm's length away from the Americans. It may be that the soldiers were following Victorian propriety in keeping a respectful distance between the sexes, but as stated earlier, their body language suggests instead an apathetic divide. In contrast, figure 10 shows Americans and Filipinos bunched together, shoulder to shoulder, a closeness that does not appear to be ironical or farcical, even though the soldiers seemed to have been enjoying a light moment while taking a break from hostilities (two of the soldiers are drinking from goblets; three are smoking). One soldier has even sought to enhance his proximity by crouching down so he is nearer in height to the Filipino beside him. This photograph was likely used to point out how American troops have been protecting helpless Filipino civilians caught in the crossfire, yet the three Filipinos pictured here do not seem too comfortable surrounded by their supposed protectors. The Filipino male, in particular, is downcast and submissive, unable to look at his new guardians or even at the camera, unlike the Filipina beside him. The photograph seems to show that despite American efforts to welcome them into their lines, the Filipinos are uneasy to be in this situation, which tends to be consistent with the psychology of many early colonial encounters.

Technological prowess is a proven fuel to colonization. Advances in nautical and military technology, for instance, facilitated the colonial expansion of many European nations, who used long-range ships, cannons, and muskets to subjugate peoples who had none of those technologies. The United States, although a latecomer to empire, was no exception, as it relied on a modern communications technology, the telegraph (figure 11), and on more effective killing machines, such as the Gatling gun (figure 12), to quickly defeat organized resistance and set up a colonial government in the Philippines. In figure 11, a young American soldier transcribes telegraph messages as other American soldiers look on. The telegraph allowed Americans to move troops quickly, first in pursuit of retreating Filipino forces under Aguinaldo and later to wage war and to secure conquered territory against Filipino guerrillas who continued their resistance. The telegraph was so essential to U.S. military efforts that Filipinos took to cutting telegraph lines to hinder American troop mobility and make them more vulnerable to guerrilla attacks. Thus, although the soldier transcribing the telegraph message appears to be performing a relatively benign activity, he was nonetheless a significant figure of imperial modernity and masculinity.

There is no such doubt about the manhood being displayed in figure 12, where five American soldiers pose almost nonchalantly beside a Gatling gun. The gun's terrible potential for "mass slaughter" had given U.S. forces great superiority in firepower as well as some psychological advantage over Filipino troops (McCoy 29). As an effective weapon for quelling resistance against U.S. rule, the Gatling gun was an object of imperial masculinity. The soldiers posing next to the gun are agents of imperial abjection who compel the regime of empire through the terror of the Gatling gun. The casual poses of the soldiers on the left and the right, their arms resting on the gun's wheel mount, highlight their confident virility, and the manliness of war is suggested by the phallic barrels of the Gatling gun.

The telegraph and the Gatling gun were first tested on Native Americans during the last of the Indian wars and were later exported to the Philippines to reprise their effective empire-building roles. The photographs of white soldiers posing with these technologies are imperial honorific portraits of U.S. agents of abjection, which were created at the same time that ethnographic images of the naked Filipino savage were being disseminated. Not coincidentally perhaps, the same dissemination of photographs of honorific white and savage Native American subjects had taken place during the Indian wars to provide a rationale to western expansion. "Seeing whiteness," particularly white imperial masculinity, reverses the gaze of the colonial camera by focusing on the spectacular male bodies that mythologize empire through race and masculinity. As photographs of abjection, these images do not have to depict actual scenes of violence or carnage, but instead represent indices of violence through the visual representation of objects of imperial warfare.

DEATH

Given the surreptitious nature of guerrilla warfare, the U.S. Army could not distinguish between civilians and rebels, and could not definitively tell who was *amigo* or *insurrecto*. A common racist phrase among soldiers, again borrowing a similar saying from the Indian wars, was "The only true *Amigo* is the dead *Amigo*."[35] It is quite probable that many soldiers were soon making good on this saying or had simply given up on trying to tell the difference between a combatant and a civilian, because Filipino civilian casualties far outnumbered combat deaths. Guerrilla war, because its morality is so contingent and its outcome so irresolute, can unnerve the nation that enjoys the superior firepower. American journalist Stephen Bonsal, who visited the Philippines for three months in 1902 during the guerrilla phase of the Philippine-American War, writes in his account that, despite American government reports, the rebellion was "chronic" and that the Filipino guerrillas were "winning" through strategies of "subterfuge and disguise,"[36] even though there were still fifty thousand U.S. troops in the Philippine Islands after the official end of the war. He describes with frustration what was then called *amigo* warfare: "When a band of insurgents in Batangas is hard pressed by our soldiers, when they have bushwhacked an army train, shot down teamsters, cut to pieces a small detachment, or murdered a lonely signal-corps man . . . they store their guns in bamboo logs, put on *amigo* clothes, and once beyond the borders of Batangas, amuse themselves with cock-fighting and fiestas, like all the other *hombres*" (Bonsal 412).

To help manage disquieting news from the Philippines and to calm national anxieties regarding the constitutionality of war and imperialism, American publications regularly displayed dead Filipino bodies. Stereograph companies even sold photographs of dead "Filipino *amigos*," using the phrase as a caption for the stereoscopic cards. Viewed by turn-of-the-century Americans through the racial and gendered frames of abjection, empire's violence was muted and even mooted by the imperative for American victory. If abjection is the symptom (the monstrous) and the sublime (the magnificence) of empire, images of the slain Filipino "enemy" are both the symptom and the sublime of empire, in photographs that are both violent and celebratory. The Filipino cadaver, rebel or civilian, becomes a sign of American nationhood and victory, an emblem of the *American imperial sublime*.

This sublime is very much in evidence in the photograph of numerous Filipino corpses in a ditch (figure 13) captioned, "After a skirmish, Singalong." Singalong is part of the district of Santa Ana in Manila, where much fighting occurred during the early months of the war. There is scant detail, apart

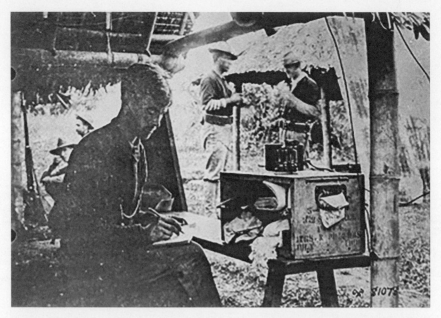

Fig. 11. White imperial masculinity: manhood and technology. No date. From the National Archives collection of the Bureau of Insular Affairs.

Fig. 12. White American imperial masculinity: the Gatling gun as object of masculinity. No date. From the National Archives collection of the Bureau of Insular Affairs.

Fig. 13. After a battle in Singalong, a town near the district of Santa Ana. No date. Original photograph taken from the National Archives collection of the Bureau of Insular Affairs.

Fig. 14: Imperial sublime: The war photograph is republished in the illustrated book *Fighting in the Philippines* (1899). The book features actual war scenes, Philippine landscapes, Filipino natives, American soldiers, and corpses of slain Filipino insurgents.

Fig. 15. Enemy corpse. Caption: "A Sacrifice to Aguinaldo's ambition—Behind the Filipino trenches after the Battle of Malabon, P.I. [Philippine Islands]. Copyright 1899." From the Library of Congress online collection.

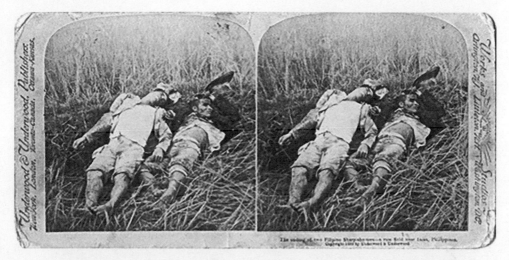

Fig. 16. Enemy corpse. Caption: "The ending of two Filipino Sharp-shooters—a rice field in Imus, Philippines. Copyright 1899." From the Library of Congress online collection.

from the photograph, about this little "skirmish" that resulted in an impressive number of enemy dead. The photograph itself is found in a National Archives folder labeled "Records of U.S. Army Overseas." The photo was then published in the illustrated book *Fighting in the Philippines* (1899) with the caption: "The American Artillery did wonderful execution in the battles with the insurgents. In a trench at Santa Ana the Tagal [*sic*] dead lay in piles. The group shown in the picture consisted of thirty-eight bodies" (Figure 14). Apart from the admirable diligence someone must have employed in painstakingly counting the number of corpses in the trench (stacked on top of each other, the dead bodies are almost impossible to tell apart in the photograph), there is also much to admire in the unabashed triumphalism of the caption. Indeed, artillery will do a "wonderful execution" of any enemy unfortunate enough to be in its range. The term "Tagal" is a misspelling of the term *Tagalog*, which was used interchangeably to refer to natives from the central region of Luzon island that includes Manila. The placement of this photograph alongside the one showing a large troop of Americans looking at stacks of railroad iron from an unfinished rebel barricade seems to imply (perhaps unwittingly) a parallelism: those who dare to stand up against Americans will end up lying dead in piles at their feet.

Figures 15 and 16 are stereo cards showing scenes taken after battle, circa 1899. In figure 15, two dead Filipino rebels lie contorted on the ground while three American soldiers look on. The Americans are in the upper half of the

Fig. 17. Taken by the "Engineering Office Department," but the name of the photographer is crossed out. The dead Filipino soldiers are in a trench close to Bagbag River in Bulacan, a town near Manila.

Fig. 18. Censorship and the undeclared second phase of the Philippine-American War: The photograph of the 1906 "Battle at Bud Dajo" (in Sulu Province) was taken four years after the Philippine "insurrection" was declared over in 1902. Over a thousand Tausug Muslims, mostly women and children, were killed by General Leonard Wood's army. The negative of this photograph was "accidentally" destroyed by an unnamed American official. Published in Oswald Garrison Villard's memoir, *Fighting Years: Memoirs of a Liberal Editor* (1939).

frame, a visual suggestion of their status as victors; the Filipino corpses occupy the lower half of the frame, suggesting their subaltern/abject status. The caption reads: "A sacrifice to Aguinaldo's ambition," belittling the death of the Filipinos as damage collateral to Aguinaldo's foolish and vain ambition to remain president of the independent Philippine Republic. The caption shifts the blame for the deaths—and, by extension, the entire war—to one man, Aguinaldo, disregarding the fact that his anticolonial ambition to live in a free country was shared by most Filipinos, and that Aguinaldo himself was an ally in the earlier U.S. war against Spain, which was partly waged to liberate Spain's colonies from its grasp.

It must be noted that the logic of abjection is often articulated in the captions of the photographs, where the visual elements—such as those of death and destruction—are interpreted so that the suffering of the enemy is minimized and the benefit to the victors is substantiated and maximized. The image delivers the spectacle of American victory while the imperial caption pal-liates whatever feelings of discomfort the spectacle might produce. The image of enemy corpses can produce an imperial "pleasure" that helps manage the nation's fear of losing the Philippine "insurrection," similar to the equanim-ity offered by Civil War photographs of dead Confederacy soldiers. As abject visuals, therefore, the Philippine-American War photographs articulate the monstrosity and magnificence of empire. They can disturb and fascinate the viewer, often at the same time. In figure 16, the caption reads: "The ending of two Filipino Sharp-shooters—a rice field in Imus, Philippines." Two Filipino corpses, bodies twisted, lie side by side, with the fighter on the right holding what appears to be a rifle above his head. The caption tries to glorify the ab-ject situation by portraying both men as "sharp-shooters," hence as dangerous enemy assets who needed to be neutralized. The captioner perhaps cannot be faulted for taking both Filipino fighters as sharpshooters—Filipino forces were so poorly equipped, and rifles and bullets so short in supply, that anyone with a rifle must surely be a sharpshooter. Neither man was even wearing a military uniform, so we have only the caption's assurance that these men, so pathetically arrayed in death, were really enemy combatants.

Figure 17, captioned "Insurgent Trenches at Bag-Bag River," shows a deep ditch, presumably dug by the "insurgents," filled with corpses of Filipino sol-diers. There is a fence, possibly made of bamboo, over the trench, which makes it likely that this was a fortified position where the Filipinos apparently made their last stand. The Bag-Bag River is in Bulacan, a province just north of Ma-nila and part of the Tagalog region, which was the center of early Filipino resis-tance. The photograph is imprinted with the seal of the "Chief Engineering Of-fice of the Philippines," but the name of the photographer who took the image has oddly and literally been covered up. Unlike in the U.S. Civil War and Indian wars, no American photographers became famous, or at least were noted, for their photographs of the Philippine "insurrection." It must have made sense that a war that received critical attention from an articulate organization such as the Anti-Imperialist League would have its chroniclers and documenters remain anonymous, especially if they had been witnesses to this kind of car-nage. Indeed, as protests and criticisms against the conquest and occupation of the Philippine Islands continued even after the declaration of the end of the Philippine-American War in 1902, censorship by the United States became in-creasingly active.

American journalists protested the censorship of the war as early as August 1899, when a correspondent from the Associated Press wrote that one censor told him he was instructed to "shut off everything that could hurt McKinley's administration." Another journalist, Oswald Garrison Villard, published his memoir *Fighting Years: Memoirs of a Liberal Editor*, which included a photograph from the undeclared "second phase" of the Philippine-American War, fought after 1902 in many parts of occupied Philippines, particularly in the Muslim Mindanao region. The photograph (figure 18) shows the infamous aftermath of the 1906 "Battle of Bud Dajo" in Jolo, Sulu Province, fought by American forces under General Leonard Wood against Tausug Muslims. In the photograph, dead bodies of dozens of Tausug Muslims, mostly women and children, are piled up in an extinct volcano crater, where a thousand Tausugs sought refuge but were massacred by Wood's troops. In his memoir, Villard writes that an unnamed but high-ranking American official "accidentally" destroyed the negative (Villard "frontis" 156). Fortunately, a copy of the photograph was eventually reprinted in American newspapers (Kramer 220). Looking back at his years as an editor and journalist for the *Nation*, Villard wrote that there was an "official repression of facts" about the war (Villard 139), citing as example the American official's attempt to suppress the Bud Dajo photograph.

Such censorship notwithstanding, anonymous photographers still managed to record images of great devastation. Figures 19 and 20 are images of decimated towns after battles between American and Filipino forces. The caption for figure 19 ("Burned district of Cavite") mentions the city of Cavite, an important port on Manila Bay and later the seat of U.S. naval forces in the Philippines. It is also right next to the town of Kawit, which was the birthplace and headquarters of General Aguinaldo, over which the flag of the independent Philippine Republic was first raised. The battle for such a historical and strategic location reduced the city to rubble; the photograph shows that only the ruins of houses and scorched tree trunks were left standing. In figure 20, a lone soldier walks through the razed town of Calumpit, Bulacan, "after American troops had passed thru" it, according to the caption.

Besides those of death and destruction, photographs of public hangings during the war were reprinted as postcards, perhaps to remind viewers of the state's power to discipline its subjects, but also to reinforce the depiction of the Philippine colony as a zone of abjection. The caption on figure 21 describes the execution of three Filipino "ladrones," the Spanish term for "bandits" or "thieves." The date, "Dec. 28, 1900," is marked on the photograph. Given the censorship by the American military authorities and the lack of information regarding the subjects of most colonial photographs in the Philippines, we could question the labeling of the three Filipinos as bandits. For one thing, we see a phalanx of American soldiers standing in front of the gallows. The sizable contingent of U.S. soldiers present during the execution might suggest that the Filipinos who were being hanged were not just petty thieves, but persons of considerable repute or notoriety.

Fig. 19. Visualizing death and abjection: The seaside province of Cavite after battle with American forces. Cavite is also the hometown of General Emilio Aguinaldo. Caption: "Burned district of Cavite." No date. From the National Archives collection of the Bureau of Insular Affairs.

Fig. 20. Visualizing death and abjection: The town of Calumpit, Bulacan Province, in ruins, with a lone American soldier walking. Caption: "After American troops had passed thru town of Calumpit." From the National Archives collection of the Bureau of Insular Affairs.

Fig. 21. The Philippine colony as a zone of abjection: photographs of public hang-
ings were used as postcards. In the image, the large presence of American soldiers in
the background suggests the importance of the execution of the Filipino "criminals."
Caption: "The execution of three Philippine *ladrones* [bandits]. Luzon, P.I. [Philippine
Islands] Dec. 28, 1900." From the National Archives collection of the Bureau of Insular
Affairs.

One important ideological achievement of the photographs in this section
is that they created what Virginia Dominguez describes as a taxonomy of enemies and allies.[37] The images during and after battle articulate the American
imperial sublime by displaying death as the inevitable consequence of racial
inferiority: U.S. soldiers standing upright and triumphant as they pose next
to multiple brown cadavers, usually shown as an tangled heap of bodies or a
tattered row of nameless dead, their humanity unrecognizable. By producing
a visual taxonomy of the enemy in death, Americans manufactured their own
imperial and racial lessons through the American photography complex—our
war is just and our war is winnable.

For many viewers, these were not images of horrific violence but were images of American modernity claiming victory over Filipino savagery. Photography brings forth the argument that the increasing destructiveness of war is, like
photography itself, nothing other than an advancement of science. American

soldiers and civilians who saw these war images were able to adopt a new "military morality" that absolves the perpetrators, since war is presented as a science enabled by technology and therefore part of the improvement of the "civilized" or Western race. This might explain why President Theodore Roosevelt sent a telegram to General Wood to congratulate him for his "brave feat of arms" for the American flag a week after the publication of the photograph of the massacre of one thousand Tausugs, including women and children, at Bud Dajo (Kramer 220).

But despite the racial and imperial ideologies at work in the photographs and American popular culture, which promoted what Kirstin Hoganson describes as the white American "manly ideal" and the "jingoist desire" for war,[38] these photographs still disturbed the peace and fueled criticisms of the Philippine War. W. J. T. Mitchell, paraphrasing Marx, writes that pictures "have lives and desires of their own" and that the meanings produced by photographic or visual images "do not always do it in the same way, nor under conditions of their own choosing" (11). In other words, war photographs do not always deliver the "correct" imperialist message or condone the violence of war under a celebratory rhetoric. Critics of the Philippine-American War in fact interpreted these war images differently. Members and supporters of the Anti-Imperialist League read these photographs not just as evidence of the atrocities committed in the service of American empire-building, but as proof of the social problem resulting from the crisis of white American masculinity being threatened by the "imperial degeneracy" of a war of conquest. To help refute these anti-imperialist arguments, the complex had to produce other images that showed Filipino docility and domesticity as benevolent consequences of American imperialism.

DOCILITY

In November 1899, when Filipino forces shifted to guerrilla warfare, American military officials, policymakers, and soldiers viewed this irregular form of warfare as a marker of the Filipinos' primitive state, since a "civilized people" would surely observe the protocols of Western warfare (Kramer 90). Facing annihilation by the Americans, poorly equipped Filipino forces had no choice but to retreat, hide in the mountains and jungle, or blend in among villagers and peasants in rural communities. Aguinaldo ordered small guerrilla units to conduct local attacks against American camps (Kramer 130). The Filipinos fought a "war of the flea," a contemporary American military term in counterinsurgency studies for guerrilla warfare, which comes from the analogy between a flea and a guerrilla, and the ability of the smaller, agile flea to exhaust, weaken, or at least

Fig. 22. Staging docility: A white schoolteacher and her Filipino students. No date. From the National Archives collection of the Bureau of Insular Affairs.

Fig. 23. Staging docility at a time of guerrilla war. Caption: "Class in the large Assembly Room of San Andres Primary School Malate, Manila." No date. From the National Archives collection of the Bureau of Insular Affairs.

Fig. 24. Staging docility. Caption: "Filipino Children outside a Native School house, Philippine Islands. Copyright 1901." From the Library of Congress online collection.

Fig. 25. Staging docility. Caption: "Class in Embroidery." No date. From the National Archives collection of the Bureau of Insular Affairs.

3587 School girls in native dress, upper garment made of hemp
gauze, Philippine Islands. Copyright 1907 by H. C. White Co.

Fig. 26. Staging docility: Caption on the stereo card: "School girls in native dress, upper garment made of hemp gauze, Philippine Islands. Copyright 1907." From the Library of Congress online collection.

harass the larger dog.[39] In a guerrilla war, the once visible body of an enemy soldier, now in disguise as an *amigo* or ally or even just a noncombatant, could no longer be identified, and the American army saw this subterfuge as a betrayal of civilized warfare. Filipino guerrilla warfare became one of the grounds for racializing Filipinos as *gugus*, referring to the Tagalog term for the coconut-oil shampoo that Filipinos typically used, and suggesting the American soldier's perception of the slippery, oily, and wily character of the Filipino "insurgent"

(Kramer 127). Since Filipinos chose to wage a guerrilla war, American soldiers viewed Filipinos as savages and used racial terms such as "gugu" and "nigger" in their letters and diaries (Kramer 139).

So in a time of guerrilla war and the treacherous "invisibility" of the Filipino insurgent, the image of the Filipino male—unless he was dead or a child or a member of a primitive indigenous tribe—dropped from circulation. In its place, two images of Filipino abjecthood were widely and popularly disseminated: the naked Filipino savage and the docile clothed colonial. The naked Filipino savage, in many ethnographic photographs taken by the colonial administrator Dean C. Worcester and others, visually recalled for American spectators the success of both the physical and "tender violence" of Progressive Era projects, which included domesticating or pacifying Native bodies through genocidal war and colonial incarceration in reservations and boarding schools. The image of the naked savage also reiterated the justness and appropriateness of America's colonial mission, which was of course to civilize him.

The second image, the clothed Filipino child or woman, references the dark or nonwhite body of American imperial modernity, continuing the long line of images of Native and black schoolchildren in institutions such as the Hampton Normal and Agricultural Institute, and images of black slaves posing in the homes of slave owners (Wexler). The image of the nonthreatening Filipino "enemy," as a naked savage or docile colonial, was produced at a time when accounts of U.S. military atrocities were being published in American newspapers. Thus the cultural work of staging Filipino savagery and docility through popular photographs, along with actual censorship of the news, rendered the brutality of American military strategies invisible and unknowable. Allan Sekula writes that photographs function metonymically as visual texts that "stand for a contextually related object or event."[40] He cites the example of how, in the nineteenth century, "solemn portraits of American Indians were made as the race was exterminated" (39). In the case of naked or clothed Filipino subjects, their solemn, scowling visages were being photographed while the Filipino race was experiencing a war of similar genocidal proportions.

Images of Filipino savagery and docility were published in dozens of illustrated travel books after 1898. The most commercially successful travel book published during the Philippine-American War was José de Olivares's *Our Islands and Their People, as Seen with Camera and Pencil* (1902), edited by William S. Bryan (Thompson 2). De Olivares was a native of California and a journalist for the *Globe Democrat* of St. Louis. Published as two oversized texts, *Our Islands and Their People* was an imperial racial spectacle that featured twelve hundred black-and-white photographs along with nineteen hand-colored photographs. The book was a commercial success, was republished in 1905, sold four hundred thousand copies, and launched an industry of illustrated books on the "insular possessions" of the United States after 1898 (Thompson 3–4).

In de Olivares's book, some photographs of naked Filipino women were displayed alongside the clothed images of lowland, or "Hispanized," Filipinas and Cuban and Puerto Rican women. These contrasting images—the clothed female colonial versus the naked Filipina—visually defined the Filipino race as a savage people in the minds of American readers, and also morphologically feminized the Philippine homeland and made it ripe for conquest. Yet it seems that the land and the women would not be as submissive and feminized as their depiction would have it, which de Olivares himself remarks in this unflattering passage on Filipino women:

> In the first place, she is the unloveliest of women. . . . After seeing Porto [*sic*] Rican and Cuban maidens, a man entering Manila will expect to be thrilled again by great, lustrous, dark eyes; but the glance of the Filipino woman will never thrill you. Her eyes are not large, but they are black and beady and un-readable. Very often hunger looks out at you; often hatred, but it is not pas-sionate hatred. . . . She cannot understand why these white men with guns intrude upon her ancient customs. She doesn't like the white man anyway. Her eyes tell him so and she wishes he were back in his own land. (590–91)

One can understand de Olivares's preference for Puerto Rican and Cuban women since he has race, culture, and history in common with them. But he definitely was not imagining the hunger and hatred he saw in Filipina's eyes, because she was truly hungry and she really hated—and de Olivares was again right in ascribing the cause of her hunger and hatred to the white man with the gun. Yet he gets it wrong when he says that she doesn't like the white man anyway, conflating a colonial misfortune (white men with guns) into a bias against all white men. Applying a flawed racial logic, he fails to see that war and occupation would turn any female caught in their grip into the unloveliest of women.

Elsewhere, de Olivares writes:

> They are a dark people—some are distinctively black—and our soldiers have fallen into the habit of calling them "niggers." . . . For all the practical pur-poses of civilization, the mirthful, easy-going African is superior to these treacherous and blood-thirsty hybrid Malays. (559)

De Olivares was a Californian of Mexican descent. He probably did not have a profound comprehension of the troubled relationship between whites and blacks, since California did not have, during his time, a large population of "Africans." What California did have was a sizable number of Asians, for whom the state was the principal disembarkation of their Pacific crossing. Racial tensions among California's Asian, Mexican, and white populations had risen greatly in the late nineteenth century, and de Olivares may have been influenced by this knotty state of affairs in his characterization of Filipinos, who—being hybrid Malays with beady unreadable eyes—were decidedly Asian.

Yet these Asians were to be America's new wards even as a guerrilla war was raging in the islands, and as wards of an emerging world power that prided itself on its democratic ideals, they needed to be educated. U.S. soldiers served as the earliest schoolteachers; in 1901, even before the official end of the Philippine-American War, the first American civilian teachers arrived in Manila. In the colonial archive, images of Filipino schoolchildren stage the pacification of the Philippines as good or docile subjects of American imperial modernity, with their white teachers automatically reprising roles of racial superiority formerly assumed by soldiers. It could be said that the military colonial government and the public education system were twin institutions that came into being almost simultaneously. Figures 22–25 are photographs and stereographs of Filipino schoolchildren taken during the first decade of U.S. rule. The large, airy classroom in figure 22 features *capiz* shell-tiled window panels that are distinctively Filipino, thus marking its Philippine setting. The schoolboys are bent over their desks, reading and writing, Western-style hats stacked on benches in front of the desks. What seem to be arithmetical equations are on blackboards on two walls of the classroom. In front of the class is the schoolteacher, a white American woman in a light long-sleeved blouse with a high-necked collar and a long skirt. The teacher is at her desk, surveying her seemingly overcrowded classroom as eight boys stand along two sides, perhaps having no desk to sit in. It's difficult to figure out the boys' ages, but some appear to be at or near puberty, and therefore able to wield a weapon in a few years. Hence, the urgency to get them into a classroom and instill American values, and not least a good amount of docility, in them so they will not turn into guerrilla fighters in the future.

Figure 23 is a photograph of an even larger "Assembly Room of San Andres Primary School, Malate, Manila." This time, rows of schoolgirls are reading their schoolbooks with hands folded on their laps, an image of discipline and concentration. An impression one might be left with is that of row upon row of neatly braided or beribboned dark hair of the schoolgirls, yet one girl on the far left has her long, shiny hair falling past her shoulders. Is this defiance or independence? It is hard to spot the teacher, who appears partly hidden in front, with two girls facing her and at least two standing behind. Although she seems to be fully occupied attending to the standing students, she still has full control over her class, who continue reading diligently. The statement being made by these images seems to be that order reigns in the new colony, indicating submission and docility among people still presumably at war with the United States.

In figure 24, young boys in simple cotton shirts and pants pose in front of a *nipa* hut, a traditional structure built from dried cogon grass leaves and wood, being used, according to the caption, as a "Native School house." This image, like figure 22, manages proexpansionist fears regarding the danger of young Filipino males who could grow up to become *insurrectos*. The image suggests that American education and colonial tutelage will eliminate the Philippine insurgency even in remote areas where makeshift structures had to suffice as schoolhouses. The stereo card was printed in 1901 when the guerrilla war was still in full swing.

In figure 25, young Filipinas are learning their lessons in the domestic arts—a "Class in Embroidery," as the handwritten caption on the photograph states. The women in front seem quite content and intent at their embroidery, looking down at what they're doing instead of at the camera. Such outward interest in home decorative arts bodes well for the American colonial effort, as it indicates a psychology among the women that does not discount a hopeful domestic future for them. A smoldering resentment resulting from war and occupation is not easily concealed, and if that can be upstaged by the placidity, however designed, of this setting, then it shows the effectiveness of what Vernadette V. Gonzalez describes as "kinder, gentler imperialism"[41] at work.

The American imperial fiction of the violent Filipino fighter or criminal—dead or alive—is transformed, by the evolved role of the United States from war combatant to colonial occupier, into another imperial fiction: that of the docile, passive, clothed Filipino colonial who submits to American military rule. Both fictions present a type of Filipino that needs civilizing—through war and violence for the first, education and benevolence for the latter, yet a hybrid of both kinds of persuasion could surely not be avoided when all the schooling was being conducted in the middle of a raging guerrilla war. These images of docile youth must be seen as an abiding visual form of the American empire, what the nation's memory had preferred to retain from such a monumental yet brutal American experience, the colonization of its first territory in Asia. In addition, the production of Filipino docility, through the image of the colonial ward, might have helped suppress the continuing Filipino resistance to American colonial rule.

It could be argued that imperial abjection resides almost seamlessly in the photographic images of clothed Filipina women that were circulated after the Philippine-American War. Photographs of Filipina women are more than

Orientalist souvenirs or commodified "visual scapes" kept by an American photographer to remember his sojourn to the Philippine colony.[42] The photographs are in fact images of *imperial sentimentalization* that valorize the ideals of American imperialism institutionalized in "schools, hospitals, prisons" and other sites of sentimental power (Wexler 103), including that of the submissive female body. These imperial sentimental photographs insinuate forms of violence against "the darky" (Wexler 108) at a time when reports of actual violence were being withheld from the American public, who had already been told that the Philippine Islands were now pacified and under U.S. military control. To quote Wexler:

> Sentimentalization was an *externalized* aggression that was sadistic, not masochistic, in flavor. The energies it developed were intended as a tool for the control of others, not merely as an aid in the conquest of the self. This element of the enterprise was not oriented toward white middle-class readers. . . . Rather, it aimed at the subjection of people of different classes and races, who were compelled to play not the leading roles but the human scenery before which the melodrama of middle-class redemption could be enacted, for the enlightenment of an audience in which they were not even included. (101)

Sentimentalization—from what Laura Wexler traces in nineteenth-century American women's fiction and photography—is a logic of American imperialism that countenances a racial and class aggression against human bodies that did not conform to the notion of the proper occupants of a "middle-class white Christian 'home'" (Wexler 103). Sentimentalization was also an imperialist narrative about bodies that lost their own homes and "traditional modes of living" after slavery and U.S. wars of conquest (Wexler 103). With the occupation of the Philippine Islands in 1898, the bodies of imperial sentiment that were brown (Native Americans), black (African Americans), and white (working-class whites or European immigrants) now included new bodies. Imperial sentimentalization thus presents colonial docility through new bodies, such as Filipina figures, that are posed as perfect candidates for modernity and educational advancement. At work in these photographs is the idea of learning the lessons of American modernity, without revealing war and carnage as the initial agents of change. Photographs of traditionally dressed Filipinas, and by extension Filipino schoolchildren, are abject images of empire, representing the fiction of the transformation of the Filipino "savage race" into modern subjects through American education and tutelage from largely middle-class noncombatants, who had arrived in the Philippines almost at the same time as U.S.

troop reinforcements for an ongoing guerrilla war. The clandestine presence of war and occupation therefore haunts these seemingly tranquil and nonviolent images.

In one of the stereo cards (figure 26) the young girls are described as "school girls in native dress, upper garment made of hemp gauze." They are sitting in a room that appears to be the house's receiving area: potted plants, wood floors, and traditional *capiz* shell window and door panels evoke the interiors of lowland and Hispanized Philippine homes of the period. Dressed in the traditional *baro't saya* (blousy tops with the gauzy butterfly sleeves—from "hemp"—and long striped skirts), with their fans on their laps, the young girls cut an elegant yet somewhat languid look. The fans mark their identities as "Hispanized" Filipinas who follow the latest fashion from Mother Spain. The young women are described as "schoolgirls," suggesting youth, femininity, and the potential for modernity. The image of these two reposeful women is supposed to represent people that are able to rest, finally settled after a time of conflict and uncertainty, and poised to learn the modern ways of their benevolent colonizers. Yet it could be argued that these women, based on the relatively high status evident from their surroundings, would have moved into modernity with the help of any agent, be they Spanish colonizers, American colonizers, or indeed even independent Filipinos.

Figure 27 shows a young Filipino woman ("a native maid") from Albay Province, Luzon who poses in a *baro't saya* with a dark *patadyong* over her long *saya*. Like the two schoolgirls in Figure 26, she holds a fan in her hands, marking her status and femininity. Her long black hair is carefully coiffed, and she wears a dark velvet necklace with a pendant. This photograph was published as the frontispiece of an obscure romance novel, Oscar Coursey's *The Woman with a Stone Heart: A Romance of the Philippine War* (which will be discussed in the concluding chapter of the book), a novel about a cross-dressing Filipina criminal. The choice of this image as a frontispiece for the novel seems an odd one because the young woman does not embody qualities related to either cross-dressing or criminality that the woman with a stone heart is supposed to have. It could be surmised that this photograph was the best the publishers could find; perhaps its rough-hewn rustic background sufficed as a proxy for one of the novel's settings, the jungle of Aguinaldo's guerrilla army, which the woman with the stone heart had joined, posing as a man. At any rate, it is heartening to know that the book publishers could find only a marginally suitable image, from the thousands that existed, for an unsympathetic fictional character, proving that de Olivares's claim that the Filipina is "the unloveliest of women" is nothing but an exaggeration.

Figure 28 is one of the rare photographs that show a profile view of the Fili-

Fig. 27. Staging docility: A Filipina with a fan in hand. Caption: "A native maid from Albay, Luzon." No date. From the National Archives collection of the Bureau of Insular Affairs.

Fig. 28. Staging docility. Caption: "Embroidery pupil, school of Household Industries, Manila 1912." From the National Archives collection of the Bureau of Insular Affairs.

pina subject. Most portraits of the period show the full face and details of the woman's dress. This young woman's left profile highlights, quite artfully, her mestiza, or mixed-race, features—fine jawline, sharp nose, high cheekbones, and obvious light skin. She wears a traditional *baro't saya* with elaborate folds, and a full complement of jewelry: earrings, bracelet, and a ring on her left ring finger, which does not mean she is married, because Filipinos of that time, if they did wear wedding rings, wore them Spanish-style on the right ring finger. She is working on a flower embroidery, as the caption, "Embroidery pupil, school of Household Industries, Manila 1912," states. This photograph was taken later than the previous embroidery photograph in figure 25, perhaps during the first decade of American colonial rule. By that time, trade and finishing schools such as the School of Household Industries had been established in Manila to prepare new Filipina colonials for a life of peaceful domesticity. Images such as this confirm that the Philippines had entered a postwar period, and that now as a settled U.S. colony it has begun to rehabilitate itself as a modern society interested in such progressive endeavors as "household industries."

VISUALIZING GOVERNMENTALITY

More than a century ago, stereographs produced visual mediations of "an American empire in the Orient," of what it takes to build it, promote it, and maintain it. A Kodak advertisement from a 1904 issue of *Harper's Weekly* (figure 29) offers a connection between photography and American imperial abjection. In the ad, a mustachioed white man in a military uniform surveys the landscape, a small notebook in hand. His mustache, uniform, and demeanor recalls the iconic look of Theodore Roosevelt the Rough Rider (and not Theodore Roosevelt, the president of the United States at the time). In the background is a rugged terrain with several mounted riders in the distance, while to his left stands a racially ambiguous, nonwhite man tending to two horses, suggesting that the latter is either a servant or guide to the white man in uniform. The ad is entitled "The Correspondent," identifying the central figure as a journalist reporting from the remote frontline of some far-off colonial war, as the ad copy makes clear:

> In war as in peace THE KODAK is at the front.
> In Cuba and the Philippines, in South Africa, in Venezuela, and now in Korea and Manchuria, the camera most in evidence is the Kodak.
> The same qualities that make it indispensable to the correspondent make it most reliable for the tourist—simplicity, freedom from darkroom bother, lightness combined with a strength that resists the wear and tear of travel.

The ad's primary purpose, of course, is to sell Kodak cameras, to tout their advantages as simple, lightweight, and reliable devices for tourists to record travel events the same way correspondents record events that happen in a war. War here is not the messy, violent, brutally destructive, and evil thing it actually is— the ad makes it to be something sexy, alluring, and adventurous, enumerating war zones (Cuba, the Philippines, South Africa . . .) as though they were the most exotic tourist destinations, as a travel ad would say, "Bangkok, Bali, and Beyond."

"In war as in peace," begins the ad, subtly making moral equivalents of peace and war. The ad's approbation of war, it could be argued, extends to support for colonialism and imperialism. It celebrates the military correspondent as a heroic figure, yet the correspondent is nothing but an imperial agent, an employee of a newspaper published in a Western colonial power and read by citizens of that colonial power. The link between photography and imperial abjection surfaces here: Photography, as represented by the correspondent, is as ubiquitous and instrumental to the colonial enterprise as war and soldiers, because it can show racial inferiority, provide proof of victory, and build consent. In giving vi-

Fig. 29. Kodak advertisement, circa 1904. David M. Rubenstein Rare Book & Manuscript Library, Duke University.

sual form to both imperial and pedestrian adventures ("In war as in peace . . ."), the camera participates fully in the imperial enterprise by producing images of the American nation's heroes, its inferior and abject colonial Others, and all the different permutations of colonial encounters between those two.

Colonial photographs are "technological mediations of vision," that performed "the cultural-political labor" of the management of the Filipino natives for American viewers (Chaudhary 80–81). Colonial bodies in the archive are not only bodies under surveillance but are also imperial indices that narrate empire as "understandable": our war in the Philippine colony is a just and benevolent war. By considering necropolitics and the American photography complex, we highlight a critical reading practice that counters the romance of empire through the ideologies imbricated upon the images. Like all Western imperial cultures, the United States in the nineteenth century "reveled in the world of images" (Chaudhary 90), and U.S. empire-building required the production of an "anthology of images" (Sontag 3) to explain America's new imperial role in world affairs. By 1899, when the Filipino revolutionary armies dug in their heels for a protracted war against the United States, stereographs and photographs of the Philippine colony helped managed American anxieties over the war with the "Filipino insurgents."

Susan Sontag famously observed that the production of images "furnishes a ruling ideology" (Sontag 178), which in turn-of-the-century United States was an ideology based on imperial modernity. By imagining an imperial archipelago (Thompson), the colonial camera silenced and rendered invisible the political and military struggle for Philippine independence. Anti-imperialist dissent, represented in the writings of Mark Twain and the rest of the Anti-Imperialist League, had dissipated by the early twentieth century with the pacification of the Islands, which coincided with the rise of photography in print culture. What emerged, for the consumption of the fin de siècle American public, was the visual spectacle of the savage and docile Filipino body. By "displaying the Filipino"[43] through the familial and familiar tropes of savagery, docility, exoticism, and racial inferiority, these colonial photographs of the Philippine Islands visually constructed American imperial power as legitimate and legible. Through stereographs, postcards, and other photographic images from the Philippine-American War, the problematic issues of colonial violence, war, and occupation ironically disappeared.

Chapter Three

Skin

*Lynching, Empire, and the Black Press
during the Philippine-American War*

In the mid-nineteenth century, Jim Crow laws were very much ingrained in every facet of American culture, including in the U.S. Army, which had begun opening its ranks to black soldiers.[1] In 1866, despite opposition from some politicians, the U.S. Congress created a new black segment of the U.S. Army: two cavalry regiments, the Ninth and the Tenth; and four infantry regiments, the Thirty-Eighth, Thirty-Ninth, Fortieth, and Forty-First (Fletcher 20). By 1869, during the era of Reconstruction, the infantry regiments were consolidated, and the four black units became the Twenty-Fourth and the Twenty-Fifth Infantries (Fletcher 21). At the time, white military leaders, and indeed many Americans, had a generally negative opinion of the fighting capabilities of African American soldiers, and so racial segregation was upheld even during times of war (Fletcher 18). As one white journalist wrote, the incidents of slave revolts dating decades back and black soldiers' mutinies were proof that "colored soldiers" could not be trusted, since they were naturally violent, murderous and had contempt toward their white officers and loyalty only to "men of their own color."[2] The creation of distinct and separate units based on race reproduced the culture of American abjection in the U.S. Army while the army was becoming an important apparatus of continental expansion and empire-building. In fact, the army was an intense site of imperial abjection because of the nationalization of racial and gender hierarchies through military cultures.

Despite segregation, African American soldiers fought in every American war.[3] In 1898, some ten thousand African American soldiers volunteered to fight in the Spanish-American War (Foner 84). But regardless of their show of patriotism, black soldiers suffered racial humiliation and violent assaults from white Americans. In training camps in the South, both black volunteers and regulars received insults and abuse and were attacked by white soldiers, civilians, and the local police (Foner 87). In one incident in Nashville, Tennessee, a train carrying black infantry men was boarded by seventy-five white policemen and two hundred white male civilians who proceeded to beat the black soldiers with clubs and pistols (Foner 87).

In 1899, more than five thousand African American soldiers were sent to the Philippine Islands to fight in the Philippine-American War.[4] In her excellent study of the history of black soldiers in the Philippines, Cynthia L. Marasigan writes that their arrival in the Philippine colony was a moment of ambivalence for the black soldiers, who were both participants of U.S. "state-sponsored violence," on the one hand, and witnesses to the "failures of Reconstruction curtailing citizenship rights" and the escalating violence of segregation, on the other.[5] By many accounts, the war was unpopular among African Americans. Given the racist climate of the segregated army and in the larger American society at the time, it was not surprising that there was vocal opposition to American imperial expansion and the Philippine-American War coming from the black community. Critic Hazel V. Carby points out that in the decade of the 1890s, a cohort of African American women writers had written against lynching and empire well before the Philippine-American War. Writers such as Anna Julia Cooper, Ida B. Wells, Pauline Hopkins, and Frances Harper critiqued American imperial expansion as "unrestrained patriarchal power" and "as bestial in its actual and potential power to devour lands and peoples."[6] The writings of these black feminists predated the work of the Anti-Imperialist League of Boston. During the Philippine-American War, however, black male journalists, academics, officers, and soldiers joined the voices of black feminist writers to carry on an African American anti-imperialist tradition of political writing.

Letters by black soldiers published in the Negro press as well as editorials written by black journalists condemned the racial nature of the war.[7] Readership for the "race papers" or the "colored press" had been increasing. From 1880 to 1890, the Negro press expanded to 154 periodicals, concentrated in urban areas in the Northeast.[8] The rise of "Negro journalism" coincided with two important events that affected black American communities: the steep drop in illiteracy rates, from 70 percent in 1880 to 44.5 percent by 1900, and the steady rise in lynchings across the country (Detweiler 61). Into these enormous changes taking place in black America came the critical voices of black soldiers who wrote to their families and to community newspapers about what they witnessed and experienced during the Philippine-American War.

African American soldiers who were sent to the islands wrote about the racist attitudes of white soldiers: how Filipinos were called "niggers," "black devils," and "gugus" by white soldiers, military wives, and officers;[9] how Filipino natives

were labeled as outlaws and bandits when they seemed to be fighting a legitimate war of independence; and how countless atrocities such as rape, massacres, looting, robbery, physical abuse, harassment, and torture were committed by the U.S. military against the Filipino people. These accounts must have
struck a familiar though uneasy chord among those whose own emancipation
was bought by war barely a generation ago and who continued to undergo racial oppression. Some saw through the hypocrisy of "Philippine annexation"
as a civilizing mission, since many black Americans continued to live with racial violence and economic discrimination even after 1865 and the abolition
of slavery.[10] In the Philippine-American War, African Americans saw a strong
connection between U.S. domestic politics and its colonial endeavors—a connection between lynching and empire—which members of the Negro press
wrote about. Black journalists across the nation were warning that the lynching
of black men, women, and children in the South was the same violence being committed against Filipino men, women, and children. As William Loren
Katz notes, at the height of U.S. overseas expansion, the lynchings escalated.
From 1899 to 1902, the years of the Philippine-American War, "Almost 2,000
black men, women and children were lynched, often with unspeakable brutality."[11] Lynchings were so common in the early part of the twentieth century that
by 1918, lynchings had occurred in all but six states.[12] From 1882 to 1968, the
Department of Archives and Records of the Tuskegee Institute documented
that there were about 3,445 lynchings of African Americans across the country
(Holden-Smith 36).

This chapter focuses on two ideas: first, that the trope of black skin, or the
abject meanings of blackness, can be traced in the writings of African American soldiers and journalists about the Philippine-American War. The trope
functioned as an anti-imperialist idea in the writings of black soldiers and journalists who argued that Filipinos were their Pacific "kith and kin" (San Buenaventura 11) and that racial violence at home was being exported as a race war
to the Philippine Islands. This discussion borrows from Hazel Carby's study of
a black feminist anti-imperialist tradition demonstrated in the writings of black
women writers in the late nineteenth century.[13] Carby argues that lynching, the
common occurrence of rapes of black women by white men in the South, and
the American expansion in the Pacific were all attempts by white supremacy
to regain control of emancipated nonwhite bodies. In the late nineteenth century, black feminist critiques against lynching and U.S. imperialism rested on
the call for social justice for all oppressed races, a political imagination that
expressed transnational solidarity. I thus consider an emergent discourse of African American modernity in the critical discussion of lynching and empire
expressed in black soldiers' letters and editorials that made the connection be-

tween the expansion of racial violence at home and "abroad" or overseas. This understanding of black modernity recalls Gilroy's discussion of the "antinomies of modernity," by considering memories of slavery and institutionalized forms of racial violence as "the primal history of modernity" and narrating modernity from the point of view of the enslaved and, by extension, the descendants of slaves and those oppressed by U.S. military rule.[14]

Second, the discourse of Filipino savagery, or Filipino blackness, that circulated in African American newspapers functioned as an abject icon of imperial modernity, an anti-imperialist representation that codified racial grammars of the darker races. This idea of the Filipino's black body, with the Filipino general Emilio Aguinaldo as an icon of blackness, functioned as an image of solidarity. In black community newspapers of the time, Aguinaldo was compared to valiant and honorable soldiers of past wars and revolutions including the Cuban revolutionary general Antonio Maceo.[15] At the same time, however, there were also black male intellectuals who believed that "colored men of the Republic" (Troy) must enlist and fight in the Philippine insurrection so that the Negro race could claim cultural citizenship in white America.[16] The erotics of empire surface in racial discourses about the Filipino native that recall earlier racial discourses of other racially abject bodies. The seemingly black figure of the Filipino insurgent will be discussed in relation to earlier grammars of American Otherness, in particular early nineteenth-century representations of "black inferiority" and "red savagery."[17] As a figure of degeneracy and savagery, a figure reviled and eroticized in the American imperial imaginary, the Filipino native thus differed from the hardworking, passive, feminized Oriental, although some American writers and politicians would describe Filipinos as "asiatics." After 1899, however, when Filipinos resisted U.S. rule, discourses of savagery and primitivism were ascribed to Filipino natives, and the idea of the Filipino savage or the black Filipino insurgent was popularized in American culture. In the early years of the war, there were U.S. congressional debates on torture as well as news reports on atrocities committed by American soldiers.[18] To manage negative news about the war and to produce support and consent for the continued military occupation of the Philippine Islands, proexpansion writers and politicians drew from the familiar vocabularies of the imperial frontier and thereby codified the idea of the Filipino savage. As Etienne Balibar reminds us, imperialism is an "extreme term" of nationalism that seeks to "subjugate" and rule by "might."[19] In studying American imperial modernity as a language, I recognize Balibar's observation that there exists an "ideological symmetry" (Balibar 45) between discourses, a symmetry based on racism's power to represent and commit violence. The language of the American empire is a palimpsest, consisting of what Balibar describes as the "presence of the past" (38) and the "repetition of themes" (41) in imperialist and anti-imperialist discourses. The "past" in my discussion refers to earlier representations of black American and Native American subjects and how these abject representations merged and coalesced in the new figure of the Filipino savage in the late nineteenth century and after.

While there were many black soldiers sent to the Philippine Islands who thought that the savagery of the Philippine-American War was fueled by the racism of white officers and soldiers, there were some who believed that enlisting to fight in the "Philippine insurrection" was a chance to prove African American loyalty to the U.S. nation that could then lead to full citizenship and equal rights for the Negro race.[20] American imperial modernity for some African Americans thus offered the possibility of cultural citizenship that had long been denied even after the abolition of slavery, and fighting an unpopular war was the Faustian pact that would allow them to become modern black American citizens rather than second-class emancipated slaves. It was an ideology they embraced and accepted because it promised citizenship as a benefit of empire-building.

AFRICAN AMERICANS AS ABJECT ICONS

Reverend Theophilus Gould Steward, chaplain and officer of the Twenty-Fifth Colored Infantry, served in the Philippine-American War from 1899 to 1902 and later became superintendent of schools in the province of Iba, Zambales, during the military occupation of Luzon island (Seraile 275–83). He was also a published author and a history professor at Wilberforce University in Ohio, one of the oldest historically black private universities in the country.

Steward was of mixed racial descent, having a white forebear, an aristocratic Englishwoman, who had lost her inheritance after marrying a colored man by the name of Gould (Seraile 272–73). The young Steward began his career as a pastor for the African Methodist Episcopal church in New Jersey, served as a teacher for the Freedmen's Bureau in South Carolina, then returned to the ministry as a pastor in New York and then in Delaware (Seraile 272–74). In the 1880s, he published theological and sociological studies that established himself as an academic. In 1891, he was appointed chaplain of the Twenty-Fifth Colored Infantry by then president Benjamin Harrison (Seraile 275). Back then, as now, the U.S. Army provided financial security for people of color. Steward in fact accepted his chaplaincy, even after the prior success he enjoyed as a pastor and scholar, because he would be "fairly situated for the rest of (his) days" with a generous salary, a 10 percent increase every five years, and a comfortable retirement (Seraile 275). Steward's distinguished military appointment, and his belief in the discipline, solidarity, and opportunities offered by the army (Seraile 276–80) did not shield him from personal experiences of racism. In Nashville, Tennessee, he and his family were refused service in a dining saloon reserved for officers; in Tampa, Florida, some members of his infantry were attacked by white soldiers and civilians (Seraile 280).

Once Steward was stationed in the Philippines, he became disturbed by the casual use of the word "nigger" by white soldiers to refer to Filipino natives (Seraile 282), and he would often encounter rudeness from white soldiers who refused to salute him or would hurl racial epithets to his face (Seraile 283). But like many black officers at the time, he believed that fighting in America's wars proved one's patriotism, and for African Americans to be considered noble and loyal sons of the Republic, they must enlist. In 1898, he supported the recruitment and mobilization of black soldiers for the Spanish-American War because he saw military service as the salvation and the education of black men (Seraille 132–33). Steward's essay "A Plea for Patriotism," published in the *Independent*, naively argued that America would bring peace "to the newly freed Cuba, Puerto Rico, and the Philippines" (Seraille 133). Steward went on to write a commissioned study of the history of black American participation in America's wars as a possible recruitment tool for the U.S. Army. This more than four-hundred-page manuscript, entitled *The Colored Regulars*, which professed "race pride" for the military prowess of the valiant black soldier (Seraille 135–36), was completed in 1899, just months before Steward's deployment in Manila as chaplain of the Twenty-Fifth Infantry, but was not published until 1904 by the African Methodist Episcopal church's publishing house, the A.M.E. Book Concern. The delayed publication of Steward's colored soldier's book suggests the book may have been "too militant for any other publisher at the turn of the century" (Seraille 136). Regardless of how militant and alarming the idea (never mind the *reality*) of colored regulars in the army might have been for most Americans, Steward's writings promoted the idea of the military as a pathway to citizenship for black men, who in turn could help the nation achieve its goals, which by then included empire-building.

Steward was therefore a patriot for empire, yet he continued to be critical of the violence of racism that occurred both within and outside the military (Seraille 132). In 1899, Steward witnessed how Jim Crow was successfully exported to the Philippine Islands (Seraille 137) and wrote an article in the *Independent* about Filipinos and black soldiers being refused service in American-owned restaurants. He also warned that "a deep revulsion will set in as soon as Filipinos come to understand what the word 'nigger' means" (Seraille 137).

Another figure of black imperial abjection was a soldier who took a different path than Steward. In the annals of the Philippine-American War, a little-known but beloved anti-imperialist figure was David Fagen, a black soldier who defected from his unit and became a general for the Filipino army.[21] During the Philippine-American War, a handful of black soldiers defected and fought as members of the Katipunan, the Philippine revolutionary army led by General Emilio Aguinaldo. Historians Michael Robinson and Frank Schubert note that there were only twenty-nine desertion cases among the four black regiments during the war (73). Defection meant cutting ties from other black soldiers while they lived in a foreign land, and there was the threat of execution or a long imprisonment (73). These frightening realities might explain the very few defections of black soldiers to the Filipino side. But as E. San Juan Jr. notes, Fagen and other black deserters are "indexical" and "pedagogical signifiers" of the politics of "self-determination for enslaved and subjugated communities" (San Juan 7), or what we might consider icons of black modernity.

In contrast to Theophilus Steward, very little is known of the life of Corporal David Fagen. He enlisted in the Twenty-Fourth Infantry in June 1898, when he was twenty-three years old (Robinson and Schubert 73). In June 1899, Fagen boarded a ship to Manila after being in the army for only a year. His military records show that during his early months in the islands, Fagen experienced difficulties with his white officers. Marasigan writes that Fagen was described as "one who thought it was smart to 'buck' the First Sergeant," a "rowdy soldier," a "bad man," and someone "given to slang and profanity" (Marasigan 81). She notes that Fagen had seven previous convictions for insubordination and was "almost constantly doing extra fatigue duty" (Marasigan 81). Fagen might have been assigned to "all sorts of dirty jobs" such as latrine cleaning and kitchen work, and his records show that he tried unsuccessfully to obtain transfers on three occasions, suggesting that he also had problems with his black sergeants (Robinson and Schubert 73). On November 17, 1899, Fagen left the Twenty-Fourth Infantry with the help of Filipino revolutionaries. As Marasigan observes, Fagen's successful desertion while he was on duty "indicated careful preparation, the establishment of trust between Fagen and the revolutionaries, and an understanding of the risks involved in Fagen's desertion" (Marasigan 80). He could have slipped away quietly and lived the rest of his life as a civilian in an obscure, secluded Filipino province. But instead he chose "the more difficult and hazardous alternatives" by joining the Katipunan (Robinson and Schubert 75) and fighting for Filipinos against his fellow Americans.

The remaining historical records highlight the abject status of African Americans like Fagen who defected and joined the Filipino side. For American military leaders, Fagen and his celebrity status were a wretched curse. His identity was revealed in an article published in the *New York Times* on October 28, 1900.[22] Fagen, whose name was misspelled as Fagin, was described as a deserter who held the rank of general in the Filipino army and had a "sworn special enmity toward his former company." In Brigadier General Frederick Funston's memoir *Memories of Two Wars* (1911), he mentions Fagen as the dastardly "American negro" whom he had hoped to capture and lynch with a "picket-rope."[23] He asserts that by 1901, during the guerrilla phase of the Philippine-American War, there were still "more than seventy thousand troops" who were remnants of the Katipunan—Filipino men and women who survived the early encounters with the better-equipped American army (Funston 385). By that time, the American troops were "worn out" but were still determined to capture Aguinaldo and to end the "Philippine insurrection." In the province of Nueva Ecija, Funston arranged for a meeting with General Urbano Lacuna, who wanted to surrender (Funston 387). During their meeting, the question of "David Fagan [*sic*]," the deserter turned general, came up. Funston told Lacuna he and his men would be treated as prisoners of war, but not Fagen, who if he surrendered would be given a court-martial and executed (Funston 431). According to Funston, Lacuna was said to have agreed to these terms.

Funston's memoir mentions that Fagan's capture became a priority for the American military command, so a reward for his capture, "dead or alive," was set at six hundred dollars (Funston 434). A call for his capture was printed in Spanish and Tagalog and posted in all towns of Nueva Ecija. On December 8, 1901, the *New York Times* published a story about the capture and beheading of Fagen by Filipino scouts working for the American colonial government.[24] Funston recalls that Fagen's head, along with some rifles, revolvers, Fagen's official papers as an officer of the Katipunan, and a West Point ring taken from a white officer, were handed over to American military authorities (Funston 434–35). On December 10, 1901, the *Times* published an account by a white officer, Lieutenant F. W. Altstaetter, recalling his experience as a prisoner taken by Fagen's army.[25] Altstaetter mentioned that it was his West Point ring that was taken by Fagen. He stated that there were about four hundred men under Fagen's command and that he vowed never to be captured alive by the U.S. Army. The white officer noted the modest but humane treatment he received: "We slept side by side, together in a little hut, and ate out of the same dish, having only one dish." He was eventually released by Fagen, who never returned his ring.

More than a century after Fagen's death, his story along with the disparate stories of the more than one thousand black soldiers who remained and lived in the Philippines after the Philippine-American War[26] continues to disturb the romantic narrative of America's benevolent assimilation of the Philippines. These abject bodies of an imperialist war produced letters and eyewitness accounts that found their way to the Negro press and provided an overseas racialized counterpart to the violence blacks were experiencing in Jim Crow America.

THE FILIPINO INSURGENT'S BLACK BODY

In 1898, racial ideas about the Filipino native were being formed in popular and political discourse. As Rick Baldoz notes, race was invoked by those for and against the military occupation and annexation of the Philippines.[27] Both white imperialists and anti-imperialists, while vigorously disagreeing on the issue of Philippine colonization, freely and interchangeably used the stereotype of the Filipino as a "savage." University of Chicago professor Harry Pratt Judson wrote in favor of colonizing the Philippines as an "annexed territory" without extending citizenship or constitutional rights to "inferior races."[28] Yale professor Theodore S. Woolsey, on the other hand, objected to the colonization of the Philippines but used the backwardness of the country to make his point that colonizing it would be fiscally unfeasible. He viewed colonization as "the burden of administration and responsibility for the conduct of seven millions of half-civilized or savage Filipinos."[29]

While journalistic essays carried on the debate about American empire-building, other literary forms, including those written by non-Americans, took on the issue as well. A popular poem by Rudyard Kipling, "The White Man's Burden," romanticized and encouraged the imperial project of colonizing the Philippines. In the poem, Filipinos were described as "fluttered folk and wild," and also as "sullen peoples, / half devil and half child." Kipling also described empire-building as a manly act, an affirmation of American manhood that, up to that moment of 1898, was unavailable to a "young" republic. He writes:

Take up the White Man's burden!
    Have done with childish days—
The lightly-proffered laurel,
    The easy ungrudged praise:
Comes now, to search your manhood
    Through all the thankless years,
Cold, edged with dear-bought wisdom,
    The judgment of your peers. (*Literary Digest* 219)

Ever the cheerleader for Anglo supremacy and expansionism, Kipling encourages the United States to join other imperial powers who have taken on the "White Man's Burden"—that of colonizing and disciplining savage races. This burden or mission is represented as a search for "manhood," and the United States is encouraged to learn from the older and more established colonial powers, which can pass on to the fledgling imperialist "the judgment of your peers."

After its publication, parodies of Kipling's proimperialist poem appeared in other papers. The London *Truth* published an anti-imperialist poem by a writer named Labouchere entitled "The Brown Man's Burden." The poem viewed colonization as the gratification of "greed" that entailed clearing away the "niggers," the racial epithet used by white American soldiers for Filipinos. Imperialism meant "piling on" more burdens upon the "brown man." To quote from the "The Brown Man's Burden":

> Pile on the brown man's burden,
>   Compel him to be free;
> Let all your manifestoes
>   Reek with philanthropy.
> And if with heathen folly
>   He dares your will dispute,
> Then in the name of freedom
>   Don't hesitate to shoot.
> Pile on the brown man's burden,
>   And if his cry be sore,
> That surely need not irk you—
>   Ye've driven slaves before.
> Seize on his ports and pastures,
>   The fields his people tread;
> Go make from them your living,
>   And mark them with his dead. (*Literary Digest* 21)

In this parody, imperial expansion is deromanticized by exposing the hypocrisy and the greed behind its facade of a civilizing mission and philanthropy. The author reminds American readers that it was Americans themselves who encouraged Filipinos to throw off the yoke of Spanish imperialism. The writer then sarcastically advises Americans to shoot the "brown man" if, after following their manifestos to be free, he dares to question Americans who have now taken over his country. The poem continues by making a reference to slavery and how the colonization of the Philippines was not a new form of racial violence.

In the *New York Times*, Ernest H. Crosby wrote another parody. In Crosby's anti-imperialist poem, some vices and diseases were not to be found in the "degenerate" tropics until they were actually brought over by America's "sturdy sons." To quote Crosby:

> Take up the White Man's burden;
>   Send forth your sturdy sons,

And load them down with whisky
    And Testaments and guns.
Throw in a few diseases
    To spread in tropic climes,
For there the healthy niggers
    Are quite behind the times. (*Literary Digest* 21)

The poem offers blistering comment about the U.S. Army; the "sturdy sons" of the United States do not in fact uplift or civilize the natives but corrupt and defile them. The poem also invokes the familiar racial epithet used by white soldiers to refer to Filipinos.

In mainstream editorial cartoons across the United States, as among white soldiers in the Philippines, Filipino savagery was conflated with blackness. Filipinos were represented as black figures, such as the image of the sword-bearing Aguinaldo with hoop earrings, and of the Filipino "native" wearing a grass skirt (figures 30 and 31). Another cartoon shows a black figure in a grass skirt carried by an American soldier who is heading toward a schoolhouse with the flag of the United States. This cartoon, entitled "The White Man's Burden" (a clear reference to the Kipling poem), suggests that colonization is the burden of the United States because it is a "civilized" nation weighted down with the task of civilizing savages through education (figure 32).

Discussions of Filipino savagery periodically appeared in print. The *Star*, published in Washington, described Filipinos as "treacherous, arrogant, stupid and vindictive, impervious to gratitude, incapable of recognizing obligations." It added, "Centuries of barbarism and subjection have made them merely cunning and dishonest. We cannot safely treat them as our equals, for the simple and sufficient reason that they could not understand it. They do not know the meaning of justice and good faith." the *Star* advocated a more brutal conduct in the war against Filipinos, who, after all, were not "moral equals" of Americans. Fighting savages meant that the rules of civilized warfare did not apply in the Philippine American War. Other publications such as the *Detroit News* recommended the suppression of all Filipino dissent against American military rule. The *News* begins by describing the Philippine revolution against the U.S. Army as merely an "insurrection" and goes on:

The insurrection began under Spanish rule must be suppressed under American rule. The men that defied the authority of Spain must be punished for transferring their defiance to the authority of the United States. The patriots of a year ago have become savages to be treated after the manner of savages—and more power to the Krag-Jörgensen rifle that does the treating.

A JOB LOT.

It is considered absolutely necessary that a first-class statesman be sent to Manila to investigate the situation there.—Cablegram.

—*The Republic, St. Louis.*

Fig. 30. The Filipino in a grass skirt. From *Literary Digest* 18.2 January–June 1899: 33.

In 1898, at the outbreak of the Spanish-American War, the United States recognized Filipinos as allies and as "patriots" for their revolution against Spanish imperialism. But when Filipinos continued their war for independence by fighting the U.S. Army—their former brothers in arms who now had turned their cannons and rifles on them, to preserve the growing American family of new territories—these same Filipinos were suddenly transformed into "savages" who needed to be treated as such. The shift from patriot to savage took less than a year, yet the image of the savage had remarkable staying power, outlasting the actual Philippine-American War many times over. The final sentence that endorses the treatment of Filipinos with the "Krag-Jörgensen rifle"

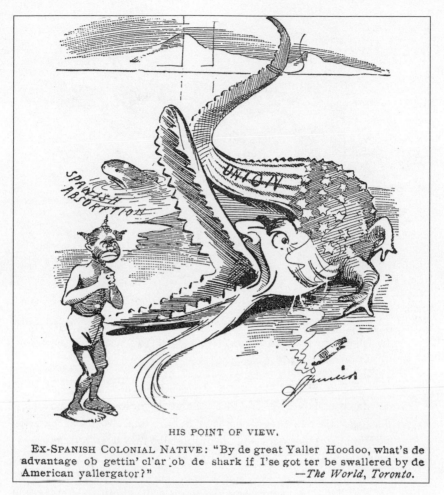

HIS POINT OF VIEW.

Ex-Spanish Colonial Native: "By de great Yaller Hoodoo, what's de advantage ob gettin' cl'ar ob de shark if I'se got ter be swallered by de American yallergator?"   —*The World, Toronto.*

Fig. 31. From *Literary Digest* 18.5 January–June 1899: 141.

suggests that savages cannot be treated any other way but through violence. A good rifle was necessary in the treatment of savages.

Not only were Filipinos seen as savages, they also were viewed as simian and treacherous. According to one account:

It is impossible for the United States to hold themselves responsible for the acts of half-wild peoples. . . . I sometimes think that this [*sic*] people are nearer the monkey than the man. Conceive, if you can, a people made up of individuals without the least consistency of character—anything to anybody at any time. One day, a Filipino may be your sworn friend, and the next day

THE WHITE MAN'S BURDEN.— *The Journal, Detroit.*

Fig. 32. The Filipino in a grass skirt. From *Literary Digest* 18.7 January–June 1899: 180.

he may stab you in the back, and that without provocation. This character is not due to volatile weakness of character, but to a total absence of character, for the Filipino is phlegmatic and unemotional in the extreme. (*Literary Digest* 18, no. 11: 297)

The claim that Filipinos are monkey-like reprises the popular stereotypes of blacks being "apelike" and "bestial," more animal than human. The repugnant comparisons extend to other nonwhite races. The Filipino as a stereotype of the treacherous and inscrutable "Oriental" surfaces elsewhere in this editorial. In another editorial published in *Harper's Weekly*, Frank D. Millet observes that Filipino treachery is comparable to red savagery. Millet wrote: "The Filipinos are intensely superstitious, inordinately vain, and, like all people of the Malay stock, treacherous—that is, they have no code of honor or morals as regards an enemy. . . . If we have to carry on a campaign against them, it will be found that they are a most harassing and difficult enemy in all the arts of uncivilized warfare—much the same as the North American Indians" (*Literary Digest* 18, no. 13: 358–59).

Other accounts exemplified Filipino treachery in unfounded and unsub-

stantiated characterizations of the leaders of the Filipino revolution. A testi-
monial by a Belgian consul to Manila Edward C. André, published in the *New
York Independent*, described Filipino general Antonio Luna as an ambitious
and unscrupulous man: "He really is the leader of the radical independents,
and is both bloodthirsty and unprincipled" (*Literary Digest* 18, no. 13: 357).
The most dangerous elements of the Filipino revolutionary army for André,
however, were not the middle-class Filipino leaders but those, like lawyer Apolinario Mabini, who came from humble origins. He wrote: "The radicals . . .
have no property. They have nothing to risk or lose, but everything to gain in
a revolution" (*Literary Digest* 358). A European diplomat who claims personal
knowledge of revolutionaries who have no standing in the government they are
fighting, and is therefore unlikely to have encountered them, is hardly a cred-
ible source.

Another common representation during the period is that of the infantilized
Filipino, incapable of most grown-up actions, least of all of governing himself.
In one editorial cartoon, Uncle Sam laughs at a small person marching in a helmet many sizes too large that comically covers his face. The "little native" holds
a sword with the name "Aguinaldo" on the scabbard (figure 33), representing
the Filipino revolutionary general Emilio Aguinaldo, who was president of the
short-lived Philippine Republic and is now depicted as impotent and laughable.
Caricatures of Aguinaldo also represented him as a wild, savage child with dark
skin, with Uncle Sam as a paternal figure. In figure 34, Uncle Sam holds Aguinaldo as he sits on a rocking chair with another weeping savage baby. The word
"Iloilo," a province occupied by Filipino revolutionaries, is partially seen on the
shirt of this second savage baby. In another cartoon, a small dark boy with two
not very menacing pistols fires at Uncle Sam, who points a bayonet to the native boy's throat (figure 35). The meaning of these images is plain: Filipinos who
resist Americans are being merely childish and unreasonable in the face of the
firm yet necessary guidance offered by their benevolent new guardians.

While these cartoons also suggest that the fledgling Philippine army would
not last long against the veteran and far more powerful U.S. Army, historical
accounts of the war show that the Filipinos, heavily outgunned, did not give
up easily. Their war lasted much longer than the recently concluded Spanish-
American War, which was fought by two more evenly matched combatants.
Filipinos—the helpless juveniles pictured in the cartoons—managed to hold an
emerging world power at bay by fighting a crafty, grown-up guerrilla war. That
was hardly child's play at all.

As early as February 1899, during the first few days of the war, some international newspapers had correctly predicted that the Philippine army would
resort to long-term guerrilla warfare (*Literary Digest* 18, no. 9: 260). The Vienna

UNCLE SAM: "Where did you get that hat?"—*The Herald, Boston.*

Fig. 33. Infantilizing Aguinaldo and the Filipino revolutionaries. "Uncle Sam: 'Where did you get that hat?'" *Literary Digest* 18.6 January–June 1899: 152.

Tageblatt wrote that even if the Philippine fighters were defeated, "a guerrilla war may be carried on for six years" (*Literary Digest* 18, no. 5: 142). Similarly, the Hong Kong *Telegraph* predicted that Filipinos "would be able to carry on a most trying guerrilla warfare for a long period." During the first week of the war, there were reports of the loss of many lives for the Filipino army. In one battle alone, 160 Filipinos were killed and eighty-seven wounded (*Literary Digest* 18, no. 5: 180). Despite these losses, Filipino men *and women* carried on their war against the new colonizers; one account by the Associated Press mentions that members of the American hospital corps were shocked to discover "several women, in masculine uniform, and with hair cropped" among those killed in action (*Literary Digest* 18, no. 5: 180). Despite many warnings to the contrary, Americans were still caught by surprise by the Filipino guerrilla war, which is perhaps what happens when you underestimate children.

In the Spanish-language Philippine newspapers circulating at the time, the Filipino revolutionaries wrote about their need to continue the fight for independence. These statements were translated from Spanish and published in the United States in publications such as the *Literary Digest*. Belying the American expectation of the rustic and unschooled "little native boy," Filipinos were able to effectively articulate their anger toward the new colonizer and their determi-

HOLDING HIS OWN.

UNCLE SAM: "This isn't exactly pleasant, but these children have got to be brought up right, and I'm not backing out on the job."

— *The Journal, Minneapolis.*

Fig. 34. Aguinaldo as a savage baby. "Holding His Own. Uncle Sam: 'This isn't exactly pleasant, but these children have got to be brought up right, and I'm not backing out on the job.'" *Literary Digest* 18.9 January–June 1899: 240.

nation to pursue independence. One statement published in *Republica Filipina* declared:

> We want independence at any price, and will not recognize the transaction by which we are sold like so many cattle. The Americans have over and over again asserted that the only object of their war with Spain was to give independence to the Spanish colonies, and the Philippine people will not rest

PHILANTHROPY UP TO DATE.

UNCLE SAM: "Consarn yer picter, I'll larn you that 'Government derives its just powers from the consent of the governed,' whether they like it or not!"   —*The Globe, Toronto.*

Fig. 35. Bayonet diplomacy. "Philanthropy Up to Date. Uncle Sam: 'Consarn yer picter, I'll larn you that Government derives its just powers from the consent of the governed, whether they like it or not!'" *Literary Digest* 18.9: 260.

until they have won that independence. The yoke of the new master will not be as irksome as that of the old, we are informed, but chains are hateful to us tho [*sic*] they be gilded. (*Literary Digest* 260)

In this statement, the Filipino revolutionaries made clear they did not recognize American authority in the Islands and reminded American readers about the motives behind the earlier U.S. war with Spain. At the time, the United States went to war with Spain to help the cause of Cuban independence. The Filipinos who wrote the statement recognized how ironic it was that the same country that fought for Cuban independence was now their own colonizer as well. Despite promises of a "benevolent" American rule of the Islands, the revolutionaries rightly believed that any rule by an external power, no matter how well intentioned, would still be a "yoke," a fetter on freedom.

The war dragged on for months, much to the U.S. military command's bedevilment, and American setbacks in the war were censored upon the orders of General Elwell Otis. In July 1899, the Manila correspondents for various American newspapers disseminated a letter of protest complaining that Otis had censored their dispatches to present instead an "ultra-optimistic view" of the war in the Philippines that would not alarm the American public. The journalists mentioned that hospital reports were prohibited from being released, thus suppressing information on how many Filipino revolutionaries and civilians and American soldiers were killed or wounded. Editorials from all over the nation followed the letter of protest and demanded to learn the truth about the war.[30]

Amid these calls for truth and more open communications from the military, racialized representations of Filipinos continued to appear in editorial cartoons and news reports. In November 1899, the *Chicago Inter Ocean* compared the war to the "Indian campaigns" and confidently predicted that the Filipinos would be defeated just as the Indians were defeated, because more than a hundred of the generals and officers in the Philippine war were "Indian veterans" who knew how to crack "Indian tactics."[31] This allusion to the "Indian wars" recalls Amy Kaplan's idea that wars "continue each other" through cyclic discourses that generate symbolic meanings that transpose and reinterpret earlier wars.[32] Appropriately, it must be noted that Filipinos were called "indios" (Indians) by their Spanish colonizers. And once the American frontier had moved overseas to the Philippines, Filipinos joined the tribes of "the Cheyennes, Arapahoes, Comanches, Modocs, Apaches, Nez Perces, Utes, Sioux and the Piutes" (*Literary Digest* 19, no. 22: 634) as stumbling blocks to Manifest Destiny, which had continued rolling westward, vanquishing savages along the way.

If military analogues in the Philippine-American War were mostly American Indian, representations of the Filipino colonial subject, and former general and president Aguinaldo in particular, remained resolutely black. Figure 36 shows Aguinaldo as a bird-man, phenotypically black with a dark face and thick lips. In another cartoon, Aguinaldo sits in a classroom, drawn as a young student with other young wards of Uncle Sam who are forced to learn the "ABC's of self-government" (figure 37). In December 1901, a cartoon shows Aguinaldo as a pickaninny with "Philippines" written on his shirt as he hangs a Christmas stocking (figure 38). A sign that reads "Funds for maintenance of government in the Philippine Islands" hangs near his Christmas stocking. In figure 39, two black figures smoke. The larger of the two represents "Cuba," holding a large cigar with the smoke of "independence" wafting in the air. "Cuba" speaks to the smaller "Philippines," in a racist depiction of the black vernacular, that he may someday enjoy independence.

From 1899 to 1902, racialized images of Aguinaldo, and by extension all

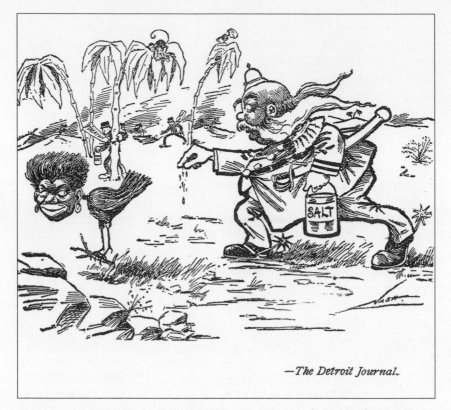

—*The Detroit Journal.*

Fig. 36. Aguinaldo as a pickaninny-bird. "The Pursuit of Aguinaldo in Cartoon." *Literary Digest* 19.22: 634.

Filipinos, circulated in newspapers across the nation as justification for the war and colonization, and also demonstrated the centrality of blackness in turn-of-the-century discourses on the U.S. empire and the Philippine colony. For most white Americans, this representation was logical and understandable, since they uniformly read blackness as primitive, savage, backward, and incorrigible, and clearly saw all these qualities in their new enemies, the Filipinos. These racial discourses, however, would be read and interpreted differently by African Americans, who at the time were struggling with their own war against white supremacy and racism.

READING LYNCHING AND IMPERIALISM

Critiques of racism and imperialism are part of an old tradition in African American political discourse. As early as 1846, Frederick Douglass wrote

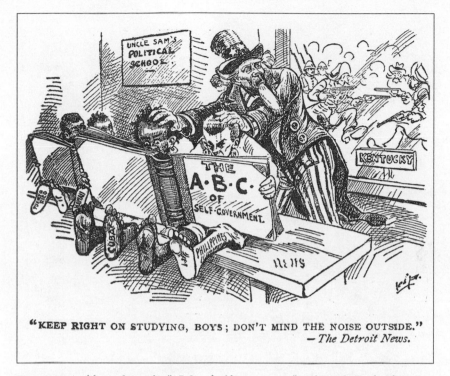

Fig. 37. Aguinaldo studying the "ABCs of self-government" with Uncle Sam's other savage pupils. "Keep right on studying, boys; don't mind the noise outside." *Literary Digest* 20.7: 204.

against the United States' war against Mexico (Katz vii). Prior to the "Philippine war," black journalists voiced their opposition to the Spanish-American War of 1898, criticizing it as unjust. On April 30, 1898, the Salt Lake City's *Broad Ax* wrote that the "Negro's main enemy is Southern lynchers," not the Spaniards (Marks 51). Similarly, the *Iowa State Bystander* in May 6, 1898 wrote, "White America's cruelty equals Spain's" in the continued lynchings of men and women "murdered by the American white people in the past 25 years" (Marks 52). Black communities, concluded Kansas's *Coffeyville Journal* on May 7, 1898, were not "spoiling for a fight" for a country that could not protect its "colored" citizens (Marks 53). The hypocrisy in patriotic rhetoric was not lost on the *Parsons Weekly Blade*. On June 11, 1898, the *Blade* argued that even as "Uncle Sam can find time to shoot Spaniards for their cruelty to Cubans," the American nation continues to ignore lynchings in places such as Louisiana, Texas, Maryland, Missouri, and Arkansas (Marks 67).

In 1899, critical voices in the Negro press focused on the Philippines and the

ANOTHER STOCKING TO FILL.
— *The Minneapolis Times.*

Fig. 38. Aguinaldo as a pickaninny. "Another stocking to fill." *Literary Digest* 23.25: 793.

"new" war. Negro newspapers at the turn of the twentieth century suggested that the Philippine-American War for many black Americans was just another imperialist war that sought to enforce Jim Crow laws on another dark race. A common theme running in editorials of proexpansion newspapers was the notion of imperialism as "assimilation." For American statesmen eager to claim the islands for the U.S. flag, Filipinos were portrayed as "orphans" separated "from their Spanish fathers and desired by other European powers."[33] To protect the "orphaned" Filipinos from the European colonialists, the United States kindly annexed the Philippines. Thus, Vicente L. Rafael describes U.S. colonization of the Philippines as "white love," particularly a love that is founded on

CUBA: "Yo' watch me, chile, mebbe yo' hab a chance yo'se'f some day."
—*The Ohio State Journal, Columbus.*

Fig. 39. Cuba and the Philippines as pickaninnies, desiring the "smoke" of independence. "Cuba: 'Yo' watch me, chile, mebbe yo' hab a chance yo'se'f some day.'" *Literary
Digest* 24.21: 703.

racial ideas of white supremacy and the racializing discourse that constructs
the dark "beloved," the natives. The idea of colonization as "white love" is a
"benign" version of Hazel Carby's fiercer interpretation of American expansion
as "white rape."

War and colonization established and maintained U.S. racial and economic
hegemony abroad; lynchings did the same at home. But while lynching and war
were both instruments of white supremacy, they were understood by most Americans as unrelated events, separated by thousands of miles and happening to two
entirely different entities. However, starting in the late nineteenth century, black
intellectuals and black soldiers saw lynching and empire as two interconnected
processes of domination over the darker races. This recognition eventually led
to a counterhegemonic interpretation of lynching and empire, an interpretation elaborating the shared histories of racial violence and economic oppression
of black Americans in the United States and colonized peoples in Asia and the

Caribbean. This "third worldist perspective," resurrected in the early writings of W. E. B. DuBois and common among Pan-Africanist intellectuals in the 1950s, was in fact already in existence in the late nineteenth century.[34]

Historian Paul Kramer writes that in the Philippines at the turn of the century, American colonial officials and anthropologists who were faced with the task of narrating or "making racial sense of the population" drew on the discourse and racial ideas of the "Negro problem."[35] By discursively representing Filipino savagery in that context, the savage conduct of the Philippine-American War was justified to the nation, just as lynching was justified as an answer to the Negro problem. Literary critic Sandra Gunning notes that there was an antiblack message in discourses at the turn of the century regarding the unassimilability of the darker races, who were deemed "inferior human species."[36] For Americans at the time, these darker races included Filipinos. As Gunning observes, in 1899 Theodore Roosevelt referred to Aguinaldo as "the typical representative of savagery, the typical foe of civilization of the American people" (Gunning 31).

The contentious debates over an American empire in Asia and the conduct of the war can be gleaned from the remarks made by an African American newspaper that supported the annexation of the Philippines by the United States. An editorial from the *Indianapolis Freeman*, dated October 7, 1899, argues:

> Those papers and prominent citizens, who said that the Negro was a fool if he espoused the cause of our government as against the Philippines, have some considerable crow to eat, or in order to be consistent, prove to be the fools themselves. The strife is no race war. It is quite time for the Negroes to quit claiming kindred with every black face from Hannibal down. Hannibal was no Negro, nor was Aguinaldo. We are to share in the glories or defeats of our country's wars, that is patriotism pure and simple. (Marks 150)

The editorial reprimanded African American intellectuals who opposed the war, reminding them that the Philippine-American War was an opportunity to prove their patriotism and choose country over skin. Pro-expansionist African Americans believed that, by professing their zealous nationalism, they would eventually be given fair treatment under the law and enjoy civil liberties. Black folks, according to this argument, should stop "claiming kindred" with other members of the darker races just because they were not white; it would be more to their advantage if they supported war and empire. By adamantly stating that Aguinaldo was "no Negro," the editorial had actually betrayed a proexpansionist worry: it recognized that most members of African American communities saw through the hypocrisy of Philippine annexation and America's imperial ambitions (Litwack 405) and knew that casting their lot with a white man's war would not improve their situation. Thus, while the dissemination of the racial image of Filipinos in proannexation newspapers, in both mainstream and black presses, was a hegemonic racial project in support of imperialism, this same racial image became a counterhegemonic racial project in the "Negro press" that allowed it to maintain anti-imperialist and antiracist positions against the war. In short, for most African Americans, Aguinaldo *was* a Negro, and the racialized representations of Filipinos only served to strengthen African Americans' identification and deepen their empathy.

The scholar George P. Marks III found, in reading editorials from 1898 to 1900, that many Negro newspapers were critical of the war and colonization. The American nation, writes Marks, "was not wise, just and democratic enough to govern people of a darker hue in the Philippines or anywhere" (Marks xviii). A recurring theme among the editorials in the anti-imperialist black press was "the interconnection between the government's domestic and foreign policy in dealing with dark-skinned people" (Marks xvii).

On December 10, 1898, a few days before the ratification of the Treaty of Paris (under which the United States purchased the Philippines from Spain), the *Parsons Weekly Blade* drew an analogy between the U.S. annexation of former Spain colonial possessions and "highway robbery." The *Blade* likened Spain's colonial subjects to children being whipped by Spain, who had wised up and rebelled, and who now needed Uncle Sam's protection from Spain. Uncle Sam, argued the *Blade*, obligingly but not altruistically "steps in and takes the children under his arm for protection"; in the Philippines' case, for example, the United States treacherously moves on to another side of the globe and "gobbles up another small kingdom." The *Blade* concludes: "All this highway robbery is done in the name of humanity and is done by a nation that shows by its actions at home that the principles of humanity are an unknown factor when the treatment of the American Negro is taken into consideration" (Marks 106). Continuing this tack, on January 7, 1899, the *Cleveland Gazette* reported that Ida Wells-Barnett, the black journalist who exposed the horrors of lynchings in the South, maintained that all black citizens should oppose expansion until the U.S. government could "protect the Negro at home" from white mob violence (Marks 109).

On February 4, 1899, the first day of the Philippine-American War, the *Washington Bee* reported that "a majority of the negroes in this country are opposed to expansion" since most blacks believed that a government that could not protect its citizens from racial violence at home had no business invading another country abroad. The *Bee* added that the status of an "American protectorate" was "nothing more than political and physical oppression" and that expansion was a fraud (Marks 112). A week later, on February 11, 1899, the *Bee* published an editorial entitled "Negroes Opposed to the Treaty of Paris." The *Bee* mentioned that the "consensus of opinion among the negro citizens of this government was naturally opposed to a ratification of the treaty," based on the grounds that black citizens were denied their rights in the United States, a circumstance that Filipinos in the Philippines would share once they were subject peoples of the United States (Marks 114).

The same day, the *Coffeyville American* published a piece against the U.S. annexation of the Philippines. The *American* reasoned that the question of the annexation was not merely confined to the right of the American government to acquire land "by purchase or conquest" but was an issue that affected all "people who belong to the dark-skinned races." The *American* pointed to the historical treatment of Indians, Chinese, and Negroes by "white Americans" and concluded that the Filipinos would be mistreated as these other nonwhites had been. American civilization had "very little to commend it," and it would be doubtful to extend it to the newly acquired territories (Marks 114–15).

The war in the Philippines was viewed by some as a "war for humanity." But, as the *Indianapolis Recorder* described it on February 18, 1899, the war had become a "slaughter" and a war for greed. During the first month of the Philippine war, the *Recorder* mentioned that "6,000 natives" had been killed and that what was being established in the Islands was "the dominating mastery of the Anglo-Saxon asserting itself; humanity—never!" (Marks 115–16) The following month, on March 4, the *Recorder* wrote that Filipinos were being "civilized" by the American army just as the North American Indians had been "civilized" through war and violence (Marks 116). Some black journalists admired the Filipino insurgents for continuing to struggle despite tremendous odds. On March 11, 1899, the *Washington Bee* wrote that Filipinos exhibited "the spirit of heroism" and that their struggle for independence proved that "all people who are oppressed will fight, and if need be, die for their liberty." The *Bee* also linked the struggles of the Filipinos for independence from the United States with the struggle of colored citizens for constitutional rights and "hence a bond of sympathy naturally springs up" (Marks 116–17).

Elsewhere, the *Recorder* on March 18, 1899, described the "bayonet-imposed civilization" of the United States:

The Americans are determined to make the Filipinos accept civilization at the point of the bayonet. The officers in command of the American forces are old Indian fighters, who owe their success to the close adherence to the theory that "a dead Indian is the best Indian." They will employ the same methods in dealing with the Filipinos. (Marks 117)

This editorial was accurate in its assessment of the racial attitudes of U.S. Army officers and their violent conduct of the war. Most of the officers assigned to the war were "Indian veterans," the same soldiers who fought the Apaches, Comanches, Kiowas, Sioux, and others. Indeed, of the generals who served the U.S. Army in the Philippines from 1898 to 1900, 87 percent had fought in the "Indian wars."[37] As noted earlier, the proexpansionist *Chicago Inter Ocean* would make a similar assertion six months hence, but in an entirely different jingoistic tone that touted the ruthless potential of Indian war tactics to achieve results. Both periodicals were correct, of course: the tactics employed in the two wars were pronouncedly alike, with predictably similar tragic results. Just as mass population transfers onto reservations ended Indian resistance, decimated their population, and eradicated their lifestyle and culture, the forced movement of Filipinos into *reconcentrados*—concentration camps—resulted in the death from hunger, disease, and overcrowding of tens of thousands of civilians. Between two hundred thousand and one million Filipino civilians were estimated to have died in the Philippine-American War.

As if on cue, a *Salt Lake City Broad Ax* editorial, dated March 25, 1899, expounds on the continuum of violence of American expansion, from the frontier to the Pacific:

> When the Pilgrim Fathers landed at Plymouth Rock, they came into contact with the law-abiding and peaceful Indians; and the blood stained pages of history record their hellish plots. The Fathers robbed, plundered the Indians and outraged their wives and daughters and murdered them, so that they could acquire their land without compensating them for it. . . . The same fate awaits Aguinaldo and his subjects if they permit themselves to be conquered. . . . For if they submit, the same treatment is in store for them which has been meted out to the Negro for over two hundred and fifty years.
>
> What right has this or any other nation to interfere with the inhabitants of those islands? What right has it to foully murder innocent women and children? . . . This war is simply being waged to satisfy the robbers, murderers, and unscrupulous monopolists who are crying for more blood! This country is not invested with any valid title to those islands. (Marks 118)

The *Broad Ax* outlines an alternative history of the United States that directly challenges the nationalist narrative of American benevolence, innocence, and exceptionalism. Instead, the history narrated here is one of American malevolence and greed. Violence, rape, racism, and capitalism, in the guise of robbers and "unscrupulous monopolists who are crying for more blood," are the forces that construct colonial "white love."

In the Negro newspapers, the ascribed "savagery" of Filipinos (as propagated by the proexpansionist press) and the actual savagery of the war against them were invoked by black journalists in their own commentaries on the savagery of life under the lynch law. On April 25, 1899, the *Broad Ax* wrote that the American people were deceived into believing that U.S. soldiers were sent to the Islands "on a mission of love and goodwill, and to carry the torch of liberty and freedom to those benighted savages." Instead, in a brief span of eighty days since the start of the war, American soldiers had killed over "6,000 of the natives—more than the Spaniards have killed in fifty years." The *Broad Ax* added, with an ironic tone, that this slaughter may have been counted as a "blessing," since Filipinos were not considered civilized "by the people of this country who believe in mob and lynch law." For the *Broad Ax*, the policy of annexation was "inhuman, blood-thirsty," and "wrong," and the American imperialists were willing to "wade in human blood and gore up to their knees in order to fasten a new policy upon the people" (Marks 124). Similarly, the *Iowa State Bystander* published an editorial on April 28, 1899, that criticized the U.S. government for its inaction on the lynchings in the South and the continuing violence being inflicted against the Filipino people:

> The recent lynchings in the Southland, especially in Georgia and the Carolinas, of colored people who are accused of a crime without a trial, evidence, or facts except the mere accusation, has become a stench upon our civilization and damnable curse on our vaunted humanity. . . . Is this civilization? Is this America's justice? Is this humanity? Are those white people insane? . . . Were Americans fighting the Spaniards to free Cuba from barbarous treatment of Spain; what thinks Spain of our barbarous treatment of our own citizens? Why are we now fighting the natives 10,000 miles away in the Philippine Islands, trying to force our flag and banner over them to civilize them? If the action of the Southern States is civilization, then away with such a government. (Marks 125)

The *Bystander* concluded that the American government had no right to ask its black citizens to serve in the Philippine war if the government could not protect them from racial violence, echoing a popular sentiment among black communities at the time that there was a connection between racial violence at home and abroad.

The black press was very much aware of the racist perspectives of white soldiers deployed to the Philippine Islands during the war, mostly as described by black soldiers in letters home and in those sent to Negro newspapers. On May 16, 1899, the editors of the *Salt Lake City Broad Ax* wrote that they were vehemently opposed to annexation due to "race prejudice": they had found out from their sources that it was a common practice among white soldiers to call Filipinos "niggers." Black soldiers writing home would complain that white soldiers had "an utter contempt 'for the niggers which they are engaged in slaying.'" The *Broad Ax* argued that Negroes with any conscience must arrive at the conclusion "that the war is being waged solely for greed and gold and not in the interest of suffering humanity" (126). The *Progress* of Omaha, Nebraska, declared in outrage: "Every soldier in the Philippines who uses the term 'nigger' does so with hell-born contempt for the negro of the United States, and it is our one desire that he be cured of his fiendish malady by a Filipino bullet" (128). On February 7, 1900, the *Reporter* of Helena, Arkansas, wished that every Negro soldier who went to the Philippines to fight in the war would get "ball-stung." The *Reporter* blisteringly wrote:

> Every colored soldier who leaves the United States and goes out to the Philippine Islands to fight the brave men there who are struggling and dying for their liberty is simply fighting to curse the country with color-phobia, jim-crow cars, disenfranchisement, and lynchers and everything that prejudice can do to blight the manhood of the darker races, and as the Filipinos belong to the darker human variety, [it is] the Negro fighting against himself. Any Negro soldier that will cross the ocean to help subjugate the Filipinos is a fool or a villain. . . . May every one of them get ball-stung is our sincere prayer." (Marks 167)

For the Negro newspapers, black soldiers fighting for the American army were really taking part in the racial subjugation of the Filipinos. The war was seen as an effort to restore the racial order of the United States in the Philippine Islands, a racist hierarchy based on white supremacy and the repression of the darker races, which was toppled, in theory but not in practice, in the U.S. Civil War.

Comparisons about the racist treatment of African Americans in the United States, and of Filipinos in the Philippines were obvious not only to most African Americans but to Filipinos themselves. In the *Indianapolis Freeman*, dated May 11, 1900, a black soldier named William Simms wrote that a Filipino child had approached him and asked him a startling question, "Why does the American Negro come from America to fight us when we are much friend to him, and me all the same as you. Why don't you fight those people in America that burn Negroes, that made a beast of you, that took the child from its mother's side and sold it?" (Marks 169) Simms was astonished by the Filipino boy's knowledge of race issues in the United States.

Near an American military camp, a placard was discovered nailed to a tree, with a message written in Spanish addressed to black soldiers. The *Richmond Planet*, dated November 11, 1899, published a translation of the placard:[38]

> To the colored American soldier. It is without honor that you are spilling your costly blood. Your masters have thrown you in the most iniquitous fight with double purposes, in order to make you the instrument of their ambition; and also your hard work will make soon the extinction of your race. Your friends, the Filipinos, give you this good warning. You must consider your situation and your history, and remember that the blood of your brothers, Sam Hose and Gray [who were lynched in the United States earlier that year], proclaims vengeance. (Marks 155)

The placard implored black soldiers to consider the lynchings in the South that happened earlier that year and discouraged black soldiers from fighting a war created by the same people who oppressed them back home. Several hundred copies of the placard, captured later on, were addressed specifically to a colored regiment, the Twenty-Fourth Infantry. This psychological warfare was successful in some cases, even resulting in desertions by African American soldiers who joined Aguinaldo's army. The most famous deserter, as mentioned earlier in the chapter, was David Fagan of the Twenty-Fourth Infantry, who became a general in the Filipino revolutionary army and fought alongside Filipinos for two years before he was captured and beheaded by the U.S. Army (Gatewood 15).

Soldiers who read the placard were disturbed by it even as they took part in the war. This anxiety is reflected in the letter of Michael H. Robinson of the Twenty-Fifth Infantry, published in two installments in the *Colored American* dated March 17 and March 24, 1900. Robinson's letter revealed the dilemma of black soldiers who recognized they were fighting a war unpopular in their own community, yet were compelled by duty to remain in their posts:

> I will say that we of the 25th Infantry feel rather discouraged over the fact that the sacrifice of life and health has to be made for a cause so unpopular among our people. Yet the fact that we are American soldiers instills within us the feeling and resolve to perform our duty, no matter what the consequence may be as to public sentiment. . . . We have been warned several

times by insurgent leaders in the shape of placards, some being placed on trees, others left mysteriously in houses we have occupied, saying to the colored soldier that while he is contending on the field of battle against a people who are struggling for recognition and freedom, your people in America are being lynched and disenfranchised by the same people who are trying to compel us to believe that their government will deal justly and fairly by us. (Gatewood 268)

And in one unsigned letter published in the *Wisconsin Weekly Advocate*, dated May 17, 1900, an anonymous black soldier recounts the maltreatment of Filipinos by white soldiers and his ambivalence at having to fight on their side. He writes:

[They] cursed them as damned niggers, steal [from] and ravish them, rob them on the street of their small change, take from the fruit vendors whatever suited their fancy, and kick the poor unfortunate if he complained, desecrate their church property, and after fighting began, looted everything in sight, burning, robbing graves. . . . But I have seen carcasses lying bare in the boiling sun, the result of raids on receptacles for the dead in search of diamonds. . . . On upbraiding some fellows one morning . . . the reply was: "Do you think we could stay over here and fight these damn niggers without making it pay all it's worth? The government only pays us $13 per month: that's starvation wages. White men can't stand it." Meaning they could not live on such small pay. . . . They talked with impunity of "niggers" to our soldiers, never once thinking that they were talking to home "niggers" and should they be brought to remember that at home this is the same vile epithet they hurl at us. . . . I want to say right here that if it were not for the sake of the 10,000,000 black people in the United States, God alone knows on which side of the subject I would be. (Gatewood 280)

The letter is a sharp indictment of the war and the racism prevalent among white soldiers, and a pained recognition of the shared condition of racial discrimination and violence among African Americans in the United States and Filipinos in the Philippines. The author even goes as far as to say that were it not for the possible repercussions of his desertion—that is, the possibility of even more lynchings if black soldiers were to leave their posts en masse—he would have immediately joined the Filipino rebels in their cause.

What these editorials and letters outline for us is a discourse of black modernity that recognized the connection between violence against Native Americans, African Americans, and colonized peoples such as Filipinos. As a shared burden, U.S. imperial expansion meant extending racial violence on emancipated black Americans and inflicting another brutal war of colonization on Filipinos, who had barely ended their war with Spain, as allies of the United States, no less, in 1898.

BLACK MODERNITY AND DUBOIS

The year 1898 was the originary moment of the circulation of racialized ideas of an American empire. Visions of an American empire began early on in the political life of the nation, with pronouncements like those of geographer Jedidiah Morse in the late eighteenth century—on an American empire "that will comprehend millions of souls" west of the Mississippi—as early expressions of American imperial modernity.[39] It was in the late nineteenth century, however, with the interconnected discourses on race, gender, and power that the ideology of empire took root and materialized as both a policy and an aesthetic. By 1893, Frederick Jackson Turner's thesis on the necessity and the natural order of expansion had taken on such force that many politicians and writers after him echoed his ideas on American expansion as an aspect of American nature. Turner's thesis was in fact, as Campomanes noted, a violent "vision and ideology" that was softened around the edges by notions of "tradition," "nature," and the "natural" order of things.[40] Simultaneous with this articulation of expansionist visions were discourses on the savagery and inferiority of the darker races, such as Native Americans, African Americans, and, later, Filipinos, who would become abject subjects of the new empire. The natural order of things required the subjugation of lesser races through laws, policies, or the violence of lynching.

In the early twentieth century, this new language of empire was being disseminated not only by American proexpansion propagandists but by literary writers as well. In the popular novel *Tarzan of the Apes* (1914) by Edgar Rice Burroughs, the character Tarzan embodies white masculinity as a result of both his Anglo Saxon heritage (his British parents) and his savage boyhood in the jungle, where he was raised by apes and, befitting his status as the only white male, ascended to be their king. Tarzan is an icon of white male hegemony and the American empire.[41] As Gail Bederman has shown, he represents white supremacy, as he is "a one-man lynch mob, a proud murderer of African men" (Bederman 223). Tarzan introduces himself to his love interest, Jane, as "TARZAN, THE KILLER OF BEASTS AND MANY BLACK MEN" (Bederman 226). Burroughs wrote this description in proud capital letters and consistently celebrated the racial violence committed by Tarzan as an essential component of his masculinity. For Burroughs, "the impulse to kill black men" was also "a racially superior man's inherent masculine instinct" (225).

While authors such as Burroughs romanticized the discourses of empire and white supremacy, others chose to challenge and expose the violence. One of these was William Edward Burghardt DuBois. W. E. B. DuBois's multigenre text *Darkwater* (1920) is an example of an American literary work that used an African American modernist perspective in identifying, analyzing, and repurposing a shared history of racism for colonized peoples in Asia and black Americans.[42] It is an articulation of black modernity from the perspective of the enslaved and the oppressed.

While *Darkwater* has been described as "a less successful sequel" to DuBois's popular and critically acclaimed autobiography, *The Souls of Black Folk* (Mostern 28), it is an important text because of its anticolonial perspective and experimental form.[43] In *Darkwater* DuBois locates the colonial world as a central part of world history (Sundquist 29), anticipating the writing of subaltern scholars who would follow decades later. Critic John Carlos Rowe observes that DuBois was one of the first American intellectuals to critique "Euro-American imperialism's reliance on hierarchies of race, gender, and class," as he did in *The Souls of Black Folk* and *Darkwater* (Rowe 215).[44] *Darkwater* is inscribed with or informed by two political formations of twentieth-century African American intellectual history—that of liberalism and Pan-Africanist Marxism (Mostern 31). As a multigenre narrative of "many strands," the text displays DuBois's "anti-colonial thinking" (Sundquist 27).

DuBois's "Pan-Colored hypothesis," or the notion of a world color line that "binds together not simply the children of Africa, but extends through yellow Asia and into the South Sea" (Sundquist 31) is a relevant framework for understanding the writings of black soldiers and journalists who were against the colonial occupation of the Philippines. DuBois's vague notion of a shared "nationhood" of people of color, that they are all united by "a common disaster" of being nonwhite, and "one long memory" of racism, certainly raises the unavoidable problems of racial essentialism and the question of nationalism (31). However, what is illuminating in DuBois's *Darkwater* is its move toward a "politicized abjection," a term I borrow loosely from queer Latino critic Alberto Sandoval-Sánchez.[45] If, for Sandoval-Sánchez, "to embrace abjection is to undo, in some part, racism, shame, homophobia, and the fear of death, allowing for a source of self-empowerment" (549), DuBois lovingly claims black skin as the basis of nationhood and racial solidarity among nonwhite peoples who are intimately aware of the violence of white supremacy and colonialism. *Darkwater* is an unapologetic attack on imperialism, racism, and capitalism and on the violence they inflict on dark-skinned peoples. Like Anna Julia Cooper, whom DuBois quotes in *Darkwater*, and the black journalists from the turn of the twentieth century, for DuBois, lynching and empire were bitter fruits of the same tree.

In *Darkwater*, DuBois describes whiteness as "the ownership of the earth forever and ever, Amen!" (Sundquist 498). He criticizes imperialism as "this new religion of whiteness" (498) and as "[the] conquest sugared with religion; mutilation and rape masquerading as culture" (501). Elsewhere, he discusses the "Authoring" of members of the "darker world" (503), noting that "white culture" disseminates the notion that "'darkies' are born beasts of burden for white folk" (503). Predating Edward Said's notion of modern or "American Orientalism" by sixty years, DuBois undercuts the theoretical concerns of a discourse in support of American empire:

> The supporting arguments grow and twist themselves in the mouths of merchant, scientist, soldier, traveler, writer, and missionary: Darker peoples are dark in mind as well as in body; of dark, uncertain, and imperfect descent . . . they are fools, illogical idiots,—"half-devil and half-child." (504)

"Half-devil and half-child" is from Kipling's poem "White Man's Burden," an ode to the annexation of the Philippines by the United States, and recalls the discourse of abjection that followed after Filipinos resisted in 1899. Natives or "darkies," then, were the "idiots" or the abject bodies in need of American civilization. In imperial discourse, skin color is a significant marker in establishing either superiority or degeneracy. DuBois argues that associated with whiteness is "everything great, good, efficient, fair and honorable" (Sundquist 505). Darkness or black skin is associated with evil: "Everything mean, bad, blundering, cheating and dishonorable is 'yellow'; a bad taste is 'brown'; and the devil is 'black'" (505). He adds that this racist discourse can be found in all forms of American culture: "The changes of this theme are continually rung in picture and story, in newspaper heading and moving-picture, in sermon and school book" (505).

DuBois links this completely institutionalized racism in the United States with imperial expansion, which provides an alternative history of the American nation that is very different from the primary narrative of exceptionalism that has always been offered. To quote from *Darkwater*:

> For two or more centuries America has marched proudly in the van of human hatred,—making bonfires of human flesh and laughing at them hid-

eously, and making the insulting of millions more than a matter of dislike,—
rather a great religion. . . . Instead of standing as a great example of the
success of democracy and the possibility of human brotherhood America
has taken her place as an awful example of its pitfalls and failures, so far as
black and brown and yellow peoples are concerned. . . . Absolutely without
excuse she established a caste system, rushed into preparation for war, and
conquered tropical colonies. (Sundquist 508)

In this radical new history of the U.S. nation, democracy is replaced by racial hatred, violence, and colonial expansion. DuBois narrates the history of
expansion and empire as an abject history of the American nation, shared by
subjugated peoples of darker skin who were unfortunate enough to have been
standing in the way of insatiable destiny and irresistible modernity. For Du-
Bois, confrontation is the only way to salvation. In writing his autobiography as
an alternative history of America, DuBois continues to hold out the possibility
of human brotherhood, but only with the consent of those who share the "common disaster" of having black or brown or yellow or red skin.

Chapter 4

The Bile of Race

White Women's Travel Writing
on the Philippine-American War

In 1903, a political pamphlet entitled *A Massachusetts Woman in the Philippines* was published and distributed out of Boston, Massachusetts, as part of the campaign of the Boston Anti-Imperialist League to shed light on the continuing war in the Philippine Islands. The essay was published anonymously to hide the identity of the author, Helen Calista Wilson, a Radcliffe-educated woman, who traveled unaccompanied to the Philippines and remained in the country for half a decade after publishing her essay. Wilson writes:

> Late in the same afternoon we stopped for a couple of hours at Taal (Batangas). Taal and Lemery form, in fact, one large town, being separated only by a river. Formerly it was the largest and one of the richest towns in the province. It was, however, burned by the Americans, and very largely destroyed, and is still in a thoroughly depressed condition. The streets are almost deserted except in the very central part of the town, and the nipa shacks built up among the ruins are an eloquent testimony to the poverty of the town.[1]

Wilson was not a woman of leisure traveling to the islands for adventure, nor was she a missionary impassioned by an evangelizing desire to bring God and civilization to the natives. As a member and representative of the Anti-Imperialist League,[2] Wilson was in the Philippines to witness firsthand the war and its colonial aftermath that she and her fellow anti-imperialists vehemently opposed.

When *A Massachusetts Woman in the Philippines* was published in the United States, the Philippine-American War had been declared over by President Theodore Roosevelt, although Filipino resistance to U.S. rule would continue for a decade through guerrilla warfare. The forty-eight-page pamphlet was published a year after accounts of military atrocities committed by American soldiers against Filipino natives were being circulated despite the heavy press censorship under the directives of the secretary of war, Elihu Root, and General Elwell Otis.[3] As early as July 17, 1899, American journalists in the Philippines tried to bring attention to escalating violence in the colony and started a petition against Secretary Root's censorship of the actual conditions of the war and "the barbarous practices" of American soldiers (Storey and Codman 10–11). The journalists alleged that the American people were being deceived by censored accounts of the war purged of reports of actual carnage. The Negro press had also exposed some of these atrocities, as discussed earlier.

The savage and racial conduct of the war was a contentious national issue that caused bitter and angry debates in the U.S. Congress and horrified the American public. In 1902, a U.S. Senate hearing was held to investigate the veracity of the reports of American atrocities. The Senate hearings, however, cleared the U.S. Army and accepted the statement of Secretary of War Elihu Root that "the war in the Philippines has been conducted by the American Army with scrupulous regard for the rule of civilized warfare, with careful and genuine consideration for the prisoner and non-combatant, with self restraint, and with humanity."[4] Critics of the war questioned the findings of the hearings, as well as the nominal punishments handed by military courts to rogue officers and soldiers accused of these atrocities.

The court-martial cases of General Jacob Smith and Major Littleton W. T. Waller were controversial events that drew media attention at the time. In late October 1901, as an act of revenge for the slaughter of forty-eight American soldiers by Filipino forces in Balangiga, Samar Province, General Smith ordered Major Waller and his troops to punish the Filipino civilian populace. General Smith gave his infamous orders: "I want no prisoners. I wish you to kill and burn. The more you kill and burn the better you will please me. . . . The interior of Samar must be made a howling wilderness."[5] Despite the gruesome details that surfaced during their court-martial cases and the national debate about torture and military atrocities committed by the U.S. Army in the Philippines, the two officers were let off with light sentences. In March 1902, Major Waller was charged and then acquitted for the execution of eleven Filipino prisoners. In April 1902, General Smith was given the lightest sentence possible for his seven-month brutal campaign in Samar Province, which involved mass executions and the burning of villages, crops, and animals and the uprooting of thousands of Filipino civilians (Bruno 42). General Smith was actually not charged for any war crimes but for "conduct" resulting from his military orders in Samar (Bruno 43). Fearing public outcry, President Theodore Roosevelt ordered General Smith to retire from active service (Bruno 43). Despite his court-martial and President Roosevelt's termination of his position, General Smith continued to receive the support of his fellow officers and some American journalists. Newspaper articles in the mainstream press and in military professional journals believed General Smith was merely a "scapegoat" in the politics of war and that he remained an exemplary soldier of the U.S. Army (Bruno 43).

By mid-1902, Democratic-leaning and independent newspapers in the United States were reporting incidents of torture in the wake of the extreme turn in the war.[6] There were reports of American soldiers cutting off the ears of Filipino corpses, massacres of Filipino civilians, including women and children, in different provinces across the country, and acts of torture such as the water cure (an early form of waterboarding) and Filipinos tied to trees to extract confessions, to name a few (Storey and Codman 10–11, 28–33). In April 1902, the U.S. Congress received a report by Major Cornelius Gardner, the civil governor of Tayabas Province (Quezon), regarding army abuses against the Filipino people, such as "burning of the barrios to lay waste the country" and "the torturing of natives by so-called water cure and other methods" (McCoy 89). In a confidential letter to the War Department, Gardner recounted more atrocities that he had left out of his report: even more accounts of torture, the rapes of Filipino women in Tayabas town, and the brutal treatment and death of two Catholic priests.

These violent accounts of the Philippine-American War serve as the background of white women's travel writing on the Philippine colony. In this chapter, the *bile of race* is the discourse of white, female travel writers who are both agents and critics of empire. Bile as an abject metaphor for race and racism can be traced in travel narratives—essays, journal articles, and memoirs—that describe scenes of resentment or resentfulness toward the Filipino natives as dirty disease carriers or ugly "beast-like" creatures; that convey irritation and annoyance regarding the tropical weather or the conditions in the colony; and that express virulence, anger, or wrath against the Filipino *insurrectos* who were challenging American military rule. Colonial racial affect, such as rage, rancor, and irritability toward the Philippine colony and "the natives," is an expression of the bile of race and is manifested, for example, as the racial and physical violence of a colonial war documented in Helen Calista Wilson's travel essay. Imperial bile then aims to debase the Filipino race and provide a justification for war and genocide, recalling the nineteenth-century social Darwinism that argues "the progress of civilization depends on the suppression or outright elimination of savage life."[7] For the purposes of this discussion, the racial origins of American travel writing on the Philippines, and by extension Asia, are war and empire, specifically the genocidal wars against Native Americans by the U.S. Army, the conquest of the Pacific Islands by European and American settlers, and the forced occupation of the Philippines at the turn of the twentieth century.

While Wilson's *A Massachusetts Woman in the Philippines* has received attention from a few scholars who discuss her work as an example of U.S. women's anti-imperialist writing (Anderson; Murphy; Kramer, *Blood of Government*; Zwick), this chapter discusses Wilson's essay as travel writing that followed and broke the bileful discourse of imperial women's travel writing.[8] Along with Wilson's essay, the other travel texts to be discussed are Mrs. Emily Bronson Conger's memoir, *An Ohio Woman in the Philippines* (1904), and Mrs. Campbell Dauncey's memoir, *An Englishwoman in the Philippines* (1906).

While Vicente Rafael and Dinah Roma-Sianturi have discussed white women's travel writings on the Philippine colony as narratives of colonial domesticity or the colonial picturesque,[9] this chapter takes a different route by discussing imperial bile in white women's travel writing. Lifting the veil off colonial picturesque discourse such as the exotic scenery and the quaint customs of the natives, we read for signs and symbols of colonial violence in the travel texts, both the overt and covert forms of racial violence and cultural taboos witnessed by white women travelers who visited and lived in the Philippines. A central argument of this chapter borrows from historian Ranajit Guha's strategy of translating historical discourse in colonial Indian documents.[10] Guha's reading tactic examines colonial documents for random and seemingly insignificant reports of Indian peasant uprisings, as the "prose of counter-insurgency." For Guha, these peasant uprisings in colonial documents are "narrative indices" and "ideological birthmarks" of colonialism: the narrative origins of colonial discourse. Accordingly, by reading the Philippine narratives of white female travelers as colonial documents, we assume that these texts are inscribed with "bias, judgment and opinion" (Guha 59) that outline the narrative indices of American colonialism through the trope of imperial bile. Put simply, travel writing by white women articulates both the violence of empire and Filipino resistance to U.S. rule, through either actual armed resistance or moments of what Homi Bhabha calls colonial ambivalence (Spurr 185, citing Homi Bhabha). Following Guha, the act of translating these Philippine colonial texts rests on the capacity of "turning things upside down" (Guha) so that familiar signs of colonial violence and power are defamiliarized. This textual rebellion, what critic Simon Gikandi has called "theoretical inversion,"[11] puts signs of colonial violence and power into question and recontextualizes representations of empire by examining the inequalities between white colonial societies and the native communities. Theoretical inversion can be mapped in specific moments or scenes from the women's narratives as the limits of imperial power where we see either native resistance or uncensored, unintentional accounts of gendered and/or racial violence against Filipino natives under U.S. rule. The narrative of an imperial witness is thus never self-evident and may contain moments of a critique of the violence of empire that may or may not have been the author's intention. In this sense, reading these narratives serves as a way to understand the violence and romance of American imperial modernity through inversion and translation. We therefore return to the notion of imperialism as a tender violence through the erotics of imperial abjection by focusing on processes of racialization and heterosexualization in the travel narratives.

My discussion of white women's texts on the Philippines thus departs from the colonial picturesque[12] by focusing on narrative moments of the visibility *and* the disembodiment of colonial violence through "the erasure of the (imperial) body."[13] As feminist scholars have noted, travel accounts by European and white women travelers were intensely aware of how their physical bodies, "as women and as Europeans," shaped their travel experiences (Helmers and Mazzeo 269). Female travel writers narrated how they were "both surveyor and surveyed," and their texts express these two experiences (Helmers and Mazzeo 269–70). Accordingly, the imperial female body has the privilege of being visible and invisible, symbolizing that the violence of empire is both visible and invisible in white women's travel writing. The physical bodies of the native or the colonial subjects of travel texts, however, are very visible, just as their racial difference, their experience of degradation, violence, or suffering, is narrated as part of the travel tale. The natives' marked presence, their savage embodiment, *is* the form of the travel text. The genre of travel writing requires the presence of savage bodies and the visible/invisible presence of the colonizer and the violence of empire. Travel texts thus function like modernity—as narratives of modernity that mask and expose its racial, gendered and imperial logics.

Given the racial dimensions of the Philippine-American War, I consider how popular culture produced during or about the time gives meaning to the imperial eye or "I" in travel writing.[14] If travel writing requires the privileges of seeing, surveilling, and narrating the colonized by the colonizer, travel culture's darker twin is the military eye or intelligence collected during war. Travel writing by white American scientists (Worcester), colonial officials (Worcester again, Barrows, and LeRoy), missionaries (Brown), and a host of white soldier-correspondents supplied images of the colony not only for the travel-hungry reading public but for U.S. military purposes as well.[15] As one historian put it, at the turn of the twentieth century, U.S. intelligence gathering on the Philippine colony relied on "short-term secondment of consultants and contractors—rotating military officers between continental and colonial service, and dispatching experts . . . to frame templates for colonial policy."[16] The travel texts for this discussion were published during the official years of the Philippine-American War, from 1899 to 1902. Others were published after 1902, at a time of Filipino guerrilla warfare and the emerging science of counterinsurgency for the U.S. military. The historical context of these travel texts makes these American narratives the prose of counterinsurgency, both literally and in Guha's sense. Analogous to Guha's subaltern strategy of translation and inversion, this discussion will focus on the American travel writings as narratives of "anticonquest," or what Mary Louise Pratt describes as "the violence of the conquest and destruction of the contact zone" glimpsed in the aftermath "in traces on bodies or in anecdotes" (52–54). In these travel texts, we will trace anti-imperialist tropes as well as imperialist logics that embody the colonial genre of white women's travel writing. This reading will focus on moments in the texts that suggest the aftermath of the "conquest and destruction" of a colonial occupation, by translating and inverting scenes of the colonial picturesque as colonial bile.

Most of the women writers discussed here, with the exception of Wilson, were spouses of colonial officials, merchants, and travelers. The colonial context of these memoirs and travelogues renders the narratives as more than popular sentimental literature; they are the prose of the ascendant American empire at the turn of the twentieth century. In these travel texts, the Filipino native became both a problem and a subject of colonial modernity, with American schoolteachers and travelers as official narrators of the American colonial experiment in the Philippine Islands. Thus the travel narratives functioned as ideological primers for ordinary Americans to embrace their "new" role as enlightened colonizers, introducing modernity through American culture and the creation of a U.S. public school system in the islands. The form and function of these travel narratives about the Philippines will be studied by analyzing the tropes of Filipino savagery and docility in travel cultures, keeping in mind that the grammar of imperial bile was informed by earlier American discourses of Otherness. Imperial bile functioned in the material realm in two ways: first, the travel texts rendered Filipino native resistance to American military rule invisible; and second, all that was "visible" or disseminated in popular culture were images of the primitive and exotic Filipino native. Thus at the moment of guerrilla warfare after 1902, the Filipino *insurrecto* practically vanished from popular imagination and was transformed into the nonthreatening but primitive native in popular travel writing. Yet the travel texts were nonetheless very aware of the furtive yet exigent Filipino peasant insurgency. This discussion highlights the panoptic sensibility of white women's travel accounts, and how accounts of imperial domesticity and the picturesque contain the violent struggle between the colonizer's view of modernity and what modernity meant for the Filipino colonial subject.

BILEFUL DEBATES AND THE ANTI-IMPERIALISTS

Leading the efforts to expose the brutalities in the Philippine-American War was the Anti-Imperialist League. In the same year as the U.S. Senate hearings on military atrocities, the League published the pamphlet *"Marked Severities" in Philippine Warfare* (1902), a collection of accounts by U.S. soldier-witnesses, compiled and written by the lawyers Moorfield Storey and Julian Codman. Storey was a former president of the American Bar Association and was the first white American president of the National Association for the Advancement of Colored People (NAACP]. In *"Marked Severities"* Storey and Codman noted that the genocidal nature of the war began early, in the first five months: "It became apparent that there was at least a considerable element in the army who despised the native inhabitants, and were willing to kill prisoners, burn villages, and to rob and murder non-combatants upon little or no provocation" (Storey and Codman 10). To support the League's claim about the racial and brutal nature of the war, they quoted letters from soldiers. L. F. Adams of Ozark, Missouri, a soldier in the Washington regiment, describes the scene of an early battle on February 4–5, 1899:

> In the path of the Washington Regiment and the Battery D of the Sixth Artillery, there were 1,008 niggers, and a great many wounded. We burned all their houses. I don't know how many men, women, and children the Tennessee boys did kill. They would not take any prisoners. (Storey and Codman 10)

Another soldier, Sergeant Howard McFarland of Company B, Forty-Third Infantry, wrote to the newspaper *Fairfield Journal* of Maine and echoed the racial horrors of the war:

> I am now stationed in a small town in charge of twenty-five men, and have a territory of twenty miles to patrol. . . . At best, this is a very rich country; and we want it. My way of getting it would be to put a regiment into a skirmish line, and blow every nigger into nigger heaven. On Thursday, March 29, eighteen of my company killed seventy-five nigger bolomen, and ten of the nigger gunners. . . . When we find one that is not dead, we have bayonets. (Storey and Codman 10)

The regular use of the racial epithet "nigger" to refer to Filipinos, as attested to by the white soldiers' accounts dating from 1899 and by letters of African American soldiers, suggests that American racism about "the darker races" was indeed exported to the Philippine colony. News of the racist attitudes of white soldiers and the brutalities they committed reinforced the notion that the war had countenanced the expansion of Jim Crow laws to the shores of the new Philippine colony, and this connection between slavery, segregation, and empire-building convinced some Americans to join the Anti-Imperialist League.

Boston reformers, including many former abolitionists, and socialists and suffragettes, founded the Anti-Imperialist League on November 1898.[17] After a year, the League grew to more than a hundred affiliated organizations, with over thirty thousand members and five hundred thousand contributors (Hoganson 12). By contrast, the National American Woman Suffrage Association (NAWSA) had less than nine thousand members in 1900.

By the late nineteenth and the early twentieth centuries, the emergence of suffragist and, later, anti-imperialist movements in the United States coincided with the rise in literacy rates among women and the growing market for sentimental or domestic fiction. By then, travel tales were no longer limited to the experiences of men but included women as travelers and authors. As some scholars have written, travel texts are narratives that are "an implicit celebration of freedom."[18] Rather than interpreting the Philippine travel texts as narratives celebrating modernity and mobility, I examine these texts from the perspective of the colonized by reading them as narratives of immobility for the dominated. In seemingly peaceful, quaint travel accounts of white women, we can read allusions or direct references to the Philippine-American War and its violence, the racialization of Filipinos, and their resistance to U.S. rule. This discussion draws much from critic Saidiya V. Hartman's theorization of "the terror of the mundane and quotidian" in historical texts or the violence of everyday life for the racially dominated.[19] In this case, the racially dominated are the Filipino women, men, and children who lived during the early years of American military occupation and colonial rule.

FILIPINO SUFFERING: HELEN CALISTA WILSON'S *A MASSACHUSETTS WOMAN IN THE PHILIPPINES* (1902)

The bile of racism is traced in the violence of the war itself. Helen Calista Wilson's travel reportage, *A Massachusetts Woman in the Philippines*, narrates politicized abjection by focusing on Filipino suffering. While the title recalls British texts such as Sophia Poole's *The Englishwoman in Egypt: Letters from Cairo* (1844) and Sarah Mytton Maury's *An Englishwoman in America* (1848), Wilson's narrative is farthest from the British imperial tradition of women's travel writing and is staunchly anti-imperialist. It was in 1903 when Wilson made her journey to the Philippine colony and wrote about the conditions there. Fiske Warren, an executive committee member of the Anti-Imperialist League, was to be the publisher and editor of her monograph and paid for her trip to Hong Kong, China, Japan, and Manila (Murphy 261). The publication of *A Massachusetts Woman in the Philippines* was part of the League's political campaign to bring the exiled leader Apolinario Mabini, Aguinaldo's adviser, to the United States to testify about the conditions in the Philippines and to bring an end to the American occupation of the Islands (Zwick 74; Kramer 292–94). Wilson's essay makes no outright references to her personal life, but we can glean from the text that she was a white New England woman fluent in Spanish who traveled to the Philippines as a young, single, and unaccompanied lady, which made her unusual for the time. Her knowledge of Spanish enabled her to associate with elite Filipino families, many of whom were members of the resistance against Spanish and, later, American rule. Her participation in the Anti-Imperialist League also afforded her common ground with most Filipinos.

Although history does not recognize Wilson as one of the more prominent Anti-Imperialists, her essay underscores the crucial role of white women in the U.S. anti-imperialist movement (Murphy 257–61). Her narrative is an important example of American anti-imperialist travel writing, considering that it was written in the actual site of imperialism. But, as Hazel Carby notes, black women writers had long before written editorials and speeches against U.S. imperialism during the Spanish-American War of 1898, not to mention the Philippine-American War of 1899.[20] Given the realities of Jim Crow laws, however, no African American women writers were able to travel to the American colony during the Philippine-American War. Accordingly, Wilson's essay stands as a unique eyewitness account that was critical of the violence of American military occupation of the Philippines. Wilson did not immediately return to the United States after she wrote her essay, and her sojourn in Manila would last for half a decade, until 1908.[21]

Her essay takes what would have been a radical position more than a hundred years ago by narrating the racial terror of the mundane and the quotidian experienced by Filipino colonial subjects. While there are passages that wax poetic about the colonial picturesque or about the tropics as "no heart of darkness but a collection of scenic spots" (Rafael 60), Wilson's travel text is in fact an inversion of the colonial picturesque by emphasizing the horrors for the colonized.

Wilson documents Philippine life under American military rule after the end of the Philippine-American War in 1902: towns reduced to rubble after being torched by American forces; poverty; the death of thousands of townsfolk from disease, starvation, and dislocation; incidents of torture committed by

American forces that include the infamous "water cure";[22] the physical abuse of both Filipino students and native schoolteachers by American schoolteachers; and the racism prevalent among American soldiers and civilians living in the colony. She also describes her meetings with the remaining Filipino revolutionaries, who recounted personal tragedies such as the torture and death of family members at the hands of Americans, the destruction of their homes, and their poverty and misery while living in exile in Canton, China.

The travel text begins with Wilson landing in Canton, a large port city that might have had regular steamships traveling to and from the Philippines in the early twentieth century (nearby Hong Kong certainly had regular steamship service to the Philippines at that time). Her essay begins in media res— our anonymous traveler, only identified as a woman from Massachusetts, does not mention how she knew the Filipinos (members of Aguinaldo's revolutionary cabinet) who lived as exiles in Hong Kong after the end of the Philippine-American War, or what her reasons were for traveling to China, Hong Kong, Japan, and the Philippines. But what are evident are her anti-imperialist politics and her sympathy for the Filipino intellectual who was most critical of American colonial rule—Apolinario Mabini, Aguinaldo's political adviser, prime minister of the failed Philippine Republic, and the architect of the first Philippine constitution. In January 1901, members of the Filipino revolutionary government were considered "irreconcilables" by the American colonial government and were forcibly deported to Guam and later relocated to Hong Kong.[23] This cohort of former political advisers and generals of Emilio Aguinaldo were considered "irreconcilables" because they did not want to pledge allegiance to the United States, an act Aguinaldo conceded to perform after his capture by the U.S. Army in 1902. In Wilson's account, she narrates the difficult circumstances of the exiled Filipinos living in Hong Kong and Canton: their poor health, poverty, and personal experiences of hardship under U.S. rule.

In Hong Kong, Wilson paid a visit to the exiled members of the Filipino "Junta." She writes:

> I am now . . . receiving calls of ceremony from the members of the Junta. I have seen Ricarte, who proves to be a thoroughly likable sort of a fellow. In regard to Mabini, there did not seem to be very much to say. When he left Guam on the Thomas, he had, it seems, no intention of taking the oath; but his health had been steadily failing for some time, and he was seasick most of the way to Manila. The Junta had sent letters to Guam, and to Manila to meet him on his arrival, but none of these ever reached him, and when he found himself in Manila, sick, crippled, absolutely destitute, supposing that the Junta in Hong Kong had long since broken up and disbanded, not know-

ing that he had a friend in the world outside of Manila, he took the oath and went to his old home in Tondo. (Wilson 7)

Here, we learn that after 1902, the year of the official declaration of the end of the Philippine-American War, the paralytic Mabini, ravaged by years of exile, was forced by personal circumstances to pledge allegiance to the United States. Wilson concludes: "He is described as being much broken by the long confinement and the unsuitable food, and he was ill on the trip to Manila, arriving in a thoroughly prostrated condition" (11). The broken, abject figure of Mabini, as a symbol of the Philippine colony under U.S. rule, is in contrast to the imperial Adamic represented by American soldiers in popular colonial narratives and images from the Philippine-American War.

Imperial power had a destructive effect on the life of former general Artemio Ricarte, one of the Filipino exiles she met in Hong Kong. Ricarte narrated to Wilson that his house was burned and his property confiscated by the U.S. Army, his wife and two daughters were left destitute, and a young male relative was taken and killed by the American soldiers (8). By documenting Ricarte's tragedies, Wilson exposes the hypocrisy of Secretary Root's humane and civilized war in the Philippines. Ricarte was not just any civilian but a general who fought in Aguinaldo's army, a man whose high position in the Philippine revolutionary army made him a reliable witness about the brutal conduct of the war.

Wilson describes the harrowing case of an American schoolmaster, Mr. Trace, whose cruelty against a Filipino child serves as an allegory of American colonial rule. Wilson describes Mr. Trace as a former sergeant of U.S. volunteers who stayed on in the Islands after the Philippine-American War to become a schoolmaster. He taught in the town of Balayan, Batangas, a town whose population had been severely reduced, "due partly to the war, partly to the cholera" (30). Wilson narrates that most of the children were very irregular in attendance. To make an example of one of the children, Mr. Trace gave one child "twenty blows" (32). The child was so affected by his punishment that it was several days before he returned to class. Wilson writes:

Mr. Trace, bent upon maintaining discipline, repeated the beating, this time increasing the number of blows to thirty. The only result was to intensify the child's aversion, and when he reappeared, after a still longer absence, Mr. Trace, now thoroughly exasperated, determined to make an end of the matter and whipped him once more, this time counting out fifty merciless blows on the little boy's body. The little fellow shrieked with the pain, and the other children, thoroughly frightened, stopped their ears, shut their eyes and wept with him. (Wilson 32)

Wilson ends the story by saying the cruel schoolmaster received merely a slap on the wrist for his cruelty, when he was sentenced by a Filipino justice to spend two weeks in jail, a sentence never carried out after the American officers in the town of Balayan pulled strings for his release. After his release Trace went on to become the principal of a normal school in Lipa, Batangas.

Wilson then narrates the case of a Filipino native who died due to the water cure torture administered by an American soldier, Lieutenant Kievaski (37). Kievaski, under orders, also flogged and tortured the town's Filipino mayor in public. Wilson writes that the official, realizing that he had only a slow and painful death to look forward to, "flung himself down a deep well" (38).

By highlighting the stories of Trace and Kievaski, Wilson brings to light two figures that symbolize the violence of American imperial modernity—the schoolteacher and the soldier. Wilson's account, however, also includes stories of colonial ambivalence represented by Americans and other foreigners who questioned the war and the occupation. She narrates her meeting with the gray-haired, distinguished-looking Mrs. Martin, a schoolteacher from Springfield, Massachusetts, who was teaching in Vigan Province, north of the Manila. Mrs. Martin confided in Wilson because of their shared background as "New Englanders" and described the culture of corruption in the colonial education bureau (Wilson 22). She advised Wilson "to trust no one" and to be cautious while doing her interviews, since she believed many of the American schoolteachers were women of "very doubtful fitness, and not a few of undoubted immorality" (Wilson 23). Wilson does not give more details other than the brief statement made by Mrs. Martin, yet her story paints a more realistic, if not unflattering and tainted, image of the imperial Eve sent to teach native schoolchildren about American culture.

Another schoolteacher, a Miss Emma Rose, revealed that the American director of the Bureau of Education, Fred Atkinson, and the director of the Philippine Commission, Bernard Moses, were so incompetent that the colonial authorities asked them to resign (Wilson 22–23). Miss Rose, who resigned to protest the conditions at the education bureau, exposed Atkinson's incompetence by leaking an account of his dismissal to the *Boston Evening Transcript*. But like many accounts of soldiers' atrocities, the story of the corrupt practices of the education bureau was suppressed and never published (Wilson 24). Miss Rose left teaching and took a job as a stenographer and later as a clerk for another office in the colonial administration. While she was critical of the American officials, her racial views about Filipinos echoed the colonial government's view of the native: "You can't trust them; the longer you stay out here the less you know about them" (Wilson 24). Miss Rose invokes the colonial stereotype of the treacherous Malay, what Guha might refer to as an "ideological birthmark" of the colonial science of U.S. counterinsurgency.

During her travels around the Philippines, Wilson had a reunion with an old Radcliffe classmate, Annette Crocker, and a Miss Magoon, both schoolteachers. She writes that her friend "Annette" desired to have more "contact with the natives" and asked to be assigned to Dagupan Province, which had the reputation of being "the dirtiest and most disagreeable town in the Islands" (26). Despite these less than favorable conditions, Annette enjoyed her work and "simply *loves* the Filipinos" (Wilson 26), whom she described as culturally "white."

Foreigners Wilson met in Manila had their own opinions about race and the American occupation. She befriended an educated young German man who invited her to a party he threw for his compatriots. During the get-together, the German bragged that he had lived in the Philippines for twenty years and believes that the country will be better off if the Americans "withdraw from the Islands" (Wilson 27). She adds that the unnamed German man was quite eager "to get acquainted very fast" with her, though she believes that he might have also been quite drunk that evening (27). She thinks that the German might have been attracted to her because of her "intellect" and not her looks: "He was of a superior social grade to the others present, but . . . in *me* he had found an intellectual equal" (27). When she mentions that she would be leaving Manila to conduct interviews in the province, the German is dramatic in his disappointment that he will not see her again soon: "My departure would throw Manila into such darkness that he feared he would 'himself the stairs down fall!'" (27–28). After the dinner party ends, Wilson is relieved that it will be a while before she will have to socialize with her German admirer (Wilson 28). This is the only instance in the travel text that mentions heterosexual male attention toward Wilson, a romantic-sexual attention that she apparently neither desired nor cultivated.

Another anti-imperialist she meets in the Philippines is Lt. Richmond and his wife, who invite Wilson as a dinner guest. During the event, Wilson talks about the war but mentions no discussion regarding the military abuses by American soldiers. This spurs Lt. Richmond to volunteer his anti-imperialist politics:

He said that he had been an anti-imperialist before he came out and his stay of four years in the Islands had only strengthened his opinion. He thought that the retention of the Islands in the first place had been a blunder; that it was almost certain that sooner or later we should leave. (34)

In July 1902 President Roosevelt declared the end of the Philippine-American War, months after the Senate committee's report that cleared American soldiers of any wrongdoing in the islands, and months after the Anti-Imperialist League circulated the pamphlet *"Marked Severities"* to contest the Roosevelt administration's sanitized version of the conditions in the Philippines. By declaring the military pacification of the islands over, Roosevelt tried to end any debates on military atrocities and torture committed by U.S. troops against Filipinos. Wilson's reportage, however, highlighted the continuing violence in the colony and suggested that despite the capture of the Filipino revolutionary leaders and their deportation to other territories as exiles, the war for Philippine independence continued.

She writes about the continuation of Filipino resistance to U.S. rule in her moving description of the funeral of Apolinario Mabini, who died in Manila on May 13, 1903, at the premature age of thirty-eight. She notices that on the day of Mabini's funeral wake, she is the lone American in a crowd of thousands. Her slight unease reminds us that white female travelers are both the imperial surveyors and the surveyed. Wilson does not dwell on her unease long and is moved by the somber procession. Following two hearses filled with flowers was a multitude of mourners:

> Crowding close but without jostling or disorder, came the Filipino people, thousands of them, many of them on foot; and, as far as the eye could reach, carriages and yet more carriages filing the wide avenue from sidewalk to sidewalk. . . . And there was something strangely and deeply impressive about the democratic simplicity of this great orderly silent gathering, rich and poor together following in the heat and dust of the street, and the throng of dark serious faces, so plainly stamped with the deeper melancholy of a long subject race,—a sadness so deep that it seems to have grown into the very modelling of their features.
>
> It seemed as though the whole city of Manila had gathered, and I could not help noticing the large proportion of strong and finely intelligent faces, especially among Mabini's intimate friends. Most noticeable also, and with certain suggestiveness for the future, was the extraordinary number of young men, many of them evidently students, keen, thoughtful and intelligent-looking. (Wilson 48)

In her description of the funeral procession, Filipino bodies are marked by their shared grief, as melancholy stemming from their position as a "subject race" stamps their faces. The Filipino crowd's dark and serious faces express pain, but what also catches Wilson's attention is the significant number of Filipino youth marching in the wake. Wilson noticed two things: first, the impressive size of the crowd that marched at Mabini's funeral procession suggests that he was held in high esteem by the rich and poor in Manila despite his years of exile in Guam; and second, the sizable number of young Filipino males marching together that afternoon could be the next generation of *insurrectos*. Anyone who reads her observations about Mabini's funeral would conclude that Filipino resistance to American imperialism was not about to fade soon and would likely be carried forward into the next generation. This was clearly the message that Wilson sought to convey to her fellow anti-imperialists, and it may have had an effect even on their opponents, for American imperialist ambitions formally ended with the Philippines, even though the United States would later use other means to extend its hegemony to many parts of the world. But the Philippines remains the only country where Americans directly and officially fought a war against a people in order to colonize them.

The impact of Wilson's travel writing on the Philippines might be gleaned from the similarly titled texts that were published after 1903, such as Conger's and Dauncey's book-length memoirs. The politics and the imperial tone of both memoirs, however, are in stark contrast to Wilson's anti-imperialist text. Wilson's trip would change her life in profound ways, eventually leading to her residence in the Philippines for five years. Accounts of her life in the Philippines after the publication of her essay, however, remain a mystery for historians and feminist scholars. A few clues suggest her continuing political involvement with Filipino causes. In 1905, a group of Filipinas headed by the Bulacan feminist Concepcion Felix-Calderon organized the first feminist organization in the Philippines, called the Asociacion Feminista de Filipinas (Tiongson 203). Wilson was a founding member of the organization, and her participation suggests her high standing among elite civic-minded Filipino women. A quarter century later, Wilson, by now fifty years of age and single, cowrote a book-length memoir, entitled *Vagabonding at Fifty: From Siberia to Turkestan* (1929), an account of living and traveling around Russia with her travel companion, Dr. Elsie Reed Mitchell, a fifty-year-old medical doctor who was also an unmarried woman. Both women lived together in Russia for five years. An advertisement for their book appeared in the *New York Times* on April 7, 1929, and mentions that they traveled "7,700 miles," "experiencing adventure without end—all for a cost of $350."[24] A brief profile of the two authors that appeared in *Time Magazine* described them as "tramps" and as "two wanderlustful spinsters" who traveled to Russia armed only with a Boy Scout hatchet, drinking cups, "knickerbockers," and an oiled tent sheet.[25] After living together for half a decade in Russia, they both retired in Greenwich Village, New York, which might suggest Wilson's nonheteronormative and possibly lesbian identity. Wilson's last travel essay appeared in the *New York Times* on July 13, 1930, on the indigenous mountain tribes living in the Caucasus region.[26] In the life of Helen Calista Wilson, we follow her transformation as a suffragette, an anti-imperialist, an early twentieth-century feminist, and an unmarried, vagabond, "wanderlustful" traveler.

FILIPINO GROTESQUERIES: MRS. EMILY BRONSON
CONGER'S *AN OHIO WOMAN IN THE PHILIPPINES* (1904)

The bile of race is the racial language of white women's travel writing that represents the "native" inhabitants of an occupied land as backward, primitive, and savage. Racial bile surfaces in narratives about Filipino inferiority as either a physical or moral condition. In white women's travel accounts on the Philippine-American War, Filipino bodies are viewed as hideous and grotesque due to malnutrition, poverty, disease, and the "primitive" conditions of the tropics or the "Orient." Filipino grotesquerie is a racial discourse that presents the abject bodies of Filipino natives in contrast to the healthy, perfect, and civilized bodies of American soldiers, along with their elite Filipino collaborators. Descriptions of the deformities of Filipino servants, the notion of Filipino treachery as demonstrated in the continuing native resistance to American rule, and the backwardness of Filipino culture construct the stereotype of the Filipino savage. Other expressions of imperial bile can be read in texts that describe the rude interruption of American colonial life in the Islands by moments of war—a military assault by Filipino guerrillas in a nearby town, accounts of Filipino civilians supporting the "insurgents," the sight of war refugees sullying the otherwise tropical landscape, or the disruption of exclusive dinner parties and other colonial socials due to a surprise attack by the Filipino rebels.

Abject Filipino bodies are described in Mrs. Emily Bronson Conger's book-length memoir, *An Ohio Woman in the Philippines* (1904), a personal narrative of a widow and a soldier's mother (her son was assigned to the Philippines). Conger spent two years in the Philippines during the Philippine-American War. Her identity as a proper, middle-class, white mother is suggested by her use of her marital status, in contrast to the anonymity of Helen Calista Wilson as the author of *A Massachusetts Woman in the Philippines*. The book's cover image highlights her partisan message: a young, half-smiling "American scout" poses in his uniform. Her book opens with a dedication to her deceased husband, Arthur Latham Conger, and she signs the dedication with the term *mizpah*, a term from the book of Genesis that refers to an emotional bond between two people severed by physical separation or death. Her travel text includes ten photographs of Japan and fourteen photographs of the Philippines that serve as tourist souvenirs and iconic symbols of imperial instruction.

The imperial sublime, expressed in bucolic images of the U.S.-occupied Philippine colony, is juxtaposed with abject images of filth, defilement, and the ugly bodies of Filipino natives. Conger's early encounter with occupied Manila begins positively. She describes the city as a "magnificent sight" with white houses with Spanish-tiled roofs (Conger 50). The "beauty" of the city is heightened when she beholds the sight of the "great warships and transports" of the American army at anchor in Manila Bay as her ship approaches the city.

A photograph of an anonymous "native lady" (Conger, frontispiece, 50) that opens the book visually suggests the Filipina as the occupied land. Yet despite the imperial sublime, the text includes moments of Filipino resistance to U.S. rule. Conger writes:

> It gave a delightful feeling of protection to see our soldiers in and about everywhere . . . the city was still under military rule, and there were constant outbreaks, little insurrections at many points, especially in the suburbs. . . . It is useless to deny that we were in constant fear even when there were soldiers by. The unsettled conditions gave us a creepy feeling that expressed itself in the anxious faces and broken words of our American women. One would say, "Oh I feel just like a fool, I am so scared." Another would say, "Dear me, don't I wish I were at home." (Conger 53)

Although Conger describes the "delightful feeling" of seeing American soldiers all over Manila, their very presence is not enough to assure the writer and other American women of their safety. Conger admits that there is constant fear among the Americans. The many "little insurrections" might suggest that brief military encounters between Filipino and American forces happened regularly. The uncertainty of their safety was notable in "the anxious faces and broken words" of white American women.

Abjection surfaces in descriptions of the bodies of Filipinos and the conditions of the colony. When Mrs. Conger sees a Filipino for the first time, she says she has a "wild desire" to take the "dirty, almost nude creatures in hand" and dip them into "some cleansing cauldron" (51). She is fascinated and revolted by the sight of a "throng of half-naked creatures that were squatting in front of the church to sell flowers, fruits, cakes, beads and other small wares" (52). When she meets Filipina women who weave the delicate native cloths from pineapple fiber and the *jusi* plant, she describes them as "poor, dirty, misshapen creatures, weaving from daylight to dark, [who] earn about fifty cents a month."

> So many of the women are deformed and unclean, both the makers and the sellers that it seemed utterly incongruous that they should handle the most delicate materials. . . . In our happy country we do not think of seeing a whole class of people diseased or maimed. In the Philippines one seldom sees a well formed person; or if the form is good, the face is disfigured by small-pox. (Conger 60)

The deformed, working-class weavers are an incongruous sight next to the beautiful textiles they make for the traditional *baro't saya* worn by Filipino women. The exploitation of the textile workers, misshapen by their backbreaking labor, presents the colony as a backward country. She insists that no such worker's exploitation happens in the U.S., "our happy country," and that most Filipinos are "poor, dirty," and "misshapen." But what Conger fails to consider are the factory conditions of white American child workers at the time, a reality documented years later in the photographs of Lewis Hine.[27]

Conger describes Filipinos through the language of colonial bile, objectifying their native bodies as curious and grotesque:

> The natives are, as a rule, small with a yellowish brown skin; noses not large, lips not thick, but teeth very poor. Many of them have cleft palate or harelip, straight hair very black, and heads rather flattened on top. (Conger 67)

The author's description of "most" natives as dark, small, and deformed ("as a rule, small with a yellowish brown skin") employs markers of racial difference at a time when popular media depictions of black Americans, Native Americans, Asians, Pacific Islanders, and other dark-skinned peoples presented them as logical subjects of racial violence. By emphasizing the "unattractive" qualities of the Filipinos, Conger's travel text erases the violence of the Philippine-American War by justifying the occupation as the introduction of American modernity to a darker race.

Conger's description of the native cook she employs is another object of Filipino grotesquerie. She describes the woman as "five feet tall, with one shoulder about four inches higher than the other, one hip dislocated, one eye crossed, a harelip, which made the teeth part in the middle, mouth and lips stained blood red with betel juice" (72). Conger adds that she had to become accustomed to the native woman's "dreadful looks," but after the cook learned to dress in Western clothes and prepare American food, she became invaluable.

Filipino *insurrectos* were equally grotesque. Conger writes, "They were a scrubby lot of hardly human things, stunted, gnarled pigmies" (131–32). In these instances, the imperial eye racializes Filipinos as grotesque and less than human. While parts of Conger's narrative focuses on the strange bodies of the natives, she herself remains invisible as an omniscient narrator. This narrative guise recalls what Mohanram observes as the erasure of the imperial white subject, whose "invisibility" is the ultimate expression of colonial power (Mohanram 270). Yet the dichotomy that has been constructed, of invisible power and the visible abject is not a perfect one—Conger's book appears two years after the official end of the Philippine-American War and during the period of guerrilla warfare conducted by the Katipunan. Up until this time, the most visible bodies of the war in American national and popular discourse were those of American soldiers engaged in various wartime transgressions, such as torture, rapes, and killings. Widespread accounts of venereal disease, atrocities committed by the American army against the Filipino people, and the troops' "lustfulness, intemperance, and other signs of degeneracy" offered a less than ideal or romantic image of the imperial white body (Hoganson 186–93). American travel texts therefore popularized the notion of the Filipino colonial's abject body, one that was the visual opposite of the "imperial white." Conger described Filipinos as the "scrubby lot of hardly human things, stunted, gnarled pigmies." Rendering this abject body onto the Philippines had the paradoxical effect of making the (already invisible) guerrilla war disappear, as well as providing justification for the continued U.S. occupation. So at the moment of the Filipino *insurrectos'* "disappearance" into irregular warfare or guerrilla war, travel writing sought to erase the continuing anticolonial struggle of Filipinos by narrating the Philippines not as an active battleground but as a subjugated colonial entity, primitive and uncivilized, and indeed ugly, but fit to be ruled.

The disciplinary mission of the colonial regime was literally expressed in public spectacles such as hangings. In her memoir, Conger mentions a hanging of a Filipino criminal that affects the entire town (74). She does not mention the name of the criminal or the offense he was accused of committing, but she describes the gallows, which were erected with "secret stations," or hiding places, for the more affluent Filipino and American women of the town so that they could watch the execution from a discreet distance. The care and discretion taken for the construction of the viewing stations might suggest that American military authorities wanted to ensure that some members of the Filipino elite witnessed the hanging. The hanging was an abject lesson of discipline offered by American military authorities to the Filipino civilian populace. The spectacle of colonial discipline is worth noting here, a spectacle that may have had a different meaning for the Filipinos. Considering that the Bandolerismo Act, instituted by the American government in 1902, defined all hostile acts against the new colonial order as simple crimes instigated by bandits or *ladrones*,[28] we have to question whether the native who was hanged was a criminal at all. Could he have been a *revolucionario*? Conger's text offers no answer to this question, although it does seem clear from her description that public hangings were commonplace during the early years of U.S. rule of the Islands. This is also suggested by postcards of public hangings in the Philippines that were circulated in the early part of the twentieth century (see chapter 2).

While the Philippine colony is described as a zone of abjection due to the rats and lizards "of every shape, every size, and every color" (Conger 65), and undernourished Filipinos who survived the Philippine-American War were described as "wasted corpses" (Conger 70), the author reserves her bile for the continuing Filipino resistance to the American occupation. Like many American writers at the time, Mrs. Conger viewed the continuing Filipino war for independence as a sign of the grotesque, with Filipino rebels as violent, monstrous butchers. When she learns how to weave the traditional Philippine cloths, she weaves and weeps as she receives news of American soldiers who were "mutilated" by the Filipino rebel army:

> The weaving was a diversion; it occupied my time when the soldiers were out of the quarters. I will not deny that yards of the fabric were watered with my tears. There was dangerous and exhausting work for our troops; and there were bad reports that many were mutilated and killed. (Conger 82)

The image of the patriotic white mother weeping while weaving cloth is imperial sentimentalism at work. Female suffering, expressed by Conger's tears, is on display as she practices a domestic art and weeps for the lost sons of empire. The "imperial project of sentimentalism," after all, aims at "the subjection of people of different classes and different races, who were compelled to play not the leading roles but human scenery" in the racial melodrama of empire (Wexler 101).

More scenes of imperial sentimentalism suggest the tensions between the imperial sublime and resistance to U.S. rule. In a chapter entitled "My First Fourth in the Philippines," Mrs. Conger decides to throw a Fourth of July feast for her son and his unit.

> I can not tell what joy it was to me to see my son and the members of the troop come riding into town alive and well after a hard campaign. . . . On the third of July, 1900, I heard that the boys were coming back on the Fourth. . . . I decided to prepare a good old-fashioned dinner myself. All night long I baked and boiled and prepared that meal; eighty-three pumpkin pies, fifty-two chickens, three hams, forty cakes, ginger-bread, 'lasses candy, pickles, cheese, coffee, and cigars. . . . We began our first Fourth in true American style, as the "Old Glory" was being raised we sang "Star Spangled Banner." (Conger 83)

The American food described by the author symbolizes her feminine labor in the service of empire, cooking a feast for her son and the troops. For her service, Mrs. Conger receives a personal note signed by the officers of the Mounted Eighteenth Infantry Scouts, who glowingly praise her as "a noble example of patriotic American womanhood" (Conger 84). The drama of a suffering and self-sacrificing mother reduces the violence of a colonial war to a racialized and gendered familial narrative. Imperial abjection erases the war for Filipino independence and instead focuses on the narrative of a white mother waiting for the return of her soldier-son fighting valiantly against the Filipino enemy.

And yet while there are such scenes that affirm the power of American imperial rule and the racialized domestic regime, Conger's text inadvertently records the continuing resistance to U.S. rule. She writes:

> Letters from home were full of surprise that we still stayed though the war was over—the newspapers said it was. For us the anxiety and struggle still went on. . . . New outbreaks of violence and cruelty were occurring, entailing upon our men harassing watch and chase. The *insurrectos* were butchers to their own people. . . . They committed many bloody deeds, then swiftly drew back to the swamps and thickets impenetrable to our men. (Conger 85–86)

While personal letters and American newspapers declared the war over, Mrs. Conger writes about the new phase of the American campaign. "Outbreaks of violence" and the practice of rebels hiding in civilian communities describe the insurgent strategies of the Filipinos who were fighting a guerrilla war. She adds that military battles between the U.S. Army and the Filipino troops would occur "almost daily" (Conger 128). For Conger, the *insurrectos* were common "butchers," in contrast with America's noble soldiers.

Even members of the educated Filipino elite were suspected (quite rightly for many, it turns out) of being sympathizers to the cause of Philippine independence. Mrs. Conger explains:

> It was evident that many of the better class of natives, in spite of oath and fair face, were directing and maintaining the murderous bands of banditti. Often letters were found that the Filipino generals had written to their women friends in Jaro, Iloilo and Molo, to sell their jewels, to sell all they could, to buy guns, ammunition, and food, and later other letters were captured full of the thanks of the Filipino army for these gifts. While the good Filipinos were taking the oath of allegiance with the uplifted right hand, the left was much busier sending supplies to the insurrectos. (Conger 117–18)

Here Mrs. Conger invokes the colonial binary popularized by the American military command at the time: the "good Filipinos," or *amigos*, who collaborated and supported U.S. military rule, and the bad Filipinos, who were described as bandits, rebels, and *insurrectos*. The Filipinos' grotesque behavior was expressed by their act of waging war against the United States, the "rightful" occupier of the Philippine Islands after the 1898 Treaty of Paris signed by the United States and Spain. But for Mrs. Conger, the "good Filipinos" were not real allies. Despite their pledge of allegiance to the United States, some elites were still secretly helping the insurrectionists by financially supporting the war. She mentions that it was common to find letters from Filipino officers who would write to their female relatives to sell their jewelry so that the Filipino revolutionary armies could buy guns and supplies. What angered the American military command and the author were the letters captured by the U.S. Army that thanked family members for their "gifts" (118).

While she fervently believed in the monstrous and murderous capacities of the Filipino insurrectionists, she rejected stories of American atrocities: "Of the many stories that were told of the cruelties our soldiers perpetrated upon the helpless Filipinos, I do not believe one word; indeed, our men were constantly assisting the natives in every way possible" (Conger 120). Instead she narrates Filipino cruelty and the betrayal committed by the Filipino rebels against the American army—the assassination of an American soldier who was planning to set up schools in the province of Panay (Conger 129); the robbery of an American missionary and the execution of the soldier who accompanied him (130); the Filipino town official who was actually a rebel officer responsible for the torture and deaths of many American soldiers (131). Throughout her travel text, she emphasizes that the Filipinos' capacity for cruelty is related to the enemy's natural capability for lying and treachery.

> Very often the troops were called out to capture these bloody bands, but it was hard to locate them or bring them to a stand. The natives knew so many circuitous ways of running to cover and they had so many friends to aid them that it was almost impossible to follow them. Whenever they were captured they were so surprised, so humiliated, so innocent, meek and subdued, that it would never occur to an honest man that they could know how to handle a bolo or a gun. But experience taught that the most guileless in looks were the worst desperadoes of all. (Conger 131)

For the author, the Filipinos were the most "treacherous people," who were capable of offering hospitality to American soldiers, then secretly planning their assassination or torture (Conger 149).

The height of her racialized fear regarding Filipinos is suggested in one scene where she washes her hands with "scrubbing brush and lye" (Conger 158). Sick of "island laziness, shiftlessness, slovenliness," and "dirt" and terrified of "sickening news" about assassinations and mutilations committed by the Filipino rebel armies, she washes her hands briskly yet takes a small dagger and revolver with her to the washroom (Conger 158–59). The Filipino domestic servants in her home stare at "the Señora washing," as she sings loudly with "tears of homesickness: "Am I a soldier of the Cross, / A follower of the Lamb? / And shall I fear to own His cause, / Or blush to speak His name?" While singing aloud and weeping, Conger imagines herself as a Christian soldier fighting the savages. As the Filipino servants watch the lady of the house wash her hands, they also look in horror at her revolver after Conger vows to use it on them if need be (Conger 159). She says to herself, while staring back at the native help, "You poor miserable creatures, utterly neglected, utterly ignorant and degraded" (159).

The narrative ends with two photographs—a photograph of two American soldiers with the captions "Collier" and "Craig"; and an image of the author as a young child with her paternal grandmother, Mary Hickox Bronson. The photograph of the two young soldiers and the accompanying text suggest that one of the soldiers is her son. The personal photographs remind the reader of the author's white imperial identities: one, as the widowed mother of an American soldier fighting the Filipino enemy; and two, her identity as a granddaughter of a white settler family. The author recalls her paternal grandmother's "pioneer days," her stories of escaping death from "the Indians" (Conger 161). These final photographic images visually affirm the imperial whiteness of the author and, by extension, of her son and the rest of the U.S. Army, in contrast with the grotesque inhabitants of the Philippine colony.

> While my dear little grandmother dreaded the Indians, I did the treacherous Filipinos; while she dreaded the wolves, bears and wild beasts, I did the stab of the ever ready bolo and stealthy natives, and the prospect of fire; she endured the pangs of hunger, so did I; and I now feel that I am worthy to be her descendant and to sit by her side. (Conger 162)

By invoking her lineage as the granddaughter of a pioneer woman, Conger links her imperialist feminine identity to its frontier source—her hardy grandmother who survived attacks from "wild beasts" and Indian savages. The photograph of the author linking her arms with her grandmother is yet another visual suggestion of how the grandmother's life experiences had prepared Conger for her own life in the Philippine colony, connecting their brave destinies to the expansion of the American empire.

THE FILTHY COLONY: MRS. CAMPBELL DAUNCEY'S
AN ENGLISHWOMAN IN THE PHILIPPINES (1906)

Mrs. Campbell Dauncey's *An Englishwoman in the Philippines* consists of forty-three chapters organized as letters. It has close to 350 pages and includes forty-two photographs of Philippine landscapes and town and country scenes and portraits of "natives" such as Filipino servants. Written by a married English-woman who lived in the Western Visayas region with her husband for nine months (from November 1904 to April 1905), the epistolary travel memoir was described by *New York Times*' senior editor Montgomery Schuyler as "a bright Englishwoman's book about the American occupation of the Philippines."[29] The book is also the longest and most acerbic of the colonial memoirs, often describing the Philippine colony as a site of filth (Cannell; Anderson; Pante; Martinez and Lowrie) and savage beauty. Her antipathy being free and unbiased, Mrs. Dauncey is also critical of U.S. colonial policies in the Philippines, announcing, in her introduction, that she is merely an impartial observer, one who holds "no brief for the Americans or the Filipinos."

When Mrs. Dauncey first arrives in Manila, she notices the floating water plants, "brilliantly green cabbages" floating on the Pasig River. She describes the plants as "extraordinary," "intensely crude and violently emerald" (3). They remind her of the emerald ring she wears, which once belonged to a former Spanish governor-general of Manila who forfeited it, through conquest, to her "paternal great-great granduncle, Admiral Cornish," who was part of the British forces that attacked, sacked, and occupied Manila in 1762 (Dauncey 4). By claiming lineage to a participant in the British occupation of Manila, Dauncey establishes her pedigree as an Englishwoman and true imperialist, and like Conger affirms her imperial white femininity, a white female body set against the darkness of the colony and the dark bodies of Filipino primitives.

She begins by expressing her disappointment with the city that was once conquered by her relative, now merely a "backwash leading to nowhere" (4), "dull, grey, ugly and depressing," "dirty and untidy," with "mean and dilapidated" buildings, badly paved streets, and with a "sort of hopeless untidiness about the place" (5). Disenchanted by the colonial capital, she mentions that there are "no traces of anything one is accustomed to think of as Spanish—no bright mule trappings, or women with mantillas, or anything gay and colored" (5). Dauncey's description of Manila as depressing, dilapidated, and untidy seems to confirm her anti-American bias. She finds the "costly luncheon parties," the long dinners, and bridge parties hosted by American women as "dreadfully dull" (132). She thinks that American colonial Manila, dubbed as the "Gayest City of the Orient," is a cultural wasteland (132), favoring the architecture and character of "old Spanish Intramuros" over the suburban areas occupied by American families and European expatriates. She writes:

> The narrow streets are cobbled, and the quaint houses, with deep, barred basement windows, have a delightful air of repose, after the half-finished, skin-deep, hustling modernity of Americanised Manila. . . . I should like to live in the Walled City [i.e., Intramuros]—that is, if I survived the awful smells—and imagine myself in an East where there were no arc-lights, no electric trams, no drinking saloons, ice-cream sodas, "Hiawatha," or Bridge, and where the natives would be humble, civil, prosperous, and happy. (131)

Dauncey sees the city's potential as being wasted under a U.S. colonial rule that has rushed to "Americanise" Manila and its inhabitants.

On their part, Filipinos are merely "mild-eyed lotus eaters" (133), indolent natives who do not care for new technology, American styles of leisure, and other American ideas. Filipinos are a backward race that would be happy with "a little rice, and a banana patch, and a nipa hut, and no priests to bother them" (134). As abject bodies, Filipinos can never be the racial equals of Westerners since they are "Malay half-breeds" who will never appreciate or understand "the institutions which it has taken the highest white races two or three thousand years to evolve" (134). Dauncey describes Filipinos as "strangely lazy, supercilious, half-bred people" (Dauncey 17), "an indolent, indifferent race" (31). She prefers hiring Filipino men as domestic help since Filipino women are "lazy" and "useless" (Dauncey 27). She mentions, as proof of their backward culture, that Catholic priests have a powerful influence over the Filipinos, who are "superstitious, childish Malays" (Dauncey 50). The Filipino is "the lazy Malay" whose innate "racial faults" cannot be reformed despite their "hasty assimilation of mathematics, electric trams and ice cream sodas" (Dauncey 171). Dauncey belittles the modernizing steps made by Filipinos and considers their American-style education a waste since the natives are merely taught "a crude wash of bad English and mathematics" when they should be working in their rice fields (Dauncey 49) or working as laborers (96). After all, Filipinos are merely "poor 'worms' that bite and sting in the dust," lower creatures who cannot benefit from Western tutelage (Dauncey 108).

Debasing Filipinos even further, she describes them as "stupid people" who are "sickeningly cruel" with "malicious cunning" (Dauncey 171). Native children, in Dauncey's eyes, are grotesque creatures. She describes malnourished children as "air-balloons set on drumsticks" (65) and sees them as "black and white imps in the moonlight" (178). Finally, Dauncey pours her sourest bile on the physical appearances of her servants and other Filipinos she meets while traveling. Dauncey tells the story of her Filipino cook, who is a "shriveled, pock-marked person, about four feet six in height with an array of immense teeth, and an air of intense importance" (28–29). At one point in the narrative, his "impudence" angers Dauncey and she refers to him as "monkey-face" (100). Another servant, the laundry woman or *lavandera*, is described as a woman with a similar simian appearance, "with a huge, almost black, pan face" (36), "cow-like and stolid" (37), and one who looked "hopelessly stupid" with a "gorilla" face (37). In general, she views Filipinos as "simple souls" who will not gain from civilizing: "What on earth can education, whisky, votes, appendicitis, electric light, a free press, frozen meat, clothes, and pianos do to such happy, simple souls?" (221).

When she moves to Iloilo, a Spanish-colonial town on Panay Island, her tone changes, evidencing the trope of the imperial sublime—the magnificence of colonial occupation that enables white travelers to enjoy their position as privileged tourists and business expatriates:

> We left Manila at three o'clock on Monday in lovely sunshine, and had a delightful voyage through scenery which was simply a miracle of beauty. The sky was intensely blue, with little white clouds; the sea calm and still more intensely blue, dotted with dreams of islands, some mauve and dim and far away. . . . We could see the great forests of bright green trees and the grassy lawns. . . . White, sandy beaches, with fringes of palm trees. . . . One after another, like a ceaseless kaleidoscope, these fairy islands slipped past all day. (Dauncey 8–9)

Here the beauty of the colony is reified through imperial abjection: Panay Island is beautiful because the landscape has not been tainted by the presence of Filipino natives. Traveling around the country without seeing or encountering "natives" allows her to wax poetic: the Philippine scenery is "simply a miracle of beauty" (8). But the fairy story turns quickly into a nightmare when she discovers that the comforts of home, in particular familiar fruits, vegetables, and meats are unavailable in Panay. Belittling American colonial rule, she concludes, "This, after six years of what we are told is the most enlightened system of colonial or tropical government yet invented" (49).

For Dauncey, the colony's state of abjection results primarily from the continuing Filipino resistance to colonial rule, and the fact that the Americans were never able to successfully end the war against the Katipunan.

> They fought, and are still fighting the Americans tooth and nail to get their own liberty. . . . If they show any signs of wanting to get rid of this American

burden and govern themselves in their own fashion, they are called Insurgents and knocked on the head or dubbed common robbers and strung up
to a tree. (51–52)

This comment refers to the Bandolerismo Act of 1902, a colonial law that crimi-
nalized any political acts against the American occupation as mere banditry, to
be punished by hanging. Yet even after the official end of the war, the Philippine
colony continued to be "honeycombed with insurrection and plots" (86). Much
to Dauncey's angry disbelief, Filipino intellectuals were openly hostile to the
continuing American occupation and published their dissent in the local press.

The fighting has never ceased; and the natives loathe the Americans and
their theories, saying so openly in their native press, and showing their dislike in every possible fashion, Their one idea is to be rid of the U.S.A. and to
have their government in their own hands, for good or evil. (86)

Dauncey adds that the country was "full of Insurrection," that many places were
"in a state of open warfare," and that war atrocities, or the more "terrible and
horrible things" about the war, were censored from the American and the Filipino public (Dauncey 181).

Perhaps even more than specter of war and insurrection, the tropical climate
oppressed the writer constantly (Dauncey 3), and she describes an evening gar-
den party hosted by a Chinese diplomat in Iloilo where the "Celestials," a colonial and racial term she uses for the Chinese officials wearing colorful silks,
mixed with well-heeled dinner guests wearing European-style clothes despite
the heat.

Of course everyone was going about in evening dress, as if in a ball-room at
home, and feeling very hot. . . . The idea of this perpetual heat soon becomes
familiar. . . . In my letters to you I can't go on saying "It is very hot," "It is very
sultry," and so on, and yet I know that you reading them at home, can have
no idea of the *setting* of all I tell you; of the terrible blazing sun all day long;
the hot nights only bearable by comparison with the day; of one's skin always
moist, if it is not actually running in little rivulets, as in a Turkish bath. . . .
And this, I am informed, is the "winter." (121)

Dauncey describes the horror of the tropics that await Victorian ladies, for
whom there is unremitting heat, noisy cicadas, the "plague" of black and red
ants, roaches "the size of mice," large spiders the size of a palm, and innumer-
able mosquitoes (Dauncey 69–73), not to mention the more palpable perils of

the Philippine tropics: "deadly snakes; poisonous, scentless plants; swamps and malaria." The monsoons and the humid weather destroy the markers of white civilization: "Steel and silver rust while you look at them; clothes come out in feverish patches of blue mould; silk and satin 'go' so that they tear like tissue paper" (265). Dauncey cringes at the thought of living in Manila with "the awful smells" (Dauncey 133) but also describes colonial Iloilo, her home, as an abject place of shit and garbage. During the monsoon, the Daunceys would smell the sewage coming from their Filipino neighbor's home: "Such neglect, such dirt, such squalor, and such smells!" (243). The Philippines, in her eyes, is "the end of the world" (99), the edge of civilization, the boundary between civilization and savagery. She writes: "I feel as if I had arrived at the end of the world, where nobody cares or knows or hears or thinks of anything" (99).

Adding to Dauncey's sense of the uncleanliness of the colony is the taboo of miscegenation. Dance socials, or *bailes*, organized by Filipino elites, would include a "mixture of races and Eurasians," and she laments that there was "no marked color distinction" that separated the white guests (Europeans and Americans) from the mixed-race or mestizo Filipinos (62). She describes an embarrassing moment in one social when a young mestiza woman "in a painfully blue satin dress, and with her face a ghastly grey-white with thick powder, sang a terrible song" (61). The *baile* scene is emblematic of the problem of race mixing in the colony, where "natives of the civilized parts of the Philippines" have been marrying members of the white or "Christian race" (62). For Dauncey, mestiza women are abject bodies, imperfect copies of white or European femininity: "They spoil their little round faces with thick layers of powder over their nice brown skins, and use perfumes that nearly knock one down" (62). She is relieved, however, that despite the mixed social gathering, there were still imperial or racial protocols that were followed in the *bailes*. So during these dances, white or European women would "keep quite apart from the coloured folk," not dancing with, let alone considering marrying, any of the Filipino men (62).

The *baile* is a space of abjection because of the mixed or "heterogeneous mass" in attendance (280), as well as the "dirty" floors with spit stains made by Filipino guests (281). Mrs. Dauncey is equally alarmed by the lack of sartorial decorum of the American and Filipino guests. In one dance, all the American men "wore day suits and boots, while many of the women had on walking shoes." The Filipina guests wore "aniline" dyed ball gowns in "blinding colors," in contrast with their "little, dark, square" faces and their "very handsome diamonds" (281).

Toward the end of her narrative, she observes that most Americans assigned to the Philippines doubt the benefits of benevolent assimilation. She writes,

"Every American I have ever yet met or seen, from the highest to the humblest is simply saving money to get away from the Philippines and back to 'God's Country'" (308). She ends with the trope of imperial abjection by describing the Philippine colony as the American empire's heart of darkness, a backward place lacking proper European culture or history. It is

> no terrestrial paradise, for one has the laziness, the heat, the apathy and the cruelty of the East, without the compensations of artistic beauty, cheapness, plenty, and luxury, which make up for those drawbacks in other countries. A shuffling, drab, discontented, thick-headed costly East—with all the worst traditions of four hundred years of the off-scourings of the Spanish monkish orders, overlaid by a veneer of a shallow cock-sureness hastily assimilated from a totally incongruous alien civilization. (345–46)

The last lines refer to the author's antipapist and anti-American politics based on racism. Dauncey sees the Philippines as a failed experiment of Old World and New World imperialism. Despite four centuries of Spanish colonial rule and the "hasty" implementation of American benevolent assimilation, Filipinos remain the lazy Malays, the lotus-eaters who will never change and will never learn the ways of white civilization.

THE VIOLENCE AND ROMANCE OF WOMEN'S TRAVEL WRITING

By the early twentieth century, travel to the Philippine colony was becoming more and more common. Like male travelers before them, expatriate women—Wilson, Conger, and Dauncey—recorded and published accounts of their Philippine sojourn, and the fin de siècle public was curious to know more about America's "Islands and Their People."[30] These white women's travel texts portrayed the traveler-authors as patriots of the American empire, exemplary citizens who risked their health and personal happiness by coming to the Islands to take part in the American civilizing mission. Their colonial desire to discipline the natives so they would transform into law-abiding, docile subjects of the American flag recalls the political rhetoric that accompanied the successful "pacification of the Indian," including the forced education of Native American children after the last of the United States' Indian wars. Representing Filipino savagery was a project of American colonization that was related to Progressive Era beliefs in the "social engineering" of the inferior races through education.

In her narrative, Wilson reveals that not all Americans living in the Philippines during the Philippine-American War believed in the righteousness of the

American imperial experiment. In fact she mentions Americans and European expatriates who recognized that some of the American officials were incompetent and corrupt. She describes in great detail and with much compassion the physical and emotional suffering experienced by Filipinos who were considered political prisoners by the U.S. military government—the members of the Aguinaldo revolutionary cabinet or the junta members living in exile in Hong Kong, Japan, and China. Her encounters with Filipino revolutionaries and their families were gracious and enlightening, and she described their personal and financial difficulties—the loss of their homes and property, their poverty while living in exile, the deaths of family members in the hands of the American army, their homesickness, their loss of morale, and the feeling of defeat after the end of the Philippine-American War—with genuine concern.

These white women's narratives document different aspects of racial bile through the imperial romance of travel. While some of the narratives echo the official position of the American military regime that believed in the necessity of violence for disciplining the natives, narratives such as Wilson's text and some passages in the other travel accounts confirm the continuing Filipino resistance to American rule, proving that the Filipino natives who were subjected to the imperial gaze were far from docile. Yet another abject body in this discussion is the mysterious figure of Helen Calista Wilson, who began her career as a young anti-imperialist activist and writer and later became an American expat and feminist in the Philippine colony, and, in her fifties, became a travel writer who lived in the remotest regions of Siberia with her female companion. Wilson's unconventional and possibly queer identity haunts her travel essay, a powerful anti-imperialist reportage on the conditions in the Philippines after the supposed end of a war that would drag on for a decade more. Wilson's essay is a forgotten travel text that turns the conventions of racial or imperialist bile on its head. In her work, we understand clearly the language of the American empire. In the texts of the other women travelers, we discern this language while decoding references to the everyday experiences of Filipinos living under U.S. rule during the first decade of the twentieth century. Reading the travel narratives requires an act of translation, recalling Guha's ideas on reading colonial narratives and texts to find instances of rebellion, insurgency, and the rupture of imperial power (Guha). By theoretically inverting the language of imperial bile, we unearth native resistance in texts that have paradoxically rendered Filipinos visible as savages but invisible as *revolucionarios*.

Some scholars have argued that historical accounts focusing on the violence of the Philippine-American War and the colonization of the Philippines by the United States that followed the war do not exist, suggesting that there was a smooth transition from Spanish colonialism to American colonialism. But by reexamining imperial texts such as travel writings, we encounter what has been repressed and forgotten in official narratives of the empire. We can decipher Filipino resistance as an inextricable part of Filipino colonial life under U.S. rule. As Gregoria de Jesus, a former Katipunero and widow of Andres Bonifacio, said in her brief autobiography: "Fear history, for it respects no secrets."[31] De Jesus's statement predates Walter Benjamin's caution that "nothing that has ever happened should be regarded as lost for history."[32] Thus, while there are few book-length accounts of life under American colonial rule written by Filipinos, we have travel accounts written by the dutiful and rebellious "daughters" of the American empire. The travel texts thus revisit the terror of American colonial rule when we read Filipino resistance in the most unlikely places.

Conclusion

Blood and Bones: The Romance of Counterinsurgency

In the twenty-first century, the camera continues to play a role in documenting images of imperial abjection. Like the older abject images of the American empire, the infamous photographs of prisoner abuse in Abu Ghraib, Iraq, reprised the horror of imperial whiteness and once again raised the persistent role of race and sex in the violent occupation of one country by a colonial power. First exposed in an article in the *New Yorker* (May 2004), the Abu Ghraib photographs showed American soldiers smiling and mugging beside naked and humiliated Iraqi prisoners.[1] One aspect of the images from Abu Ghraib seemed familial and familiar: youthful cheeks, toothy grins, and an "all American thumbs-up."[2] But this wholesome American optimism is jarringly posed alongside bruised dark faces screaming in fear, corpses in body bags, blood on prison floors, and naked human "pyramids" of Iraqi prisoners. The photographs of tortured Iraqi prisoners returned us to the idea of imperial abjection, with the Iraqi body (along with the Afghani, Arab, or Muslim) as the abject body of the archive of the War on Terror.[3] Covered in blood, bile, or filth, the Iraqi body visually invokes other abject images from American history—the cadavers of Native Americans and Filipinos; the lynched bodies of black men, women, and children; and the massacres of Vietnamese villagers in My Lai, to name a few.[4] The body of the tortured or dead Iraqi is the dark negative of the white American soldier, the same way that abject images from other periods of U.S. history were visual contrasts to white superiority. The White Adam of the American imperial imagination was again embodied in the figure of the American soldier (male and female), this time in the Middle East with Iraq as the new twenty-first-century frontier.

When the Abu Ghraib photographs were published in print and online media, journalists, scholars, and writers historicized the significance of the photographs by recalling other U.S.-sponsored race wars—some fittingly placing the photographs within the archive of abjection that has grown with American expansion since the birth of the nation in 1776. The Abu Ghraib photographs ensured that the Iraq War became a moment for once again remembering the war in the Philippine colony.[5]

The Iraq War has also given rise to problematic "misreadings and misrecognitions" of the Philippine-American War, as Allan Punzalan Isaac and Sharon Delmendo note.[6] In October 2003, President George W. Bush returned to the former American colony to speak before the Philippine Congress, and was greeted by thousands of angry Filipino activists, who marched in the streets, burning American flags and an effigy of the president.[7] It was evident that the Filipino descendants of colonialism had not forgotten the treachery of the war of 1899, especially in the context of the U.S. unjustified aggression in Iraq that the president had declared completed, just six months earlier, as a "mission accomplished." Not disappointing the protesters, in a speech delivered with no irony, Bush made comparisons between the U.S. occupation of Iraq and its occupation of the Philippines one hundred years earlier. By describing the Iraq War as a war for freedom and democracy (which it was not) and linking it to an earlier "successful" American colonization that eventually led to Philippine democracy, Bush was able to find what he thought was an optimistic precedent, albeit one enabled by historical amnesia, for his invasion and occupation of Iraq. However, Bush failed to mention fierce Filipino resistance to U.S. rule, which turned into a protracted and bloody guerrilla war fought by remnants of the Katipunan and by Filipino peasants.[8] When a commander-in-chief makes comparisons to an ongoing conflict, he might do well not to bring up an earlier war that was associated with so much brutality and human and financial cost, and so damaged U.S. exceptionalism and self-esteem, that it was virtually expunged from American popular memory. But vanished history has a tendency to return, and Bush's comparison of his Iraq war to the Philippine-American War turned out to be apt, but for the wrong reason. The United States became mired in a long and expensive war in Iraq, much like what happened in its war in the Philippines. And while the president may have rued the inadvertent prescience of his Iraq-Philippines analogy, his commanders perhaps had better sense in studying a fitter historical parallel, the role of counterinsurgency in the Iraq and Philippine-American wars. At about the same time Bush was giving his speech, U.S. Army historians and war strategists were discussing the Philippine occupation at the turn of the twentieth century as a case study of successful American counterinsurgency.[9] They understood, better than their own commander-in-chief, that their war in Iraq was far from a "mission accomplished" and needed a counterinsurgency strategy to avoid ending up as a failure.

CARNAGE WITHOUT CORPSES

Even before Iraq, the histories of American conflicts in the Philippines and Vietnam offered important lessons in the field of military science known as "irregular warfare" or counterinsurgency.[10] As a field of military science, counterinsurgency requires the narration of an efficient and effective way of conducting war against combatants who look like ordinary civilians. This narration requires abjection as a structure of its discourse—i.e., waging war without humanizing enemy casualties, abstracting or erasing blood and bones by turning actual bodies into body counts and statistics, and emphasizing military victory over ethical or moral concerns. Thus abjection shapes the discourse of counterinsurgency studies by narrating death without carnage. Of course, no combat death is possible without carnage, but what abjection does is turn casualties of war from a very identifiable and empathetic form of human tragedy into a justified, and therefore abstracted, expediency. It works in an almost paradoxical way: abjection emphasizes what is unique, hence distinctly human, in a group of people and inflates it into grotesquerie and otherness, to the point that what was once human becomes inhuman. When this happens, it becomes easier to conduct wholesale killing; with their humanity denied, multiple casualties are just body counts. Counterinsurgency is best pursued in this deadly yet sanitized manner, so as not to unduly rouse the populace of the rebel side, and to comfort and reassure the counterinsurgents' side that they are winning.

While some American military historians cite the nineteenth-century Indian wars or the Civil War as the origins of counterinsurgency (Cassidy 42–43), new studies point to wars in Southeast Asia as the testing grounds for perfecting American counterinsurgency methods. In the American popular imagination, Southeast Asia is "the jungle of Snakes,"[11] where memories of genocidal campaigns conducted by the U.S. military, and the guerrilla wars against the American army, still haunt the nightmares of survivors, refugees, and combatants. The image of a snake-infested jungle suggests deadly terrain as well as an American racial idea—the figure of the treacherous, ignoble native who lives in the jungles while participating in an insurgency against a more powerful Western army. It also suggests a terrain where the law of the jungle prevails, allowing more savage warfare. Finally, it is in the jungles where the irregular combatants have the greatest advantage of concealment, as they can quickly disappear into the undergrowth like snakes, very much like Iraqi insurgents (even though in an urban setting) who could easily slither through the countless fissures and alleyways of their ancient cities.

Essays by soldier historians and counterinsurgency experts argue for studying the Philippine-American War as prologue to Iraq.[12] Lt. Colonel Robert Cassidy uses the military phrase "winning the war of the flea" to refer to counterinsurgencies and to illustrate the necessity of learning from past guerrilla wars fought by the United States army. The Philippine-American War was the first overseas war fought by the United States against a nonimperial, non-European country, whose disadvantage in firepower was so massive it was like a flea worrying a dog (Cassidy 41). Another essay by Colonel Timothy K. Deady describes the Philippine-American War as a model counterinsurgency operation since it was arguably the first to suggest a novel strategy: deploy political tactics along with punitive military measures.[13] Deady, who draws from military historian Brian McAlister Linn's work,[14] narrates the war of 1899 as the introduction of American modernity to the Philippines and mentions the accounts of atrocities committed by the U.S. Army during the war, which the postwar colonial government tried to ameliorate through public works innovations such as road-building, telegraph lines, disease management, clean water programs, and waste disposal, as well as by paying high wages to Filipino civil servants (Deady 61). Deady believes that significant lessons of the Philippine-American War are applicable to the counterinsurgency operations in Iraq: the army must separate the civilians from the insurgents, reward collaborators, and punish rebels and sympathizers (Deady 67). Another essay, by military historian Andrew J. Birtle, argues that the Philippine war and the Vietnam War demonstrate both "force and persuasion, of severity and moderation" are keys for eliminating an insurgency.[15] Birtle brings up the abject body of the Filipino when he describes Brigadier General Franklin Bell's belief in stern forms of pacification—herding Filipino villagers into detention camps called *reconcentrados*, imposing fines, carrying out executions, and burning villages, thus creating an atmosphere of fear (Birtle 48). Pacifying the Filipino native required both physical violence and subtle coercion through colonial occupation.

Contemporary accounts of the Philippine-American War in the era of the War on Terror emphasize the efficient elimination of an insurgency as the endgame of any American operation. An essay by Thomas Bruno published in *Army History* in 2011, for example, recounts the infamous "Burning of Samar Province,"[16] rewriting that brutal campaign as a strategic lesson for a successful counterinsurgency. The court-martialed and disgraced General Jacob Smith, who ordered his men to turn Samar into "a howling wilderness," is rehabilitated by Bruno as an innovative yet misunderstood counterinsurgency tactician, whose razing of villages and massacre of civilians, including ten-year-old boys shot for being suspected rebels, were extenuated because they led—and how could they not?—to the pacification of the entire Samar Island.

In the language of counterinsurgency studies, the deaths of non-Americans are abject. Filtered through Kristeva and scholars who do not share the worldview of counterinsurgency, these abject deaths are meaningless and yet significant, "something" but "not nothing either." This dualism is acknowledged by counterinsurgency science, which recognizes that the use of military force alone will not destroy the enemy completely (although there are those like Howlin' Jake Smith who have tried and very nearly succeeded). Other means of persuasion are necessary to win over the population; in Southeast Asia, this took the form of benevolence, or benevolent assimilation, or "winning hearts and minds," even while combat was taking place. This dynamic of creation-destruction is also a function of abjection, whenever the impulse to destroy the other is arrested by the desire to possess the exotic.

In the colonial archive, this fascination and fear of the brown enemy is abundantly represented in romances set around the time of the Philippine-American War, which kept U.S. readers titillated with all the danger and excitement of "the prose of counterinsurgency,"[17] where the fate of the empire lay, literally, in winning hearts.

FORGOTTEN RACE ROMANCES

Specific types of romances, according to literary and cultural studies scholars, are artifacts of empire.[18] Anglophone "race romances," in particular, are popular American narratives from the mid-nineteenth century that are inscribed with notions of white domesticity, female subjectivity, empire, and nation-building. Race romances staged and managed the political anxieties of the mid-nineteenth century, such as American territorial expansion, slavery, miscegenation, white imperial identities, racial and gender relations, and "the entanglements of the foreign and the domestic" (Streeby 115). Romances produced notions of what was "foreign" and "domestic," conveniently collapsing the differences between them so that the takeover or occupation of some fictional, distant land gently masked the grim realities of colonial warfare. The construction of the exotic and the foreign, against tableaux of non-Western lands and people, is abjection in performance. The romance narrative focused on the extraordinary actions and adventures of a heterosexual male hero who was a metaphor for the imperial nation or empire (Hebard 806) and whose exploits produced a convergence between the imaginary of the American imperial nation and "the imaginary of the romance" (806). Given the aesthetic and discursive connections between the romance genre and American imperialism, it is no wonder that romances were popular in the late nineteenth century, during the Spanish-American War and the Philippine-American War that followed it (Kaplan). Romances were narratives that linked to a national culture of imperial expansion and violence, invoking legal and administrative structures that legitimated imperial violence (Hebard 805).

Reading these forgotten romances today, we see how well the romance mode accommodates the logic of counterinsurgency, set as they are in the Philippines during the war of 1899. These "Philippine romances" narrate the life of the heroic white American protagonist tested by the extraordinary circumstances of a colonial war and military occupation of the Philippine Islands. The soldier-hero is a character of counterinsurgency and white imperial masculinity, while the Filipinos in the novels are mainly abject bodies relegated to savage or docile roles. In the digital version of Geoffrey D. Smith's bibliography *American Fiction 1901–1925*, there are no less than a dozen works of fiction (novels and short stories) that come up when the search words "Philippines" and "romance"[19] are used. Some of these Philippine romances can still be found in the New York Public Library, although there are no abstracts available, nor secondary sources on the authors and their fiction. Scholars of U.S. imperial culture have largely overlooked these texts.[20]

My attention was drawn to the longest novel, *Daniel Everton, Volunteer-Regular: A Romance of the Philippines* (1902) by Israel Putnam. The book is close to four hundred pages long, with twenty-six chapters. I found no definitive information on the author, other than he shared the name of a famous war hero, Israel Putnam, a celebrated officer of the French and Indian Wars and the American Revolution. In the novel, the eponymous Daniel Everton, a son of a wealthy New York businessman, volunteers for the U.S. Army and is sent to the Philippine Islands during the Philippine American War. Daniel Everton is the archetypal white Adam, an American soldier-hero—dashing, ethical, and impeccably dressed in his blue military uniform despite the humid tropical weather of the islands. While others in his unit frequent the saloons, carouse with Filipino women of ill repute, and speak in coarse American vernaculars, the well-mannered Daniel speaks proper English, avoids racial epithets against Filipinos, and carries himself like "a gentleman" and "a college man." The racialized masculinities of other American soldiers and the Filipino male characters dramatize the roles of hero and enemy. White American officers such as Sergeants Cassidy and Redder drink alcohol, have lecherous discussions about the merits of native women, and refer to Filipinos as "niggers" or "naygurs" (Putnam 77). These rough manners mark their race and class but also emphasize their masculinity and, by extension, their superiority, as soldiers, over effete Filipino rebels such as Jose Mispall and Captain Rigon, who are shown planning the kidnap and murder of the Filipino sugar plantation owner, Isidro Paris, over rice cakes and hot chocolate (Putnam 58–59). The American sergeants, Cassidy and Redder, are more manly characters, hardened veterans who have proven their manhood in the "Indian campaign" (Putnam 67), thus linking the histories of counterinsurgency in the frontier and the Philippines through their fictional characters.

Miscegenation, racialized sexuality, and counterinsurgency are central elements of the story. The taboo of miscegenation can be traced in the racial language of white soldiers and civilians (i.e., the wife of an American officer, female relatives of soldiers, and an Englishman visiting Manila). At dinners and other socials, the Americans and the Englishman debate whether Filipinos are "niggers," "coons," or "Orientals," where the exclusivity of the discussions secures the boundaries of racial and gender hierarchies that support the privileges of white supremacy yet allows a curiosity about the degrees of impurity that might make racial mixing possible. Elsewhere, it is clear that miscegenation dominates the novel's thematic interests. In one scene, American soldiers exchange their views about marrying a "nigger," and they all agree that they would marry outside of their race if it meant that a wealthy Filipina wife could give them class status and all the comforts money can buy (Putnam 158–64). This scene prepares us for Daniel's marriage to the lovely, mixed-race Mercedes Paris, daughter of an elite mestizo or mixed-race Filipino family that owns a sugar plantation (hacienda) on Negros Island, south of the Philippine capital of Manila. Despite breaking the taboo of miscegenation, Daniel remains a loyal son of the American empire and the racial order. After all, he agrees to marry Mercedes only to save his elderly, sick father (a lawyer in New York) from financial ruin. During moments when he thinks of his beloved Constance Fairchild, his true love, he feels revulsion toward his native wife, Mercedes, whose bloodline is tainted by "the touch of the tar brush," a historical English derogation that refers to someone with black or mixed ancestry (Putnam 223). In Daniel's eyes, and for some of the other American characters in the novel, Mercedes's mixed heritage bars her from real beauty and complete respectability, even though she is from an elite Filipino family.

The white imperial masculinity of Daniel Everton is set against the abject bodies of the Filipino characters. Popular racial theories about Filipino natives were in circulation at the time, and Putnam's novel reflects these abject discourses: the Filipino masses are "superstitious, passive and ignorant," while the Filipino elites and nationalists are "venal, corrupt and abusive" (Kramer 198).

These discourses were imperial fictions created and popularized by the colonial administrator, Dean C. Worcester, who will be discussed in the last section. For example, the character Isidro Paris, the mestizo patriarch and *haciendero*, is viewed by both the American authorities and the Filipinos as a treacherous, venal man who claims loyalty to the American military government but is suspected of supporting the Filipino rebels (Putnam 40–41). Another character, Jose Mispall, the scion of a wealthy Filipino family, is a gambler, an ill-tempered drunk, and also a secret member of the Filipino rebellion against the United States. Far from being a revolutionary, Jose wants to marry Mercedes to pay off his gambling debts and keep his class status, rather than change the political situation of his occupied country. Similarly, the Filipino rebels symbolized by the character of Captain Rigon are spoiled, vain men with elite backgrounds and appearances.

In the novel, one working-class Filipino character is a spy for the Americans. The elderly house servant, Benita Llopis, is an abused maid who betrays her cruel employer, Jose Mispall, to the Americans so that she can get back at him for all the years he beat her. Benita, who nursed Jose as a child, has seen him grow to become an ill-tempered, violent drunk, and her maternal suffering suggests the dilemma of Filipino civilians who are forced to follow and support the ongoing insurgency against the United States led by men like Jose Mispall. But while her actions benefit the Americans, she is still, like all her fellow Filipinos, treacherous to the end, as she betrays her own. All the Filipino characters in the novel suffer in comparison to Daniel Everton and the other Americans, who are noble sons and daughters of empire with blameless natures. While Constance Fairchild is presented as a white, beautiful, educated, white, and upper-class woman, Mercedes Paris is portrayed as a spoiled, childish, unstable young woman who commits adultery after a few months of marriage to Daniel. Mercedes's primitiveness is attributed to her mixed heritage, as she is both native and tainted by "Spanish crudeness" (Putnam 131), although her light skin makes her look almost like a proper white woman (Putnam 135). The novel's singular risqué scene describes Mercedes's seduction by Jose Mispall's lies and flirtations, as she gives in to his "violent love-making" (Putnam 318). This sexualization of the mixed-race Filipina borrows from the figure of the mixed-race woman, the tragic mulatta of American fiction.[21]

The Manichaean portrayal of American heroism and Filipino criminality mimics the logic of irregular warfare that supplies the novel's plot and engenders the novel's politics. The logic of counterinsurgency that threads through the novel highlights or privileges American military victory over the histories of Filipino anticolonialism and nationalism, the loss of human lives, or the human cost of war. In other words, American victory is all that matters, and Filipino criminals/rebels do not. The American Adam or soldier-hero is not a figure of genocidal war or death, but a noble son, a gentleman soldier, and an ethical man tested by the vagaries of a colonial war. Daniel's act of heroism—that is, rescuing Isidro Paris from kidnap and murder at the hands of the Filipino rebels— wins the heart and mind of the mestizo patriarch. Isidro Paris then hires Daniel as the overseer of his hacienda and offers his daughter Mercedes for marriage. Symbolically, Isidro Paris represents the Filipino elites who embrace the occupation of the Philippines in exchange for the promise of imperial modernity offered by American colonization and tutelage. The union of the dashing imperial hero to the charming, submissive, mixed-race Filipina becomes an analogy for the necessity and inevitability of American colonial rule of the Philippines (Putnam 129–31). For her Filipino father, Mercedes would be better off with the American soldier Daniel Everton than with a corrupt and morally questionable Filipino male who might have ties to the "violent" Katipunan. In other words, the Philippines would have a better future with the Americans than with the Filipino nationalists. The novel presents the romance of counterinsurgency through the necessary union of a white soldier and a Filipina mestiza, but it is a marriage of convenience, not true love. When Mercedes and her insurgent lover Jose are killed toward the end of the novel, Daniel happily announces to Constance he is single again. The novel ends with the reinstatement of the racial order of the American empire, as Daniel, the American Adam, reunites with his white "Eve," Constance, his earlier sexual union (with the Filipina wife) having produced no mixed-race children. The novel offers a clear imperial message: the American Adam, a metaphor of the American imperial nation, is victorious in counterinsurgency and heterosexual love.

In contrast to Putnam's novel, Oscar William Coursey's *The Woman with a Stone Heart: A Romance of the Philippine War* (1914) is a shorter novel of 170 pages. By the time Coursey's romance novel was published, it had been more than a decade since the declaration of the end of the war by Theodore Roosevelt, and images and ideas about the Filipino native had been circulating in American culture for that long. The author, Coursey, served as a soldier during the Philippine-American War and dedicates the novel to his "soldier wife, Julia," who was a new bride when he was called to serve in the Philippines. The novel is set in Manila in 1898, a few months before the outbreak of the Philippine-American War. The novel follows the life and adventures of Marie Sampalit, a cross-dressing Filipina insurgent, described in the story as a "she-devil," and someone who plunged into "the abyss of vain glory." The representation of Filipino rebels as foolish, conceited, and vain recalls the depiction of the

Filipino rebels in Putnam's novel. Implicit in this representation is the idea that the cause of Philippine independence from the United States is a fool's errand, one led by vain Filipino elites.

The novel is an example of the American romance tradition known as the female picaresque novel that gained popularity during the U.S.-Mexico War of 1848 (Streeby 90–91). The female picaresque narrative is part of American story-paper literature from the 1840s, popular narratives for reading audiences from different social classes. The stories of "the picara" were about a cross-dressing female passing as a criminal, a soldier, or spy (Streeby 90–91). During the years of the U.S.-Mexico War, debates about the annexation of Mexico included the national anxieties over the scope of the new territories and the incorporation of "foreign" peoples (Streeby 91). The imperial appeal of the female picaresque story was in the management of those anxieties through the popularization of the discourse of "imperial U.S. American manhood," in the figure of the soldier-hero who would always triumph over the "unmanly" foreign villains (Streeby 91). Coursey's novel returns to this narrative genre, replacing Mexico with the Philippine colony.

Coursey's Filipina *picara* is seventeen-year-old Marie Sampalit, a working-class Filipina who loses her fiancé, Rolando Diminguez, after the authorities arrest him for the attempted murder of the Spanish governor-general. Driven by grief and the desire to avenge her lover's death, she cuts her hair, dresses like a man, and joins Emilio Aguinaldo's army, the Katipunan, to fight the new invaders, the Americans. The novel follows some stylistic conventions of the story-paper, suggesting that a general audience was intended for this Philippine romance. It has ten illustrations, including five black-and-white photographs, a map of Manila Bay and nearby regions, and four artist's sketches captioned as images "courtesy of *McClure's Magazine*." The frontispiece of Coursey's romantic tale is a photograph of a young Filipina, available in the Bureau of Insular Affairs collection in the National Archives in Maryland. The original caption on the photograph says: "A native maid from Albay Province, Luzon," with no date or the name of the subject. The frontispiece stages abjection by reducing an actual living person into an image, that of a fictional cross-dressing Filipina criminal.

The use of Philippine photographs along with artist's sketches references stereographic images, books, and essays published in the early years of the occupation of the Philippine colony. More than a decade after the occupation, images of the "Philippine Islands" still registered certain bodies and objects in the minds of American readers, and these recognizable figures of Filipino savagery and docility had remained indices of colonial intimacy. The frontispiece shows a young woman with long black hair wearing formal Filipino clothes (the *baro't saya*, a blouse with voluminous sleeves and a long skirt, with a *patadyong* or apron-like cloth that accentuates the waist and hips). She also wears what appears to be a velvet choker with an ornate pendant. The caption reads, "Marie Sampalit, the Woman with a Stone Heart." In this image, the photograph of an actual but anonymous Filipina stands in for a fictional Filipina criminal and rogue, who fought for the Filipino rebels during the Philippine-American War. The blurring of lines between fact and fiction returns us to the notion of imperial abjection, with the unknown Filipina as an image of femininity and docility being made to represent a fictional character who chooses to become manly and savage in order to fight her country's invaders. If abjection is that which does not respect boundaries or borders, the Other that disturbs the national imaginary, then the charming Filipina maiden is the representation of the charming and dangerous Philippine colony, a place of mystery, beauty, danger, and death.

Filipina savagery is the central theme of Coursey's novel, embodied in Marie's emotional instability, her capacity for cruelty and torture, her criminal acts of robbery and murder, and her "unnatural" disposition for cross-dressing. Marie is driven by her grief and rage against the Spanish and later the American colonizers, the "foreign devils" who must all be slain (Coursey 63). Her participation in the war against the United States is presented as a personal grudge rather than an anticolonial politics. In contrast to the white masculine soldier-hero, driven by honor and patriotism to discipline the unruly savage Filipinos through war and occupation, Marie is a native female insurgent driven by feminine emotions. Thus in this romance of counterinsurgency, the Philippine-American War is not a war for national liberation but an irrational war for personal revenge. The abject history of the war is the misrepresentation of the resistance as vendetta rather than as a continuation of the Filipino peoples' struggle for independence against colonial rule. The fictionalized character of Emilio Aguinaldo summarizes this colonial revenge fantasy to Marie:

> They killed your husband. They shot Rizal. They strangled Diminguez. They tortured to death several hundred of our young fellows in the dungeon. They have left ridges of dead wherever their armies have moved among us. I tell you they deserved all they got. (Coursey 66–67)

This passage is interesting not just because it intertwines fiction (the execution of Diminguez, Marie's fiancé) and fact (Rizal and torture and the "ridges of death"), but also weaves together revenge and righteous nationalist outrage at not just America and Spain, but the whole practice of imperialism and colonization. Thus, in this imperialist romance, we have a moment of slippage or

excess—where the abject history of the Philippine-American War is accidentally narrated in a scene that blurs the fictional and the factual accounts of the war
of 1899—that actually provides a fairly compelling and well-reasoned, while
still emotional, defense of Filipinos' fight against their colonial oppressors.

If the tarbrush of race disfigures the beauty of the not-quite-white Mercedes
Paris in *Daniel Everton*, it is the tarbrush of both gender and race that stains
Marie Sampalit in Coursey's *The Woman with a Stone Heart*. In this race romance, there is no plot involving miscegenation or an interracial romance, but
the novel presents the racial discourses of Filipina savagery and American imperial masculinity. Marie is an abject, monstrous figure, while the white American soldiers in the novel are virtuous, ethical men who just happen to be doing
the dirty business of war. In Coursey's novel, Marie is presented as a Filipino
criminal, a deviant and a freak because she is not a proper woman who follows
the strict social scripts of Filipina womanhood. Marie's criminal and unusual
actions define her as a woman with no gentle "heart," but one made of stone.
Rather than grieve and mourn femininely after the execution of her fiancé Rolando, Marie transforms herself into an agent of rage and violence by dressing
like a man, cutting her hair short, and enlisting as a "full-fledged soldier" of the
Katipunan, Aguinaldo's army (Coursey 104). She is a torturer who throws Spanish prisoners into a pit and uses them for live target practice (55). She is a rogue
who steals jewelry from an elderly Filipino couple, possibly thieves themselves,
who offer her food and shelter (89). Every Filipino seems to be a thief in this
novel, including rebels who come across an abandoned church (160) and inside
find a metallic box that contains the remains of a Spanish priest along with
other "valuables," such as a gilded cup that Marie hangs on her belt as a trophy
(164). In this scene, Marie and the other Filipino soldiers commit the ultimate
desecration by ransacking the blessed grounds of a Catholic church, a shocking
transgression that would horrify any Christian reader of the novel. This was, in
fact, a complete reversal of actual accounts of looting done by American soldiers, which were investigated in hearings by the U.S. Congress.[22] Marie is also
an accomplished killer who shoots an elderly Filipino man who chases after her
once the couple discovers her theft (Coursey 91), and she shoots General Lawton, the acclaimed "war hero," so she can claim the ten-thousand-dollar bounty
offered by the Filipino government in exile (137–38).

In the chapter "Death of General Lawton," the general's final hours are spent
mounted on a horse, where he cuts a "tall figure," wearing a "resplendent uniform and large white helmet" (Coursey 137–38) and is therefore an easy target for Marie. She takes perfect aim, and the general expires elegantly: "'Bang!'
went her rifle, and at that very moment this peerless leader of men, this hero of

several wars, was shot through the heart and fell dead in the arms of his aide"
(138). The deed done, the uncouth, stone-cold killer exclaims: "See that! What
did I tell you? . . . I told you I'd get him! Now for my dinero" (138). The real-
life Major General Henry Ware Lawton died in circumstances no less bizarre.
Lawton was a professional soldier whose career tied together the histories of
internecine warfare and counterinsurgencies on the North American continent
and the Pacific—the Civil War, the Indian wars, and the Philippine-American
War.[23] He served as a Union soldier in the Civil War and was a decorated army
captain during the Indian wars, where he became famous for capturing the
native chief Geronimo. Lawton died in the Philippines in a battle against Filipino forces led by a general also named Geronimo, in this case General Licerio
Gerónimo.[24] Thus, the famous Filipino twister: "Geronimo was captured by
Lawton, who was killed by Gerónimo." This curious and little-known historical
coincidence in Lawton's life is mentioned in Coursey's novel, which placed the
fictional Marie among Gerónimo's forces.

The novel includes other heroic white American soldiers who suffer the cruelties of Marie Sampalit and the Filipino rebels, contrasting American valor
with Filipino savagery. The only scene that shows American cruelty is one that
briefly mentions the "water cure," the form of torture that was the predecessor
to waterboarding. In that passage, some Filipino villagers in the town of San
Isidro are tortured using the water cure so they will reveal the whereabouts
of General Aguinaldo (Coursey 146). After Marie witnesses this spectacle, she
vows to continue her war against the Americans.

The novel ends with Marie's capture and death. It is Christmas Eve 1900,
and the American soldiers arrest a young "amigo" who refuses to speak during
his trial (173). The Americans are unaware that the young insurgent is actually
the nineteen-year-old Marie Sampalit. The novel ends with a poem entitled "A
Christmas Court Martial," written by one of the American soldiers in the firing
squad that killed the young *amigo*. After the nameless youth is shot, the American soldiers inspect the corpse. The youth's shirt accidentally falls opens, exposing Marie's young breasts, and the sight of her female body underneath her
male clothes shocks her American executioners (Coursey 178). The sight of "a
Woman's tender breast" (178) becomes a moment of imperial abjection where
the accidental disrobing of an abject Filipina body—really that of a capable
insurgent—belongs in the same category as the Filipina savages photographed
in the nude during the early years of Philippine colonial rule. Naked Filipina
breasts are again placed on display as indices of savagery. The sensational story
of Marie Sampalit telegraphs the American national anxieties regarding the
Filipino native, who appears "semicivilized" (suggested visually by the novel's

frontispiece) yet remains a savage at heart. The novel represents the attitudes and debates that were prominent in the early American colonial era regarding the fate of the Philippine colony as it transitioned to limited Filipino civilian control, putting in question the assimilability of Filipinos and their aptitude for self-government and independence. The message of Coursey's novel is that even after more than a decade of American tutelage, the colony is still a savage country.

THE VAMPIRE'S PHOTOGRAPHS

The archive of an empire is a site of abjection, an analytic for disassembling and reconfiguring colonial ideologies and fantasies in cultural texts. Many writers, soldiers, scientists, and artists helped create the archive of the Philippine-American War.

But there is one remarkable American colonial administrator who contributed many images of the Philippine Islands to the archive: Dean C. Worcester. His Philippine career spanned three decades, and Worcester's legacies can be traced in war strategies, in colonial policies, in mining and industry in the colony, and in U.S. popular culture from the era. Worcester had the longest tenure of any colonial official in the Philippines, serving as secretary of the interior from 1901 to 1913. He was also a pioneer of counterinsurgency. A zoologist by training, he used his scientific skills and photography to gather data and classify information about the Philippine Islands and the Filipino people, less for the purposes of science, however, than for those of military surveillance, war, and the maintenance of empire in the islands. When he died in 1924, he left behind a massive personal photographic archive that included sixteen thousand black-and-white photographs and 4,775 original glass plate negatives, now held by the Museum of Anthropology of the University of Michigan, his alma mater (Sinopoli 1). M. Bianet Castellanos says that of the five thousand photographs of Filipino women in the University of Michigan collection, many were nudes from the "non-Christian tribes."[25] Given the size of Worcester's collection, some of the photographs from the Bureau of Insular Affairs and the War Department discussed in chapter 2 might have been images taken by Worcester and his associates. What is certain is that Worcester was the most influential architect of war and empire of his time in the Philippines. However, his reputation, his body of work, and his legacy are known only by a few scholars in the fields of Philippine studies and American studies. This once-prominent architect of empire and his massive photographic archive have remained in the shadows.

Worcester established himself early on as a Philippine expert even before the war (McCoy 100), since he had visited the Philippines in 1887 for a scientific expedition to study zoological specimens.[26] After the United States invaded the islands, he consolidated his reputation through various public lectures, academic essays, and the publication of his book, *The Philippine Islands and Their People*, which made him famous and influential. He served on two presidential commissions, known as "Philippine Commissions," that made recommendations regarding the Philippine Islands to President William McKinley. At the beginning of the Philippine-American War, U.S. commander General Elwell Otis recognized that his intelligence service lacked linguists who could develop a "spy system" to infiltrate Filipino communities (McCoy 100–101). Worcester joined this spy system for the American military and, by July 1899, became head of an intelligence section. Every morning, Worcester would cull the local newspapers and type his notes on Filipinos (and some Americans) of interest to the American colonial government, such as Filipino nationalists, collaborators, and elite families (McCoy 101–4). His data gathering became the foundation for an effective system of counterintelligence that would prove helpful to counterinsurgency efforts once guerrilla war by Filipinos began.

Worcester's racial theories regarding Filipinos were chillingly simple: "non-Christian" Filipinos were savages who lived in "tribes," while lowland or Christianized Filipinos were corrupt. His racial theories on Filipino savagery and corruption were disseminated in different media and forums—U.S. government reports, war studies, books, magazines and academic articles, public lectures, and later moving films. As a race scientist of the era, he was greatly influenced by late nineteenth-century theories on race and blood (Fogelin 4). He believed that Filipinos were racially incapable of self-government, even lowland or Christianized Filipinos, such as the Tagalogs, who were semicivilized because of their mixed racial background (Sinopoli). Worcester's strong dislike of the Tagalogs can be read in the Philippine Commission's first report in 1900, where he first popularized the notion that the leaders of the Philippine Republic (or the Katipunan) were "inept, corrupt and unpopular" and that the insurrection against the United States was only limited to the Tagalog provinces (Sinopoli 5). The term "Philippine insurrection," then, reduces the full-fledged revolutions led by the Katipunan against Spain and later the United States to insignificant rebellions. Worcester's publications and lectures thus had a hand in discrediting the Katipunan and the short-lived Philippine Republic, and even the long and ruinous war fought against the United States was known, for many decades, as the "Philippine insurrection" or the "Philippine campaign."

Worcester's binary racial views of Filipinos served him well politically and financially. He became a famous lecturer of Philippine topics, a popular author, and a wealthy government official after he was appointed as secretary of the interior, in charge of the "Non-Christian Tribes." In October 1908, Filipino nationalists, such as journalist Fidel A. Reyes, published an editorial in the nationalist newspaper *El Renacimiento* that referred to Worcester's business ventures—mining, lumber, cattle ranching—in Benguet and other provinces as having thrived because of the advantages he enjoyed as secretary of the interior, as well as all the insider information he was able to acquire when traveling in that capacity. In the editorial, "Aves de Rapiña," Worcester, who was unnamed, was likened to a rapacious "bird of prey":

> But there is a man who, besides being like the eagle, also has the character-istics of the vulture, the owl and the vampire.
>
> He ascends the mountains of Benguet ostensibly to classify and measure Igorot skulls, to study and to civilize the Igorots; but at the same time, he also espies during his flight, with the keen eye of the bird of prey, where are located large deposits of gold, which is the real prey concealed in the lonely mountains, in order to appropriate them for himself afterwards, thanks to the legal facilities he can make and unmake, at will, always, however, re-dounding to his own benefit. . . .
>
> He gives laudable impetus to the search for rich lodes in Mindanao, in Mindoro, and in other virgin regions of the archipelago, a search undertak-en with the people's money and with excuse of its being for the public good; when in strict truth, his purpose is to obtain data and discover the keys to the national wealth for his essentially personal benefit, as proved by the acquisition of immense properties registered under the names of others.[27]

For Filipino nationalists in Manila, Worcester was "the vampire." Described by his critics as an imperious and vindictive man, Worcester did not take kindly to his nicknames and filed a libel suit against Reyes and the publishers of the paper, Teodoro Kalaw and Martin Ocampo, and its staff. The colonial courts sided in Worcester's favor and gave prison sentences to Kalaw, Ocampo, Reyes, and almost all of the staff. Some were in prison for six months.[28] The libel suit dragged on for years and bankrupted *El Renacimiento*. Much to Worcester's irritation, the publishers, Kalaw and Ocampo, never served a day in jail, since President Woodrow Wilson pardoned them in 1914. Fidel Reyes became a ce-lebrity and was elected to the Philippine Assembly.[29] By the time Worcester retired from government office in 1915, he was a fabulously wealthy man. He became the manager of the Visayan Refining Company and owned 17,500 acres of land in Bukidnon Province and a cattle ranch (Sinopoli 8).

But as Mark Rice notes, his most influential role was as a culture warrior for empire.[30] Worcester understood the power of image making as a tactic of war and used his ethnographic portraits to make a visual case for war and the occupation of the Philippine Islands. His archive was republished in official war reports, government reports, academic journals such as the *Philippine Journal of Science,* and popular magazines such as *National Geographic* (Rice 71). In public lectures, he would show lantern slides or his own "moving pictures" (Rice 69).

A fraction of Worcester's archive can be found in the CD *Imperial Imaginings: The Dean C. Worcester Photographic Collection of the Philippines, 1890–1913,* edited by Carla M. Sinopoli and Lars Fogelin. The CD contains more than a thousand images—just a fraction of the total—from the Worcester collection, bringing a small but significant part of the shadow archive to light. These artifacts from the imperial archive of an influential colonial figure are an important development in reexamining a forgotten war. This accessibility, however, while truly salutary, can lead to a mistaken belief that photographs and their captions are unimpeachable empirical evidence of the past or are "truthful."

In Rice's most recent essay, he cautions readers of historical images against concluding that what they read in an archive, in particular the captions of archival photographs, corresponds to historical fact. He reveals Worcester's photographic practice of "fabrication," manipulation, and lies (Rice 74). His practice of fabrication included the omission of data regarding his photographic subjects ("lies of omission") and manipulating images to suit his message of Filipino savagery (lies of "commission") (Rice 74). Given the limitations of historical information and the fabrication of data in Worcester's archive, reading abjection in the images enables us to detect the lies but not unfortunately to uncover the truth.

The erotics of imperial abjection filters through the Worcester archive. Worcester instructed Filipino indigenous women to disrobe and pose naked for his camera (Castellanos 9; Rice 71–72). Some of the photographs show women wearing traditional clothes, followed by another photograph without their clothes. What is noticeable in some photographs is the unease that registers in the faces of the women (Rice 71–72). In figures 40 and 41, three Benguet Province girls pose initially in their traditional woven blouses and skirts. The first photograph (figure 40) shows the young women looking directly at the camera. But the next photograph (figure 41) shows the girls without their blouses, and at least two of them looking slightly downward or looking away. Worcester's camera placed special attention on women's breasts, in particular adolescent breasts (Castellanos 9). In these abject images, we see the violence of Worcester's cam-

Fig. 40. "1907 Benguet girls." From the Dean C. Worcester photographic collection at the University of Michigan Museum of Anthropology.

Fig. 41. "1907 Benguet girls." From the Dean C. Worcester photographic collection at the University of Michigan Museum of Anthropology.

era at work by recognizing the unease on the faces of the young Benguet girls. The photographs return to the notion that savage breasts are metaphors of colonial power, race, and sex; in particular, these images portray the Philippine colony as possession, articulating the "sublime" pleasure of viewing female native bodies. As later variants of photographs of Native American women that circulated as postcards in the early twentieth century, these abject photographs link the violence of counterinsurgencies, wars of conquest, the violation of women and children, and the occupation of native or indigenous land.

Many adult women were also photographed by Worcester, and some were photographed completely naked, posing without their traditional attire (figures 40 and 41). Figure 42 shows two women from Benguet Province posing by large rocks. Both women crouch and cover their privates, with the woman on the right pushing back her hair with her left hand, striking a strangely seductive pose as her arm frames the side of her face as a professional magazine model would. Benguet Province in the early part of the twentieth century was still largely wild and remote, and the woman may not have posed that way unless it was suggested by Worcester or his associate. Very little is known of Worcester's female subjects, and as Mark Rice reminds us, Worcester either excised information about his subjects or fabricated them. Left thus in the dark about his subjects, we can view these images of Benguet women and consider that they reflect the monstrous and the sublime of empire. By using the word "monstrous," we assess the creator of these images, his career as counterinsurgency expert, imperial ideologue, colonial administrator, and opportunistic businessman. Worcester, "the vampire," embodied the power and violence of the U.S. empire, and his photographs of Filipino women codify his and the empire's power. As articulations of the sublime or the pleasures of empire, these abject bodies recall the interconnected histories of Western expansion, visual culture, and pornography. The race sciences of the late nineteenth and early twentieth centuries produced and popularized the image of the naked savage for the pleasure of Western viewers and for the management of national anxieties regarding war and occupation. "Proper white women" of Worcester's time looked nothing like these abject women. And so to see the body of a Filipina savage was an act of enjoying the pleasures of empire.

As a final example, following nineteenth-century Western portraits of race and criminality, Worcester photographed "limbs and body parts" in isolation, using a white cloth as a backdrop, to guide the viewer's gaze and thinking (figure 44) (Castellanos 9). By isolating human beings from their surroundings and community, by focusing on a limb or human part, and by photographing everyday objects that belonged to indigenous people, Worcester's camera reduced living people and their cultures to scientific objects for visual consump-

Fig. 42. "1904 Benguet women." From the Dean C. Worcester photographic collection at the University of Michigan Museum of Anthropology.

Fig. 43. "1904 Benguet women." From the Dean C. Worcester photographic collection at the University of Michigan Museum of Anthropology.

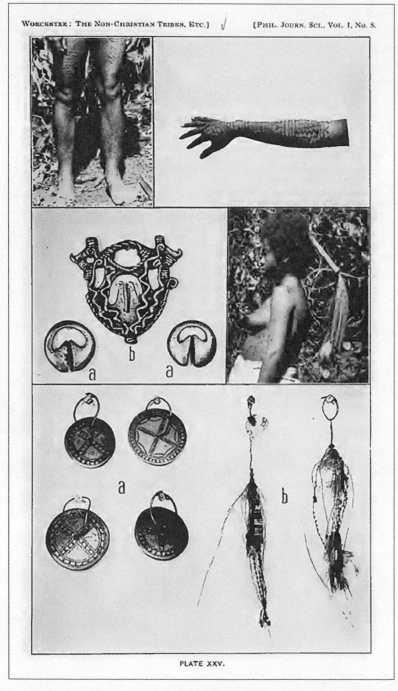

PLATE XXV.

Fig. 44. Body parts: Worcester's article in the *Philippine Journal of Science* shows indigenous objects and cropped body parts of native subjects.

tion and erased the photographs' context of war and occupation. But by considering abjection, we see more than just picturesque or exotic images. We begin to sense the violence of provenance, that is, the long period of the undeclared and ongoing Philippine-American War. Abjection shatters the imperial myth of Filipino objecthood and returns us to abjecthood. Thus, in figure 36, through the lens of abjection, we see Worcester's photographs, from his 1906 journal article, as the blood and bones of empire, relics connected to his personal history as an architect of empire and war.

Given his long Philippine career and the "lives" his racial theories continue to lead via recirculations then and now, Worcester's archive reminds us of American imperialism's abject logic of reducing living beings to body parts and bodies that were reproduced in popular culture to convey the messages of empire. Colonial images from an imperial archive like Worcester's transmit quiet and gentle forms of dehumanization, offering clues to empire's acts of violation and death. Reading abjection, we are able to sense imperial violence in these otherwise innocuous images of the Philippines by taking the image apart, by acknowledging the authorial anonymity or obscurity of the images as an articulation of empire's violence, by tracing the Philippine colony's past in different cultural texts, and by accepting that the brutal history of the American empire is connected to other histories of war, genocide, and occupation.

In our digital age, the electronic circulation of American imperial images rewrites Heidegger's notion of the world as a "world picture," or "the world conceived and grasped as a picture."[31] Imperial images, however, underscore that certain images from formerly colonized countries have always been *empire's pictures*, icons that reproduce the colonial relations of the metropole and the colony, with the colony as a visual object of study and as a military target. Abjection is a practice of reading images of the Philippines through figures, repetitions, patterns, and histories that reveal the American romance of counterinsurgency and war.

Worcester, "the vampire," was certainly an influential and frightening figure during the Philippine-American War and the years of U.S. rule. It is the hope of this study that abjection, as a critical optic for viewing America's imperial archive, brings the violence committed by the vampire, and other imperial shapers like him, into the light of day.

Notes

INTRODUCTION

1. Mitchell, W. J. T. *What Do Pictures Want? The Lives and Loves of Images.* Chicago: University of Chicago Press, 2005. Print. 155.

2. Lowe, Lisa. "The International within the National: American Studies and Asian American Critique." *Cultural Critique* 40 Autumn (1998): 29–47. Print. 29–30.

3. Taruc, Luis. *Born of the People.* New York: International Publishers, 1953. Print. 7.

4. See Wolff, Leon. *Little Brown Brother: America's Forgotten Bid for Empire Which Cost 250,000 Lives.* London: Longmans, 1961. Print.

5. See Carlson, Keith Thor. "Born Again of the People: Luis Taruc and Peasant Ideology in Philippine Revolutionary Politics." *Historie Sociale / Social History* 41.82 (2008): 417–58. Print. 419–20.

6. Saldívar, Jose David. "Looking Awry at 1898: Roosevelt, Montejo, Paredes, and Mariscal." *American Literary History* 12.3 (2000): 386–406. Print. 389.

7. Kramer, Paul A. "The Water Cure." *New Yorker* February 25, 2008: 38–43. Print.

8. Harris, Charles Kassel. *How to Write a Popular Song.* New York: Charles K. Harris, 1906. Print.

9. Wertheim, Arthur Frank, and Barbara Bair, eds. *The Papers of Will Rogers.* Vol. 2. Norman: University of Oklahoma Press, 2000. Print. Mason, Jeffrey D., and J. Ellen Gainor. *Performing America: Cultural Nationalism in American Theater.* Ann Arbor: University of Michigan Press, 1999. Print.

10. Kibler M. Alison. *Rank Ladies: Gender and Cultural Hierarchy in American Vaudeville.* Chapel Hill: University of North Carolina Press, 1999. Print.

11. The term "vestiges of war" is from Shaw and Francia. See Shaw, Angel Velasco, and Luis H. Francia. *Vestiges of War: The Philippine-American War and the Aftermath of an Imperial Dream, 1899–1999.* New York: New York University Press, 2002. Print.

12. McClintock, Anne. *Imperial Leather: Race, Gender and Sexuality in the Colonial Conquest.* New York: Routledge, 1995. Print. 72.

13. For American racial discourses on "red savagery" and "black docility," see Almaguer, Tomas. *Racial Fault Lines: The Historical Origins of White Supremacy in California.* Berkeley: University of California Press, 1994. Print.

14. LaFeber, Walter. *The New Empire: An Interpretation of American Expansion, 1860–1898.* 1998 ed. Ithaca, NY: Cornell University Press, 1963. Print.

15. See, Sarita Echavez. *The Decolonized Eye: Filipino American Art and Performance.* Minneapolis: University of Minnesota Press, 2009. Print.

16. Baldoz, Rick. *The Third Asiatic Invasion: Empire and Migration in Filipino America, 1898–1946.* New York: New York University Press, 2011. Print. Tolentino, Cynthia H. *America's Experts: Race and the Fictions of Sociology.* Minneapolis: University of Minnesota Press, 2009. Print. Baldoz, Rick. "The Racial Vectors of Empire: Classification and Competing Master Narratives in the Colonial Philippines." *Du Bois Review* 5.1 (2008): 69–94. Print.

17. Gikandi cited in Agnani, Sunil, et al. "The End of Postcolonial Theory?" *PMLA* 122.3 (2007): 633–51. Print. 635.

18. Campomanes, Oscar V. "The New Empire's Forgetful and Forgotten Citizens: Unrepresentability and Unassimilability in Filipino-American Postcolonialities." *Hitting Critical Mass* 2.2 (1995): 145–200. Print. 147.

19. According to a 2009 U.S. Homeland Security study, Filipinos are the largest undocumented Asian immigrant population. The largest undocumented immigrant population is Latinos. See Hoeffer, Michael, Nancy Rytina, and Bryan C. Baker. "Estimates of the Unauthorized Immigrant Population Residing in the United States: January 2008." *Population Estimates.* Ed. Security, U.S. Homeland: Office of Immigration Statistics, 2009. Print.

20. Isaac, Allan Punzalan. *American Tropics: Articulating Filipino America.* Minneapolis: University of Minnesota Press, 2006. Print. xxv.

21. Diaz-Quinones, Arcadio. "1898." *Hispanic American Historical Review* 78.4 (1998): 557–81. Print.

22. The term "archive-centered approach" and the notion of studying the colonial archive as imperial object are from Morillo-Alicea, Javier. "Aquel Laberinto de Oficinas: Ways of Knowing Empire in Late-Nineteenth Century Spain." *After Spanish Rule: Postcolonial Predicaments of the Americas.* Eds. Thurner, Mark and Andres Guerrero. Durham: Duke University Press, 2003. 111–40. Print. 115.

23. Richards, Thomas. *The Imperial Archive: Knowledge and Fantasy of Empire.* London: Verso, 1993. Print.

24. Sekula, Allan. "On the Invention of Photographic Meaning." *Artforum* January 1975: 37–45. Print.

25. Ardis, Anne L. "Introduction." *Women's Experience of Modernity: 1875–1945.* Eds. Ardis, Anne L. and Leslie W. Lewis. Baltimore: Johns Hopkins University Press, 2003. Print.

26. Gilroy, Paul. *The Black Atlantic: Modernity and Double Consciousness*. Cambridge: Harvard University Press, 1993. Print.

27. See Sekula, Allan. "The Body and the Archive." *October* 39 (1986): 3–64. Print.

28. Wexler, Laura. *Tender Violence: Domestic Visions in an Age of U.S. Imperialism*. Chapel Hill: University of North Carolina Press, 2000. Print. 1–51.

29. My ideas on U.S. imperial modernity are influenced by Lowe's discussion on British and French Orientalisms. On Orientalism as "heterogeneous and contradictory" discourse, see Lowe, Lisa. *Critical Terrains: French and British Orientalism*. 1991. Ithaca: Cornell University Press, 1994. Print. 5.

30. Early accounts of Filipino American history that focused on the experience of migrant farmworkers include De Witt, Howard. *Violence in the Fields: California Filipino Farm Labor Unionization during the Great Depression*. Saratoga: Century Twenty One Publications, 1980. Print. Cordova, Fred, Dorothy Laigo Cordova, and Albert A. Acena. *Filipinos, Forgotten Asian Americans: A Pictorial Essay, 1763-Circa 1963*. Dubuque, Iowa: Kendall/Hunt, 1983. Print. Scharlin, Craig, and Lilia V. Villanueva, eds. *Philip Vera Cruz: A Personal History of Filipino Immigrants and the Farmworkers Movement*. Los Angeles: UCLA Labor Center, 1992. Print.

31. San Juan Jr., E. "Mapping the Boundaries: The Filipino Writer in the U.S.A." *Journal of Ethnic Studies* 19.1 (1991): 117–31. Print. Carlos Bulosan. *On Becoming Filipino: Selected Writings of Carlos Bulosan*. Ed. San Juan Jr., E. Philadelphia: Temple University Press, 1995. Print. Carlos Bulosan. *The Cry and the Dedication*. Ed. San Juan Jr., E. Philadelphia: Temple University Press, 1995. Print. San Juan Jr., E. *From Exile to Diaspora: Versions of the Filipino Experience in the United States*. Boulder, CO: Westview Press, 1998. Print. San Juan Jr., E. *After Postcolonialism: Remapping Philippines-United States Confrontations*. Lanham, MD: Rowman and Littlefield, 2000. Print.

32. Tiongson, Antonio T., Edgardo V. Gutierrez, and Ricardo V. Gutierrez, eds. *Positively No Filipinos Allowed: Building Communities and Discourse*. Philadelphia: Temple University Press, 2006. Print. Gonzalves, Theodore S. *The Day the Dancers Stayed: Performing in the Filipino/American Diaspora*. Philadelphia: Temple University Press, 2009. Print.

33. Cordova, Fred, Dorothy Laigo Cordova, and Albert A. Acena. *Filipinos, Forgotten Asian Americans: A Pictorial Essay, 1763-Circa 1963*. Dubuque, Iowa: Kendall/Hunt, 1983. Print.

34. "The American Community—Asians: 2004, American Community Survey Reports." Ed. U.S. Bureau of the Census. Washington, DC: U.S. Census Bureau, 2007. Print. 2.

35. Hoeffer, Michael, Nancy Rytina, and Bryan C. Baker. "Estimates of the Unauthorized Immigrant Population Residing in the United States: January 2008." *Population Estimates*. Ed. U.S. Department of Homeland Security: Office of Immigration Statistics, 2009. Print. 4.

36. Mbembe, Achille. *On the Postcolony*. Berkeley: University of California Press, 2001. Print.

37. Edwards, Brian T. "Preposterous Encounters: Interrupting American Studies with

the (Post)Colonial, or Casablanca in the American Century." *Comparative Studies of South Asia, Africa and the Middle East* 23.1–2 (2003): 70–86. Print.

38. Salanga, Alfrredo Navarro. "They Don't Think Much about Us in America." *Flippin': Filipinos on America*. Ed. Luis H. Francia and Eric Gamalinda. New York: Asian American Writers' Workshop, 1996. Print. 251–52.

39. Vergès, Françoise. *Monsters and Revolutionaries: Colonial Family Romance and Metissage*. Durham: Duke University Press, 1999. Print. xii.

40. Isaac, Allan Punzalan *American Tropics: Articulating Filipino America*. Minneapolis: University of Minnesota Press, 2006. Print. 17.

41. See Kaplan, Amy, and Donald E. Pease, eds. *Cultures of United States Imperialism*. Durham: Duke University Press, 1993. Print.

42. Streeby, Shelley. *American Sensations: Class, Empire, and the Production of Popular Culture*. Berkeley: University of California Press, 2002. Print.

43. Chakrabarty, Dipesh. *Provincializing Europe: Postcolonial Thought and Historical Difference*. Princeton, NJ: Princeton University Press, 2000. Print.

44. Blanco, John D. *Frontier Constitutions: Christianity and Colonial Empire in the 19th Century Philippines*. Berkeley: University of California Press, 2009. Print.

45. Makdisi, Saree. "Postcolonial Literature in a Neocolonial World: Modern Arabic Culture and the End of Modernity." *The Pre-occupation of Postcolonial Studies*. Eds. Afzal-Khan, Fawzia and Kalpana Seshadri-Crooks. Durham: Duke University Press, 2000. 266–91. Print.

46. Lowe, Lisa. *Immigrant Acts: On Asian American Cultural Politics*. Durham: Duke University Press, 1996. Print. 103.

47. White, Hayden. *Tropics of Discourse: Essays in Cultural Criticism*. Baltimore: Johns Hopkins University Press, 1978. Print.

CHAPTER 1

1. Dinerstein, Joel. "Technology and Its Discontents: On the Verge of the Posthuman." *American Quarterly* 58.3 (2006): 569–95. Print. 575.

2. Chow, Rey. *The Age of the World Target: Self-Referentiality in War, Theory and Comparative Work*. Durham: Duke University Press, 2006. Print.

3. McClintock, Anne. *Imperial Leather: Race, Gender and Sexuality in the Colonial Conquest*. New York and London: Routledge, 1995. Print. 71.

4. Kristeva, Julia. *Powers of Horror: An Essay on Abjection*. Trans. Roudiez, Leon S. New York: Columbia University Press, 1982. Print. Shimakawa, Karen. *National Abjection: The Asian American Body Onstage*. Durham: Duke University Press, 2002. Print. Scott, Darieck. *Extravagant Abjection: Blackness, Power, and Sexuality in the African American Literary Imagination*. New York: New York University Press, 2010. Print. Sandoval-Sánchez, Alberto. "Politicizing Abjection: In the Manner of a Prologue for the Articulation of AIDS Latino Queer Identities." *American Literary History* 17.3 (2005): 542–49. Print.

5. By *discourse*, I refer to Hayden White's work on discourse as that which "moves 'to and fro' between received encodings of experience and the clutter of phenomena which refuses incorporation into conventionalized notions of 'reality,' 'truth,' or 'possibility'" (White 3–4), from the Latin term *discurrere*. In other words, discourse is language that shuttles back and forth between experience, phenomena, and common perceptions or "conventionalized notions of truth." Discourse is a model of "the processes of consciousness" (White 5) that incorporates knowledge through tropes. By *trope* I refer to Srinivas Aravamudan's discussion of the term's eighteenth-century usage as a metaphor or "a word or expression used in a different sense from what it properly signifies. Or, a word changed from its proper and natural signification to another" (1).

A trope is an early English word rooted in the word *tropus*, which in classical Latin meant "'metaphor' or 'figure of speech'" (White 2). In this study, I argue that American imperial abjection is a discourse that works on a tropological level whereby the dissemination of ideas in support of U.S. imperialism takes the form of metaphorical figures. To quote Hayden White: "Understanding is a process of rendering the unfamiliar, or the 'uncanny' in Freud's sense of that term, familiar. . . . This process of understanding can only be tropological in nature, for what is involved in the rendering of the unfamiliar into the familiar is a troping that is generally figurative" (5). Tropes are integral to the language of American imperialism because metaphors enable the visualization and familiarity of a certain idea. The unfamiliar becomes familiar or understandable through tropes, and this familiarity or recognition allows for the resilience not only of the tropes but the idea behind it. The idea of an American empire in the Pacific, and later as a global empire, was made possible by abject tropes that generated positive feelings and ideas of American superiority and exceptionalism.

See White, Hayden. *Tropics of Discourse: Essays in Cultural Criticism*. Baltimore: Johns Hopkins University Press, 1978. Print. See also Aravamudan, Srinivas. *Tropicopolitans: Colonialism and Agency, 1688–1804*. Durham: Duke University Press, 1999. Print.

6. Spurr, David. *The Rhetoric of Empire: Colonial Journalism, Travel Writing, and Imperial Administration*. Durham: Duke University Press, 1993. Print. 79.

7. The African American newspaper *Wisconsin Weekly Advocate* reported on the cost of the war. See "Cost of the War. Filipino Insurrection Entailed Expense of $48,928,060." *Wisconsin Weekly Advocate* March 8, 1900. Print.

8. Rydell, Robert W. *All the World's a Fair: Visions of Empire at American International Expositions, 1876–1916*. Chicago: University of Chicago Press, 1984. Print. 5.

9. See Isaac, Allan Punzalan. *American Tropics: Articulating Filipino America*. Minneapolis: University of Minnesota Press, 2006. Print. Tiongson, Antonio T., Edgardo V. Gutierrez, and Ricardo V. Gutierrez, eds. *Positively No Filipinos Allowed: Building Communities and Discourse*. Philadelphia: Temple University Press, 2006. Print. See, Sarita Echavez. *The Decolonized Eye: Filipino American Art and Performance*. Minneapolis: University of Minnesota Press, 2009. Print. Rodriguez, Dylan. *Suspended Apocalypse: White Supremacy, Genocide and the Filipino Condition*. Minneapolis: University of Minnesota Press, 2009. Print. Gonzalves, Theodore S. *The Day the Dancers Stayed: Perform-*

ing in the Filipino/American Diaspora. Philadelphia: Temple University Press, 2009. Print.

10. Huhndorf, Shari M. *Going Native: Indians in the American Cultural Imagination.* Ithaca: Cornell University Press, 2001. Print. 23.

11. McCoy, Alfred W. *Policing America's Empire: The United States, the Philippines, and the Rise of the Surveillance State.* Madison: University of Wisconsin Press, 2009. Print. 27.

12. Campomanes, Oscar V. "Casualty Figures of the American Soldier and the Other: Post-1898 Allegories of Imperial Nation-Building as 'Love and War.'" *Vestiges of War: The Philippine-American War and the Aftermath of an Imperial Dream, 1899–1999.* Eds. Shaw, Angel Velasco and Luis H. Francia. New York: New York University Press, 2002. 134–62. Print. 144–51.

13. Hoganson, Kristin. *Fighting for American Manhood: How Gender Politics Provoked the Spanish-American and Philippine-American Wars.* New Haven: Yale University Press, 1998. Print. 6.

14. Campomanes, Oscar V. "The New Empire's Forgetful and Forgotten Citizens: Unrepresentability and Unassimilability in Filipino-American Postcolonialities." *Hitting Critical Mass* 2.2 (1995): 145–200. Print.

15. Kramer, Paul A. *The Blood of Government: Race, Empire, the United States and the Philippines.* Chapel Hill: University of North Carolina Press, 2006. Print. 157.

16. Francisco, Luzviminda. "The First Vietnam: The Philippine-American War of 1899–1902." *Bulletin of Concerned Asian Scholars* 5 (1973): 2–16. Print.

17. Twain, Mark. *Mark Twain's Weapons of Satire: Anti-Imperialist Writings on the Philippine-American War.* Ed. Zwick, Jim. New York: Syracuse University Press, 1992. Print. 103.

18. Zwick, Jim. "The Anti-Imperialist League and the Origins of Filipino-American Oppositional Solidarity." *Amerasia Journal* 24.2 (1998): 65–85. Print.

19. Jacobson, Matthew Frye. "Imperial Amnesia: Teddy Roosevelt, the Philippines, and the Modern Art of Forgetting." *Radical History Review* 73 (1999): 116–27. Print. 116–18.

20. Kaplan, Amy, and Donald E. Pease, eds. *Cultures of United States Imperialism.* Durham: Duke University Press, 1993. Print.

21. Rowe, John Carlos. *Literary Culture and U.S. Imperialism: From the Revolution to World War II.* New York: Oxford University Press, 2000. Print.

22. Mitchell, W. J. T. *What Do Pictures Want? The Lives and Loves of Images.* Chicago: University of Chicago Press, 2005. Print. 155.

23. Said, Edward W. *Culture and Imperialism.* New York: Vintage, 1993. Print.

24. Colonial subjectivity has been explored at length by Fanon and recently by Campomanes and Mbembe in different postcolonial histories.

25. Said, Edward W. *Orientalism.* New York: Vintage, 1978. Print. 40.

26. Mbembe, Achille. *On the Postcolony.* Berkeley: University of California Press, 2001. Print. 1–2.

27. Foucault, Michel. *Discipline and Punish: The Birth of the Prison.* Trans. Sheridan, Alan. New York: Vintage Books, 1975. Print. 27.

28. Lowe, Lisa. *Critical Terrains: French and British Orientalism.* 1991. Ithaca: Cornell University Press, 1994. Print. 12.

29. Behdad, Ali. *Belated Travelers: Orientalism in the Age of Colonial Dissolution.* Durham: Duke University Press, 1994. Print. 6.

30. Ileto, Reynaldo C. "Philippine Wars and the Politics of Memory." *Positions: East Asia Cultures Critique* 13 (2005): 215–34. Print.

31. The "intimacies of empire" is from Stoler. See Stoler, Ann Laura, ed. *Haunted by Empire: Geographies of Intimacy in North American History.* Durham: Duke University Press, 2006. Print. 1–4.

32. Go, Julian. *American Empire and the Politics of Meaning: Elite Political Culture in the Philippines and Puerto Rico during U.S. Colonialism.* Durham: Duke University Press, 2008. Print. 53.

33. Mignolo, Walter. "(Post)Occidentalism, (Post)Coloniality, and (Post) Subaltern Rationality." *The Pre-Occupation of Postcolonial Studies.* Eds. Afzal-Khan, Fawzia and Kalpana Seshadri-Crooks. Durham: Duke University Press, 2000. 86–118. Print. 109.

34. Gilroy, Paul. *The Black Atlantic: Modernity and Double Consciousness.* Cambridge: Harvard University Press, 1993. Print. 44.

35. Smith, Sherry L. *Reimagining Indians: Native Americans through Anglo Eyes, 1880–1940.* New York: Oxford University Press, 2000. Print.

36. Eric Lott, *Love and Theft: Blackface Minstrelsy and the American Working Class.* New York: Oxford University Press, 1993. Print. 4.

37. Turner, Frederick Jackson. *The Frontier in American History.* 1920. New York: Henry Holt, 1947. Print. 38.

38. Campomanes, Oscar V. "1898 and the Nature of the New Empire." *Radical History Review* 73 (1999): 130–46. Print. 133.

39. Wexler, Laura. *Tender Violence: Domestic Visions in an Age of U.S. Imperialism.* Chapel Hill: University of North Carolina Press, 2000. Print. 22.

40. Bederman, Gail. *Manliness and Civilization: A Cultural History of Gender and Race in the United States, 1880–1917.* Chicago: University of Chicago Press, 1995. Print. 12–13.

41. Kaplan, Amy. *The Anarchy of Empire in the Making of U.S. Culture.* Cambridge: Harvard University Press, 2002. Print. 25.

42. Smith, Shawn Michelle. *American Archives: Gender, Race, and Class in Visual Culture.* Princeton, NJ: Princeton University Press, 1999. Print. 8.

43. The colonial camera in 19th century England was used in anthropometry (the measurement of the human body) and physiognomy (the measurement of human skulls) to visually "document" criminality, insanity and racial inferiority among the lesser races. See Levine, Philippa. "States of Undress: Nakedness and the Colonial Imagination." *Victorian Studies* 50.2 (2008): 189–219. Print. On the "criminal body," see Smith: 68–93.

44. Limón, José Eduardo. *American Encounters: Greater Mexico, the United States and the Erotics of Culture*. Boston: Beacon Press, 1998. Print.

45. Foucault, Michel. *The History of Sexuality*. Vol. 2: *The Use of Pleasure*. Trans. Hurley, Robert. 1985. New York: Vintage, 1990. Print. 189.

46. Mengay, Donald H. "Arabian Rites: T.E. Lawrence's 'Seven Pillars of Wisdom' and the Erotics of Empire." *Genre* 27 Winter (1994): 395–416. Print.

47. Wallace, Lee. *Sexual Encounters: Pacific Texts, Modern Sexualities*. Ithaca: Cornell University Press, 2003. Print. 1–10.

48. Jonathan Goldberg quoted in Wallace 24. See Goldberg, Jonathan. *Sodometries: Renaissance Texts, Modern Sexualities*. Stanford: Stanford University Press, 1992. Print.

49. Sharpley-Whiting, T. Denean. *Sexualized Savages, Primal Fears and Primitive Narratives in French*. Durham: Duke University Press, 1999. Print.

50. Leon, W. M. Consuelo. "Foundations of the American Image of the Pacific." *Asia/Pacific as Space of Cultural Production*. Eds. Wilson, Rob and Arif Dirlik. Durham: Duke University Press, 1995. 17–29. Print.

51. Lyons, Paul. "Opening Accounts in the South Seas: Poe's Pym and American Pacific Orientalism." *ESQ: A Journal of the American Renaissance* 42.4 (1996): 291–326. Print.

52. Clark, Ella Elizabeth, and Margot Edmonds. *Sacagawea of the Lewis and Clark Expedition*. Berkeley: University of California, 1979. Print. 1–13. I am indebted to Native cultural critic Shari Huhndorf for information and sources on Sacagawea and Pocahontas.

53. See Tilton, Robert S. *Pocahontas: The Evolution of an American Narrative*. Cambridge: Cambridge University Press, 1994. Print. Thanks to Shari Huhndorf for this citation.

54. Kidwell, Clara Sue. "What Would Pocahontas Think? Women and Cultural Persistence." *Callaloo* 17.1 (1994): 149–59. Print.

55. See also Nash, Gary B. "The Hidden History of Mestizo America." *Journal of American History* 82.3 (1995): 941–64. Print.

56. Stoler, Ann Laura. "Making Empire Respectable: The Politics of Race and Sexual Morality in Twentieth-Century Colonial Cultures." *Dangerous Liaisons: Gender, Nation and Postcolonial Perspectives*. Eds. McClintock, Anne, Aamir Mufti, and Ella Shohat. Minneapolis: University of Minnesota Press, 1997. Print.

57. Smith, Andrea. *Conquest: Sexual Violence and American Indian Genocide*. Cambridge, MA: South End Press, 2005. Print.

58. Stoler, Ann Laura. *Carnal Knowledge and Imperial Power: Race and the Intimate in Colonial Rule*. Berkeley: University of California Press, 2002. Print. 43.

CHAPTER 2

1. Ray, Charles. "Following a War with the Camera." *Royal Magazine* 3.18 (1900): 475–81. Print.

2. Ileto, Reynaldo C. *Knowing America's Colony: A Hundred Years from the Philippine War*. Honolulu: University of Hawai'i at Manoa, 1999. Print.

3. Worcester, Dean C. *The Philippines, Past and Present*. Vols. 1 and 2. New York: Macmillan, 1914. Print. Le Roy, James. *Philippine Life in Town and Country*. 1973 ed. New York: Oriole Editions, 1905. Print.

4. Barrett, Terry. "Photographs and Contexts." *Journal of Aesthetic Education* 19.3 (1985): 51–64. Print. 53.

5. Trachtenberg, Alan. "Albums of War: Reading Civil War Photographs." *Representations* 9 (1985): 1–32. Print.

6. Kristeva, Julia. *Powers of Horror: An Essay on Abjection*. Trans. Roudiez, Leon S. New York: Columbia University Press, 1982. Print. 3.

7. Jimmie Durham, quoted by Holt, Jonathan. "The Subjective Image." *Third Text* 10.37 (1996): 104–6. Print. 104.

8. See Mieder, Wolfgang. "The Only Good Indian Is a Dead Indian: History and Meaning of a Proverbial Stereotype." *Journal of American Folklore* 106.419 (1993): 38–60. Print. 46.

9. Linfield, Susie. *The Cruel Radiance: Photography and Political Violence*. Chicago: University of Chicago Press, 2010. Print. 33.

10. Mitchell, W. J. T. *What Do Pictures Want? The Lives and Loves of Images*. Chicago: University of Chicago Press, 2005. Print. 11.

11. The significance of the name "Geronimo" and the life of General Lawton will be discussed in the conclusion on the romance of counterinsurgency.

12. Morris, Rosalind C., ed. *Photographies East: The Camera and Its Histories in East and Southeast Asia*. Durham: Duke University Press, 2009. Print. 19.

13. Neely, F. Tennyson. *Fighting in the Philippines, Authentic Original Photos*. New York: F. Tennyson Neely, 1899. Print.

14. *Liberty Poems: Inspired by the Crisis of 1898–1900*. Boston: James H. West, 1900. Print.

15. Best, Jonathan. *A Philippine Album: American Era Photographs, 1900–1930*. Manila: Bookmark, 1998. Print.

16. See also Rafael, Vicente L. "Nationalism, Imagery and the Filipino Intelligentsia in the Nineteenth Century." *Discrepant Histories: Translocal Essays on Filipino Cultures*. Ed. Rafael, Vicente L. Philadelphia: Temple University Press, 1995. 133–58. Print.

17. Waldsmith, John S. *Stereo Views: An Illustrated History and Price Guide*. Radnor, PA: Wallace-Homestead Book Company, 1991. Print. 135. I am indebted to the late Jim Zwick for this reference.

18. Darrah, William C. *The World of Stereographs*. Nashville: Land Yacht Press, 1977. Print. 50. Reference from the late Jim Zwick.

19. Smith, Shawn Michelle. *American Archives: Gender, Race, and Class in Visual Culture*. Princeton, NJ: Princeton University Press, 1999. Print. 158.

20. Williams, William Appleman. *Empire as a Way of Life: An Essay on the Causes and Character of America's Present Predicament along with a Few Thoughts about an Alternative*. Oxford: Oxford University Press, 1980. Print.

21. The term "technology of vision" is from Smith. See Smith, Shawn Michelle. *American Archives: Gender, Race, and Class in Visual Culture*. Princeton, NJ: Princeton University Press, 1999. Print. 5.

22. Wexler, Laura. *Tender Violence: Domestic Visions in an Age of U.S. Imperialism*. Chapel Hill: University of North Carolina Press, 2000. Print. 21.

23. The term "imperial archipelago" is from Thompson, Lanny. "Representation and Rule in the Imperial Archipelago: Cuba, Puerto Rico, Hawai'i and the Philippines under U.S. Dominion after 1898." *American Studies Asia* 1.1 (2002): 3–39. Print.

24. Goldthwaite, W. M. *The United States of the World*. Chicago: International View Company, 1902. Print. 7.

25. Mbembe, Achille. "Necropolitics." *Public Culture* 15.1 (2003): 11–40. Print.

26. Chaudhary, Zahid R. *Afterimage of Empire: Photography in Nineteenth Century India*. Minneapolis: University of Minnesota Press, 2012. Print. 32.

27. Hevia, James L. "The Photography Complex: Exposing the Boxer-Era China (1900–1901), Making Civilization." *Photographies East: The Camera and Its Histories in East and Southeast Asia*. Ed. Morris, Rosalind C. Durham: Duke University Press, 2009. 79–119. Print. 87–88.

28. Sekula, Allan. "The Body and the Archive." *The Contest of Meaning: Critical Histories of Photography*. Ed. Bolton, Richard. Cambridge: MIT Press, 1989. 343–88. Print. 345.

29. Mohanram, Radhika. *Imperial White: Race, Diaspora and the British Empire*. Minneapolis: University of Minnesota Press, 2007. Print. 25.

30. Analogies between the military conquest of Native Americans and the Philippine-American War have been studied by U.S. historians. See Williams, Walter L. "United States Indian Policy and the Debate over Philippine Annexation: Implications for the Origins of American Imperialism." *Journal of American History* (1980): 810–31. Print. Miller, Stuart Creighton. *"Benevolent Assimilation": The American Conquest of the Philippines, 1899–1903*. New Haven: Yale University Press, 1982. Print. Paulet, Anne. "The Only Good Indian Is a Dead Indian: The Use of United States Indian Policy as a Guide for the Conquest and Occupation of the Philippines, 1898–1905." Dissertation. Rutgers University, 1995. Print.

31. Blount, James. *The American Occupation of the Philippines, 1898–1912*. New York: G. P. Putnam's Sons, 1913. Print.

32. Farrell, John T. "An Abandoned Approach to Philippine History: John R. M. Taylor and the Philippine Insurrection Records." *Catholic Historical Review* 39.4 (1954): 385–407. Print. 392.

33. Gates, John M. "The Official Historian and the Well-Placed Critic: James A. Leroy's Assessment of John R. M. Taylor's *The Philippine Insurrection against the United States*." *Public Historian* 7.3 (1985): 57–67. Print. 59–66.

34. Larkin, John A. "The Philippine Insurrection against the United States." *American Historical Review* 81.4 (1976): 945–46. Print. Hart, Donn V. "*The Philippine Insurrection against the United States. A Compilation of Documents with Notes and Introduction by John R. M. Taylor* by Renato Constantino." *Journal of Asian Studies* 33.3 (1974): 503. Print.

35. Welch, Richard E. "American Atrocities in the Philippines: The Indictment and the Response." *Pacific Historical Review* 43.2 (1974): 233-53. Print. 238.

36. Bonsal, Stephen. "The Philippines: After an Earthquake." *North American Review* 174.544 (1902): 409-21. Print. 410.

37. Dominguez, Virginia R. "When the Enemy Is Unclear: U.S. Censuses and Photographs of Cuba, Puerto Rico, and the Philippines from the Beginning of the 20th Century." *Comparative American Studies* 5.2 (2007): 173-203. Print.

38. Hoganson, Kristin. *Fighting for American Manhood: How Gender Politics Provoked the Spanish-American and Philippine-American Wars.* New Haven: Yale University Press, 1998. Print. 15-42.

39. Cassidy, Lieutenant Colonel Robert M. "Winning the War of the Flea: Lessons from Guerrilla Warfare." *Military Review* September-October (2004): 41-46. Print. 41.

40. Sekula, Allan. "On the Invention of Photographic Meaning." *Artforum* January (1975): 37-45. Print.

41. Gonzalez, Vernadette V. "Military Bases, Royalty Trips, and Imperial Modernities: Gendered and Racialized Labor in the Postcolonial Philippines." *Frontiers* 28.3 (2007): 28-59. Print. 42.

42. Brody, David. *Visualizing American Empire: Orientalism and Imperialism in the Philippines.* Chicago: University of Chicago Press, 2010. Print. 25.

43. Vergara Jr., Benito M. *Displaying Filipinos: Photography and Colonialism in Early 20th Century Philippines.* Quezon City: University of the Philippines, 1995. Print.

CHAPTER 3

1. Fletcher, Marvin. *The Black Soldier and Officer in the United States Army, 1891–1917.* Columbia: University of Missouri Press, 1974. Print. 61.

2. Bonsal, Stephen. "The Negro Soldier in War and Peace." *North American Review* 185.616 (1902): 321-27. Print. 327.

3. Foner, Jack D. *Blacks and the Military in American History: A New Perspective.* New York: Praeger, 1974. Print. vii.

4. Robinson, Michael C., and Frank N. Schubert. "David Fagen: An Afro-American Rebel in the Philippines, 1899-1901." *Pacific Historical Review* 44.1 (1975): 68-83. Print. 73.

5. Marasigan, Cynthia L. "*Between the Devil and the Deep Sea*: Ambivalence, Violence, and African American Soldiers in the Philippine-American War and Its Aftermath." Dissertation. University of Michigan, 2010. Print. 3.

6. Carby, Hazel V. "On the Threshold of Woman's Era: Lynching, Empire, and Sexuality in Black Feminist Theory." *Race, Writing and Difference.* Ed. Gates Jr., Henry Louis. Chicago: University of Chicago Press, 1986. 301-16. Print. 304.

7. Marks III, George P. *The Black Press Views American Imperialism (1898-1900).* New York: Arno Press and New York Times, 1971. Print.

8. Detweiler, Frederick G. *The Negro Press in the United States.* Chicago: University of Chicago Press, 1922. Print. 60.

9. Robinson, Michael C., and Frank N. Schubert. "David Fagen: An Afro-American Rebel in the Philippines, 1899–1901." *Pacific Historical Review* 44.1 (1975): 68–83. Print. 71. Ngozi-Brown, Scot. "African American Soldiers and Filipinos: Racial Imperialism, Jim Crow and Social Relations." *Journal of Negro History* 82.1 (1997): 42–53. Print. San Buenaventura, Steffi. "The Colors of Manifest Destiny: Filipinos and the American Other(s)." *Amerasia Journal* 23.3 (1998): 1–26. Print. San Juan Jr., E. "An African American Soldier in the Philippine Revolution: An Homage to David Fagen." *Cultural Logic* (2009): 1–36. Print.

10. Litwack, Leon F. *Trouble in Mind: Black Southerners in the Age of Jim Crow*. New York: Vintage Books, 1998. Print. 405.

11. Katz, William. "Preface." *The Black Press Views American Imperialism (1898–1900)*. Ed. Marks III, George P. New York: Arno Press and New York Times, 1971. Print. viii.

Orlando Patterson echoes this observation in his study of lynching as a blood ritual influenced by ideas of Christian religion, human sacrifice, and cannibalism. Charts used by Patterson show a dramatic increase in lynchings of African Americans in the 1890s. See Patterson, Orlando. *Rituals of Blood: Consequences of Slavery in Two American Centuries*. Washington, DC: Civitas, 1998. Print. See 175 and 177 for charts on lynching. For a discussion on lynching, ritual, and religion, see chapter 2, "Feast of Blood: 'Race,' Religion and Human Sacrifice in the Postbellum South," 171–232.

12. Holden-Smith, Barbara. "Lynching, Federalism, and the Intersection of Race and Gender in the Progressive Era." *Yale Journal of Law and Feminism* 8.31 (1996): 31–78. Print. 36.

13. The conceptual framework and ideas of this essay have largely been informed by the writings of Carby. Carby claims that writers like Anna Julia Cooper had a global perspective on domestic racial oppression and U.S. expansion in the Pacific, though I would add that Cooper wrote her prescient ideas seven years before the Philippine-American War.

See Carby, Hazel V. "On the Threshold of Woman's Era: Lynching, Empire, and Sexuality in Black Feminist Theory." *Race, Writing and Difference*. Ed. Gates Jr., Henry Louis. Chicago: University of Chicago Press, 1986. 301–16. Print. See also by Carby, *Reconstructing Womanhood: The Emergence of the Afro-American Woman Novelist*. New York: Oxford University Press, 1987. Print. 95–120.

14. Gilroy, Paul. *The Black Atlantic: Modernity and Double Consciousness*. Cambridge: Harvard University Press, 1993. Print. 55.

15. Troy, Rev. William. *Loyalty of the Colored Man to the United States Government, the Late Conflict with Cuba, the Spanish Government and the Philippines, Containing Brief Accounts of the Life of General Antonio Maceo and General Aguinaldo*. Philadelphia: Christian Banner Print. 1900. Print.

16. See Lynk, Miles V. *The Black Troopers, or the Daring Heroism of the Negro Soldiers in the Spanish-American War*. Jackson, TN: M.V. Lynk Publishing House, 1899. Print. Also Fletcher, Marvin. "The Black Volunteers in the Spanish-American War." *Military Affairs* (1974): 48–53. Print. Steward, Theophilus Gould. *The Colored Regulars in the United States Army*. 1904 ed. New York: Arno Press and New York Times, 1969. Print.

17. Almaguer, Tomas. *Racial Fault Lines: The Historical Origins of White Supremacy in California*. Berkeley: University of California Press, 1994. Print.

18. Storey, Moorfield, and Julian Codman. *"Marked Severities" in Philippine Warfare: An Analysis of the Law and Facts Bearing on the Action and Utterances of President Roosevelt and Secretary Root*. Boston: Geo. H. Ellis Company, 1902. Print. 10–53.

19. Balibar, Etienne. "Racism and Nationalism." *Race, Nation, Class: Ambiguous Identities*. Eds. Balibar, Etienne and Immanuel Wallerstein. London: Verso, 1991. 37–67. Print. 45–47.

20. Seraile, William. "Theophilus G. Steward, Intellectual Chaplain, 25th U.S. Colored Infantry." *Nebraska History* 66 (1985): 272–93. Print. 277 and 281.

21. Ngozi-Brown, Scot. "David Fagen." *American National Biography Online*. (2000). Web. March 8, 2013.

22. "American Deserter a Filipino General." *New York Times* October 28, 1900. Print.

23. Funston, Brigadier-General Frederick. *Memories of Two Wars: Cuban and Philippine Experiences*. New York: Charles Scribner's Sons, 1911. Print. 376.

24. "Negro Deserter Beheaded." *New York Times* December 8, 1901. Print.

25. "Lieut. Alstaetter Talks of David Fagin." *New York Times* December 10, 1901. Print.

26. Bell Thompson, Era. "Veterans Who Never Came Home." *Ebony* October 1972: 105–15. Print.

27. Baldoz, Rick. *The Third Asiatic Invasion: Empire and Migration in Filipino America, 1898–1946*. New York: New York University Press, 2011. Print. 23–38.

28. "Three Views of the Philippine Problem." *Literary Digest* 18.1 (1899): 1, Print.

29. "Three Views of the Philippine Problem." 2.

30. "Protest against Manila Censorship." *Literary Digest* 19.5 (1900): 121–23. Print. "More Foreign Criticism of the Philippine War." *Literary Digest* 19.5 (1900): 143–44. Print.

31. "Our Indian Fighters Are There." *Literary Digest* 19.22 (1900): 633–34. Print.

32. Kaplan, Amy. "Black and Blue on San Juan Hill." *Cultures of United States Imperialism*. Eds. Kaplan, Amy and Donald E. Pease. Durham: Duke University Press, 1993. 219–36. Print. 219.

33. Rafael, Vicente L. "White Love: Surveillance and Nationalist Resistance in the U.S. Colonization of the Philippines." *Cultures of the United States Imperialism*. Eds. Kaplan, Amy and Donald E. Pease. Durham: Duke University Press, 1993. 185–218. Print. 185.

34. Mostern, Kenneth. "Three Theories of the Race of W.E.B. Du Bois." *Cultural Critique* Fall (1996): 27–63. Print. 39.

35. Kramer, Paul A. "The Pragmatic Empire: U.S. Anthropology and Colonial Politics in the Occupied Philippines, 1898–1916." Dissertation. Princeton University, 1998. Print.

36. Gunning, Sandra. *Race, Rape, and Lynching: The Red Record of American Literature, 1890–1912*. New York: Oxford University Press, 1996. Print. 31.

37. Williams, Walter L. "United States Indian Policy and the Debate over Philippine

Annexation: Implications for the Origins of American Imperialism." *Journal of American History* (1980): 810–31. Print.

38. Cited in Gatewood Jr., Willard B., ed. *"Smoked Yankees" and the Struggle for Empire: Letters from Negro Soldiers, 1898–1902.* Fayetteville: University of Arkansas Press, 1987. Print. 258–59. See also Marks III, George P. *The Black Press Views American Imperialism (1898–1900).* New York: Arno Press and New York Times, 1971. Print. 155.

39. Horseman, Reginald. *Race and Manifest Destiny: The Origins of American Racial Anglo-Saxonism.* Cambridge: Harvard University Press, 1981. Print. 86.

40. Campomanes, Oscar V. "1898 and the Nature of the New Empire." *Radical History Review* 73 (1999): 130–46. Print.

41. See Bederman, Gail. *Manliness and Civilization: A Cultural History of Gender and Race in the United States, 1880–1917.* Chicago: University of Chicago Press, 1995. Print. 217–39.

42. Sundquist, Eric J., ed. *The Oxford W.E.B. Du Bois Reader.* New York: Oxford University Press, 1996. Print.

43. For a summary of debates on Du Bois's adherence to Stalinism, which affected his position among scholars, see Cain, William E. "From Liberalism to Communism: The Political Thought of W.E.B Du Bois." *The Cultures of United States Imperialism.* Eds. Kaplan, Amy and Donald E. Pease. Durham: Duke University Press, 1993. 456–71. Print.

44. Rowe, John Carlos. *Literary Culture and U.S. Imperialism: From the Revolution to World War II.* New York: Oxford University Press, 2000. Print. 204–16.

45. Sandoval-Sánchez, Alberto. "Politicizing Abjection: In the Manner of a Prologue for the Articulation of AIDS Latino Queer Identities." *American Literary History* 17.3 (2005): 542–49. Print.

CHAPTER 4

1. Wilson, Helen Calista. "A Massachusetts Woman in the Philippines." Boston: [Fiske Warren], 1903. Print. 40.

2. Zwick, Jim. "The Anti-Imperialist League and the Origins of Filipino-American Oppositional Solidarity." *Amerasia Journal* 24.2 (1998): 65–85. Print. Murphy, Erin L. "Women's Anti-imperialism, 'the White Man's Burden,' and the Philippine-American War: Theorizing Masculinist Ambivalence in Protest." *Gender and Society* 23.2 (2009): 244–70. Print.

3. "Protest against Manila Censorship." *Literary Digest* 19.5 (1900): 121–23. Print. See also Storey, Moorfield, and Julian Codman. *"Marked Severities" in Philippine Warfare: An Analysis of the Law and Facts Bearing on the Action and Utterances of President Roosevelt and Secretary Root.* Boston: Geo. H. Ellis Company, 1902. Print. 10.

4. U.S. Congress, 57th. "Charges of Cruelty, Etc. To the Natives of the Philippine Islands." War Department, 1902. 1–57. Print. 2–3.

5. Bruno, Thomas A. "The Violent End of Insurgency on Samar 1901–1902." *Army History* 79 Spring (2011): 31–46. Print. 39.

6. Kramer, Paul A. *The Blood of Government: Race, Empire, the United States and the Philippines*. Chapel Hill: University of North Carolina Press, 2006. Print. 145.

7. Spurr, David. *The Rhetoric of Empire: Colonial Journalism, Travel Writing, and Imperial Administration*. Durham: Duke University Press, 1993. Print. 82.

8. Funston, Eda Blankart. "A Soldier's Wife in the Philippines." *Cosmopolitan* 29.1 (1900): 65–72. Print. Benjamin, Anna Northend. "Some Filipino Characteristics." *Outlook* (1901): 1003–8. Print. Wilson, "Massachusetts Woman." Conger, Emily Bronson. *An Ohio Woman in the Philippines*. N.p.: n.p., 1904. Print. Dauncey, Mrs. Campbell. *An Englishwoman in the Philippines*. New York: E.P. Dutton, 1906. Print.

9. Rafael, Vicente L. "Colonial Domesticity: White Women and United States Rule in the Philippines." *American Literature* 67.4 (1995): 639–66. Print. Roma-Sianturi, Dinah. "At Home in the Cordillera Wilds: Colonial Domesticity in the Letters of Maud Huntley Jenks, 1901–1903." *Asia-Pacific Social Science Review* 7.1 (2008): 59–74. Roma-Sianturi, Dinah. "Pedagogic Invasion: The Thomasites in Occupied Philippines." *Kritika Kultura* 12 (2009): 5–26. Print. Roma-Sianturi, Dinah. "Not Just an Ordinary Tourist: American Women's Travel Writings on the Philippines, 1900s to 1930s." Print.

10. See Guha, Ranajit. "The Prose of Counter-insurgency." *Selected Subaltern Studies*. Eds. Guha, Ranajit and Gayatri Chakravorty Spivak. New York: Oxford University Press, 1988. 56–61. Print.

11. Gikandi, Simon. *Maps of Englishness: Writing Identity in the Culture of Colonialism*. New York: Columbia University Press, 1996. Print.16.

12. Rafael, Vicente L. *White Love and Other Events in Filipino History*. Durham: Duke University Press, 2000. Print. 60.

13. Helmers and Mazzeo citing Radhika Mohanram. See Helmers, Marguerite H., and Tilar J. Mazzeo. "Introduction: Travel and the Body." *Journal of Narrative Theory* 35.3 (2005): 267–76. Print. 269.

14. Pratt, Mary Louise. *Imperial Eyes: Travel Writing and Transculturation*. London: Routledge, 1992. Print.

15. Worcester, Dean C. "Notes on Some Primitive Tribes." *National Geographic Magazine* June 1898: 284–304. Print. Worcester, Dean C. *The Philippine Islands and Their People*. New York: Macmillan, 1898. Print. Barrows, David P. *A History of the Philippines*. New York: American Book Company, 1905. Print. LeRoy, James A. *Philippine Life in Town and Country*. 1973 ed. New York: Oriole Editions, 1905. Print. Brown, Arthur J. *The New Era in the Philippines*. New York: F. H. Revell, 1903. Print.

16. McCoy, Alfred W. *Policing America's Empire: The United States, the Philippines, and the Rise of the Surveillance State*. Madison: University of Wisconsin Press, 2009. Print. 43.

17. Hoganson, Kristin. "As Badly Off as the Filipinos: U.S. Women's Suffragists and the Imperial Issue at the Turn of the Twentieth Century." *Journal of Women's History* 13.2 (2001): 12–13. Print.

18. Paul Fussell cited by Stevenson, Catherine Barnes. *Victorian Women Travel Writers in Africa*. Boston: Twayne, 1982. Print. 3.

19. Hartman, Saidiya V. *Scenes of Subjection: Terror, Slavery, and Self-Making in Nineteenth-Century America*. New York: Oxford University Press, 1997. Print. 10–14.

20. Carby, Hazel V. "On the Threshold of Woman's Era: Lynching, Empire, and Sexuality in Black Feminist Theory." *Race, Writing and Difference.* Ed. Gates Jr., Henry Louis. Chicago: University of Chicago Press, 1986. 301–16. Print.

21. Tiongson, Nicanor G. *The Women of Malolos.* Quezon City, Philippines: Ateneo de Manila University Press, 2004. Print. 203.

22. Kramer, Paul A. "The Water Cure." *New Yorker* February 25, 2008: 38–43. Print.

23. Constantino, Renato, and Letizia R. Constantino. *The Philippines: A Past Revisited.* Manila: Renato Constantino, 1975. Print. 270.

24. "Vagabonding at Fifty." Advertisement. *New York Times* April 7, 1929: BR 7. Print.

25. "Miscellany." *Time Magazine* April 29, 1929. Print.

26. Wilson, Helen Calista. "In the Caucasus, Where Two Ages Meet." *New York Times* July 13, 1930: 15, 23. Print.

27. See Chinn, Sarah. *Inventing Modern Adolescence: The Children of Immigrants in Turn-of-the-Century America.* Piscataway, NJ: Rutgers University Press, 2008. Print.

28. Ileto, Reynaldo C. *Pasyon and Revolution: Popular Movements in the Philippines, 1840–1910.* Manila: Ateneo University Press, 1979. Print. 172.

29. Schuyler, Montgomery. "The Philippines: A Bright Woman's Book about the American Occupation." Book review. *New York Times* August 25, 1906. Print.

30. De Olivares, José. *Our Islands and Their People, as Seen with Camera and Pencil.* St. Louis: N.D. Thompson Publishing Company, 1902. Print.

31. Alzona, Encarnacion. *Julio Nakpil and the Philippine Revolution, with the Autobiography of Gregoria De Jesus.* Rizal: Carmelo and Bauermann, 1964. Print. 171.

32. Benjamin, Walter. *Illuminations.* Ed. Arendt, Hannah. Trans. Zohn, Harry. New York: Schocken, 1955. Print. 254.

CONCLUSION

1. Hersh, Seymour M. "Torture at Abu Ghraib." *New Yorker* May 10, 2004: 42–47. Print.

2. Henderson, Schuyler W. "Disregarding the Suffering of Others: Narrative, Comedy and Torture." *Literature and Medicine* 24.2 (2005): 181–208. Print.

3. Puar, Jasbir. *Terrorist Assemblages: Homonationalism in Queer Times.* Durham: Duke University Press, 2007. Print.

4. McClintock, Anne. "Paranoid Empire: Specters from Guantanamo and Abu Ghraib." *Small Axe* 28 (2009): 50–74. Print. Linfield, Susie. *The Cruel Radiance: Photography and Political Violence.* Chicago: University of Chicago Press, 2010. Print. Carby, Hazel V. "A Strange and Bitter Crop: The Spectacle of Torture." *openDemocracy* (2004): 1–4. Print.

5. Bankoff, Greg. "A Tale of Two Wars: The Other Story of America's Role in the Philippines." *Foreign Affairs* 81.6 (2002): 179–81. Print. Bagley, Will. "Philippines Lesson: The Peace Was More Lethal Than the War." *Salt Lake Tribune* April 27, 2003, sec. Final: B2. Diokno, Ed. "Building an Empire Is Much Harder Than It Looks; the Philippines of 100 Years Ago Can Be a Lesson for the United States in Dealing with Iraq Today." *Con-*

tra Costa Times May 25, 2003, sec. Opinion: P06. Print. "Have We Learned Nothing?" *Akron Beacon Journal (Ohio)* February 22, 2004, sec. Editorial: B3. Print. Levins, Harry. "War Redux." *St. Louis Post-Dispatch* July 18, 2004, sec. Newswatch: B01. Print. Benson, Lee. "Philippine Insurrection Rings Familiar." *Deseret Morning News* October 24, 2005. Print. Farrell, John Aloysius. "History Could Have Helped Us in Iraq." *Denver Post* May 7, 2006, sec. Perspective: E-03. Print.

6. Isaac, Allan Punzalan *American Tropics: Articulating Filipino America.* Minneapolis: University of Minnesota Press, 2006. Print. 179–80. Delmendo, Sharon. *The Star-Entangled Banner: One Hundred Years of America in the Philippines.* Quezon City: University of the Philippines Press, 2005. Print. 4–5.

7. Hutcheson, Ron. "In Philipines, Bush Vows to Root Out Terror." *Philadelphia Inquirer* October 19, 2003. Print.

8. Ileto, Reynaldo C. "Philippine Wars and the Politics of Memory." *Positions: East Asia Cultures Critique* 13 (2005): 215–34. Print.

9. Crean, Colonel Peter D. "The Chief's Corner." *Army History* 79 Spring (2011): 3, 60. Print.

10. Cassidy, Lieutenant Colonel Robert M. "Winning the War of the Flea: Lessons from Guerrilla Warfare." *Military Review* September–October (2004): 41–46. Print. Byler, Charles. "Pacifying the Moros: American Military Government in the Southern Philippines, 1899–1913." *Military Review* May–June (2005): 41–45. Print.

11. Arnold, James R. *Jungle of Snakes: A Century of Counterinsurgency Warfare from the Philippines to Iraq.* New York: Bloomsbury, 2010. Print.

12. Ramsey III, Robert D. "A Masterpiece of Counterguerrilla Warfare: Brigadier General J. Franklin Bell in the Philippines 1901–1902." Washington, DC: Combat Studies Institute Press, 2007. Print. Ramsey III, Robert D. *Savage Wars of Peace: Case Studies of Pacification in the Philippines, 1900–1902.* Washington, DC: Combat Studies Institute Press, 2007. Print. Leepson, Marc. "The Philippine War." *Military History* November (2007): 60–67. Print.

13. Deady, Timothy K. "Lessons from a Successful Counterinsurgency: The Philippines, 1899–1902." *Parameters* 35.1 (2005): 53–68. Print.

14. Linn, Brian McAlister. *The U.S. Army Counterinsurgency in the Philippine War, 1899–1902.* Chapel Hill: University of North Carolina Press, 1989. Print.

15. Birtle, Andrew J. "Persuasion and Coercion in Counterinsurgency Warfare." *Military Review* 88.4 (2008): 45–53. Print.

16. Bruno, Thomas A. "The Violent End of Insurgency on Samar 1901–1902." *Army History* 79 Spring (2011): 31–46. Print.

17. Guha, Ranajit. "The Prose of Counter-insurgency." *Selected Subaltern Studies.* Eds. Guha, Ranajit and Gayatri Chakravorty Spivak. New York: Oxford University Press, 1988. 45–84. Print.

18. Hebard, Andrew. "Romantic Sovereignty: Popular Romances and the American Imperial State in the Philippines." *American Quarterly* 57.3 (2006): 805–30. Print. Kaplan, Amy. "Romancing the Empire: The Embodiment of American Masculinity in the Popular Historical Novel of the 1890s." *American Literary History* 2.4 Winter (1990):

659–90. Print. Streeby, Shelley. *American Sensations: Class, Empire, and the Production of Popular Culture*. Berkeley: University of California Press, 2002. Print.

19. Smith, Geoffrey D., ed. *American Fiction 1901–1925: A Bibliography*. 1997. Web.

20. These Philippine-themed texts are overlooked in Rowe's study. See Rowe, John Carlos. *Literary Culture and U.S. Imperialism: From the Revolution to World War II*. New York: Oxford University Press, 2000. Print.

21. Streeter, Caroline A. "Was Your Mama Mulatto? Notes toward a Theory of Racialized Sexuality in Gayl Jones's *Corregidora* and Julie Dash's *Daughters of the Dust*." *Callaloo* 27.3 (2004): 768–87. Print. Brody, Jennifer De Vere. *Impossible Purities: Blackness, Femininity and Victorian Culture*. Durham: Duke University Press, 1998. Print. Sharpley-Whiting, T. Denean. *Sexualized Savages, Primal Fears and Primitive Narratives in French*. Durham: Duke University Press, 1999. Print.

22. U.S. Congress, 57th. "Charges of Cruelty, Etc. To the Natives of the Philippine Islands." War Department, 1902. 1–57. Print. 8, 42–44. See also Storey, Moorfield, and Julian Codman. *"Marked Severities" in Philippine Warfare: An Analysis of the Law and Facts Bearing on the Action and Utterances of President Roosevelt and Secretary Root*. Boston: Geo. H. Ellis Company, 1902. Print. 130, 135–38.

23. Denger, Mark J. "Californians and the Military: Major-General Henry Ware Lawton, U.S.Volunteers." *The California Military Museum: Preserving California's Military Heritage*. Web.

24. Dumindin, Arnaldo. "Dec. 19, 1899: General Henry Lawton Dies at San Mateo." *Philippine-American War, 1899–1902*. 2006. Web.

25. Castellanos, M. Bianet. *Photography and the Philippines*. Ed. Sinopoli, Carla M. and Lars Fogelin. 1998. *Imperial Imaginings: The Dean C. Worcester Photographic Collection of the Philippines, 1890–1913*. Web. 9.

26. Sinopoli, Carla M. *Dean Worcester and the Philippines*. Ed. Sinopoli, Carla M. and Lars Fogelin. 1998. *Imperial Imaginings: The Dean C. Worcester Photographic Collection of the Philippines, 1890–1913*. Web. 5. Fogelin, Lars. *Dean C. Worcester, Race and the Philippines. Imperial Imaginings: The Dean C. Worcester Photographic Collection of the Philippines, 1890–1913*. Eds. Sinopoli, Carla M. and Lars Fogelin. CD. Ann Arbor: University of Michigan, Museum of Anthropology, 1998. Print. 3.

27. Reyes, Fidel A. "Birds of Prey." *Filipino Nationalism: 1872–1970*. Ed. Agoncillo, Teodoro A. Quezon City, Manila: R. P. Garcia Publishing Company, 1974. 251–54. Print. 252.

28. Cano, Gloria. "Filipino Press between Two Empires: *El Renacimiento*, a Newspaper with Too Much *Alma Filipina*." *Southeast Asian Studies* 49 (2011): 395–430. Print. 426.

29. National Historical Commission of the Philippines. "Reyes, Fidel A." 2008. Web.

30. Rice, Mark. "His Name Was Don Francisco Muro: Reconstructing an Image of American Imperialism." *American Quarterly* 62.1 (2010): 49–76. Print.

31. Chow, Rey. *The Age of the World Target: Self-Referentiality in War, Theory and Comparative Work*. Durham: Duke University Press, 2006. Print. 30–31.

Works Cited

INTRODUCTION

Agnani, Sunil, et al. "The End of Postcolonial Theory?" *PMLA* 122.3 (2007): 633–51. Print.

Almaguer, Tomas. *Racial Fault Lines: The Historical Origins of White Supremacy in California*. Berkeley: University of California Press, 1994. Print.

"The American Community—Asians: 2004, American Community Survey Reports." Washington, DC: U.S. Census Bureau, 2007. Print.

Ardis, Anne L. "Introduction." *Women's Experience of Modernity: 1875–1945*. Eds. Ardis, Anne L. and Leslie W. Lewis. Baltimore: Johns Hopkins University Press, 2003. Print.

Baldoz, Rick. "The Racial Vectors of Empire: Classification and Competing Master Narratives in the Colonial Philippines." *Du Bois Review* 5.1 (2008): 69–94. Print.

Baldoz, Rick. *The Third Asiatic Invasion: Empire and Migration in Filipino America, 1898–1946*. New York: New York University Press, 2011. Print.

Blanco, John D. *Frontier Constitutions: Christianity and Colonial Empire in the 19th Century Philippines*. Berkeley: University of California Press, 2009. Print.

Bulosan, Carlos. *The Cry and the Dedication*. Ed. San Juan Jr., E. Philadelphia: Temple University Press, 1995. Print.

Bulosan, Carlos. *On Becoming Filipino: Selected Writings of Carlos Bulosan*. Ed. San Juan Jr., E. Philadelphia: Temple University Press, 1995. Print.

Campomanes, Oscar V. "The New Empire's Forgetful and Forgotten Citizens: Unrepresentability and Unassimilability in Filipino-American Postcolonialities." *Hitting Critical Mass* 2.2 (1995): 145–200. Print.

Carlson, Keith Thor. "Born Again of the People: Luis Taruc and Peasant Ideology in Philippine Revolutionary Politics." *Historie Sociale / Social History* 41.82 (2008): 417–58. Print.

Chakrabarty, Dipesh. *Provincializing Europe: Postcolonial Thought and Historical Difference*. Princeton, NJ: Princeton University Press, 2000. Print.

Cordova, Fred, Dorothy Laigo Cordova, and Albert A. Acena. *Filipinos, Forgotten Asian Americans: A Pictorial Essay, 1763–circa 1963*. Dubuque, Iowa: Kendall/Hunt, 1983. Print.

De Witt, Howard. *Violence in the Fields: California Filipino Farm Labor Unionization during the Great Depression*. Saratoga: Century Twenty One Publications, 1980. Print.

Diaz-Quinones, Arcadio. "1898." *Hispanic American Historical Review* 78.4 (1998): 557–81. Print.

Edwards, Brian T. "Preposterous Encounters: Interrupting American Studies with the (Post)Colonial, or Casablanca in the American Century." *Comparative Studies of South Asia, Africa and the Middle East* 23.1–2 (2003): 70–86. Print.

Gilroy, Paul. *The Black Atlantic: Modernity and Double Consciousness*. Cambridge: Harvard University Press, 1993. Print.

Gonzalves, Theodore S. *The Day the Dancers Stayed: Performing in the Filipino/American Diaspora*. Philadelphia: Temple University Press, 2009. Print.

Harris, Charles Kassel. *How to Write a Popular Song*. New York: Charles K. Harris, 1906. Print.

Hoeffer, Michael, Nancy Rytina, and Bryan C. Baker. "Estimates of the Unauthorized Immigrant Population Residing in the United States: January 2008." *Population Estimates*. U.S. Department of Homeland Security, Office of Immigration Statistics, 2009. Print.

Isaac, Allan Punzalan. *American Tropics: Articulating Filipino America*. Minneapolis: University of Minnesota Press, 2006. Print.

Kaplan, Amy, and Donald E. Pease, eds. *Cultures of United States Imperialism*. Durham: Duke University Press, 1993. Print.

Kibler, M. Alison. *Rank Ladies: Gender and Cultural Hierarchy in American Vaudeville*. Chapel Hill: University of North Carolina Press, 1999. Print.

Kramer, Paul A. "The Water Cure." *New Yorker* February 25, 2008: 38–43. Print.

LaFeber, Walter. *The New Empire: An Interpretation of American Expansion, 1860–1898*. 1998 ed. Ithaca, NY: Cornell University Press, 1963. Print.

Lowe, Lisa. *Critical Terrains: French and British Orientalism*. 1991. Ithaca, NY: Cornell University Press, 1994. Print.

Lowe, Lisa. *Immigrant Acts: On Asian American Cultural Politics*. Durham: Duke University Press, 1996. Print.

Lowe, Lisa. "The International within the National: American Studies and Asian American Critique." *Cultural Critique* 40 Autumn (1998): 29–47. Print.

Makdisi, Saree. "Postcolonial Literature in a Neocolonial World: Modern Arabic Culture and the End of Modernity." *The Pre-occupation of Postcolonial Studies*. Eds. Afzal-Khan, Fawzia and Kalpana Seshadri-Crooks. Durham: Duke University Press, 2000. 266–91. Print.

Mason, Jeffrey D., and J. Ellen Gainor, eds. *Performing America: Cultural Nationalism in American Theater*. Ann Arbor: University of Michigan Press, 1999. Print.

Mbembe, Achille. *On the Postcolony*. Berkeley: University of California Press, 2001. Print.

McClintock, Anne. *Imperial Leather: Race, Gender and Sexuality in the Colonial Conquest*. New York: Routledge, 1995. Print.

Mitchell, W. J. T. *What Do Pictures Want? The Lives and Loves of Images*. Chicago: University of Chicago Press, 2005. Print.

Morillo-Alicea, Javier. "Aquel Laberinto de Oficinas: Ways of Knowing Empire in Late-Nineteenth Century Spain." *After Spanish Rule: Postcolonial Predicaments of the Americas*. Eds. Thurner, Mark and Andres Guerrero. Durham: Duke University Press, 2003. 111–40. Print.

Richards, Thomas. *The Imperial Archive: Knowledge and Fantasy of Empire*. London: Verso, 1993. Print.

Salanga, Alfrredo Navarro. "They Don't Think Much about Us in America." *Flippin': Filipinos on America*. Ed. Luis H. Francia and Eric Gamalinda. New York: Asian American Writers' Workshop, 1996. 251–52. Print.

Saldivar, Jose David. "Looking Awry at 1898: Roosevelt, Montejo, Paredes, and Mariscal." *American Literary History* 12.3 (2000): 386–406. Print.

San Juan Jr., E. *After Postcolonialism: Remapping Philippines–United States Confrontations*. Lanham, MD: Rowman and Littlefield, 2000. Print.

San Juan Jr., E. *From Exile to Diaspora: Versions of the Filipino Experience in the United States*. Boulder, CO: Westview Press, 1998. Print.

San Juan Jr., E. "Mapping the Boundaries: The Filipino Writer in the U.S.A." *Journal of Ethnic Studies* 19.1 Spring (1991): 117–31. Print.

Scharlin, Craig, and Lilia V. Villanueva, eds. *Philip Vera Cruz: A Personal History of Filipino Immigrants and the Farmworkers Movement*. Los Angeles: UCLA Labor Center, 1992. Print.

See, Sarita Echavez. *The Decolonized Eye: Filipino American Art and Performance*. Minneapolis: University of Minnesota Press, 2009. Print.

Sekula, Allan. "The Body and the Archive." *October* 39 (1986): 3–64. Print.

Sekula, Allan. "On the Invention of Photographic Meaning." *Artforum* January (1975): 37–45. Print.

Shaw, Angel Velasco, and Luis H. Francia. *Vestiges of War: The Philippine-American War and the Aftermath of an Imperial Dream, 1899–1999*. New York: New York University Press, 2002. Print.

Streeby, Shelley. *American Sensations: Class, Empire, and the Production of Popular Culture*. Berkeley: University of California Press, 2002. Print.

Taruc, Luis. *Born of the People*. New York: International Publishers, 1953. Print.

Tiongson, Antonio T., Edgardo V. Gutierrez, and Ricardo V. Gutierrez, eds. *Positively No Filipinos Allowed: Building Communities and Discourse*. Philadelphia: Temple University Press, 2006. Print.

Tolentino, Cynthia H. *America's Experts: Race and the Fictions of Sociology*. Minneapolis: University of Minnesota Press, 2009. Print.

Vergès, Françoise. *Monsters and Revolutionaries: Colonial Family Romance and Metissage*. Durham: Duke University Press, 1999. Print.

Wertheim, Arthur Frank, and Barbara Bair, eds. *The Papers of Will Rogers*. Vol. 2. Norman: University of Oklahoma Press, 2000. Print.

Wexler, Laura. *Tender Violence: Domestic Visions in an Age of U.S. Imperialism*. Chapel Hill: University of North Carolina Press, 2000. Print.

White, Hayden. *Tropics of Discourse: Essays in Cultural Criticism*. Baltimore: Johns Hopkins University Press, 1978. Print.

Wolff, Leon. *Little Brown Brother: America's Forgotten Bid for Empire Which Cost 250,000 Lives*. London: Longmans, 1961. Print.

CHAPTER 1

Aravamudan, Srinivas. *Tropicopolitans: Colonialism and Agency, 1688–1804*. Durham: Duke University Press, 1999. Print.

Bederman, Gail. *Manliness and Civilization: A Cultural History of Gender and Race in the United States, 1880–1917*. Chicago: University of Chicago Press, 1995. Print.

Behdad, Ali. *Belated Travelers: Orientalism in the Age of Colonial Dissolution*. Durham: Duke University Press, 1994. Print.

Campomanes, Oscar V. "1898 and the Nature of the New Empire." *Radical History Review* 73 (1999): 130–46. Print.

Campomanes, Oscar V. "Casualty Figures of the American Soldier and the Other: Post-1898 Allegories of Imperial Nation-Building as 'Love and War.'" *Vestiges of War: The Philippine-American War and the Aftermath of an Imperial Dream 1899–1999*. Eds. Shaw, Angel Velasco and Luis H. Francia. New York: New York University Press, 2002. 134–62. Print.

Campomanes, Oscar V. "The New Empire's Forgetful and Forgotten Citizens: Unrepresentability and Unassimilability in Filipino-American Postcolonialities." *Hitting Critical Mass* 2.2 (1995): 145–200. Print.

Chow, Rey. *The Age of the World Target: Self-Referentiality in War, Theory and Comparative Work*. Durham: Duke University Press, 2006. Print.

Clark, Ella Elizabeth, and Margot Edmonds. *Sacagawea of the Lewis and Clark Expedition*. Berkeley: University of California, 1979. Print.

"Cost of the War. Filipino Insurrection Entailed Expense of $48,928,060." *Wisconsin Weekly Advocate* March 8, 1900. Print.

Dinerstein, Joel. "Technology and Its Discontents: On the Verge of the Posthuman." *American Quarterly* 58.3 (2006): 569–95. Print.

Foucault, Michel. *Discipline and Punish: The Birth of the Prison*. Trans. Sheridan, Alan. New York: Vintage Books, 1975. Print.

Foucault, Michel. *The History of Sexuality*. Vol. 2: *The Use of Pleasure* Trans. Hurley, Robert. 1985. New York: Vintage, 1990. Print.

Francisco, Luzviminda. "The First Vietnam: The Philippine-American War of 1899–1902." *Bulletin of Concerned Asian Scholars* 5 (1973): 2–16. Print.

Gilroy, Paul. *The Black Atlantic: Modernity and Double Consciousness*. Cambridge: Harvard University Press, 1993. Print.

Go, Julian. *American Empire and the Politics of Meaning: Elite Political Culture in the Philippines and Puerto Rico During U.S. Colonialism*. Durham: Duke University Press, 2008. Print.

Goldberg, Jonathan. *Sodometries: Renaissance Texts, Modern Sexualities*. Stanford: Stanford University Press, 1992. Print.

Gonzalves, Theodore S. *The Day the Dancers Stayed: Performing in the Filipino/American Diaspora*. Philadelphia: Temple University Press, 2009. Print.

Hoganson, Kristin. *Fighting for American Manhood: How Gender Politics Provoked the Spanish-American and Philippine-American Wars*. New Haven: Yale University Press, 1998. Print.

Huhndorf, Shari M. *Going Native: Indians in the American Cultural Imagination*. Ithaca, NY: Cornell University Press, 2001. Print.

Ileto, Reynaldo C. "Philippine Wars and the Politics of Memory." *Positions: East Asia Cultures Critique* 13 (2005): 215–34. Print.

Isaac, Allan Punzalan. *American Tropics: Articulating Filipino America*. Minneapolis: University of Minnesota Press, 2006. Print.

Jacobson, Matthew Frye. "Imperial Amnesia: Teddy Roosevelt, the Philippines, and the Modern Art of Forgetting." *Radical History Review* 73 (1999): 116–27. Print.

Kaplan, Amy. *The Anarchy of Empire in the Making of U.S. Culture*. Cambridge: Harvard University Press, 2002. Print.

Kaplan, Amy, and Donald E. Pease, eds. *Cultures of United States Imperialism*. Durham: Duke University Press, 1993. Print.

Kidwell, Clara Sue. "What Would Pocahontas Think? Women and Cultural Persistence." *Callaloo* 17.1 (1994): 149–59. Print.

Kramer, Paul A. *The Blood of Government: Race, Empire, the United States and the Philippines*. Chapel Hill: University of North Carolina Press, 2006. Print.

Kristeva, Julia. *Powers of Horror: An Essay on Abjection*. Trans. Roudiez, Leon S. New York: Columbia University Press, 1982. Print.

Leon, W. M. Consuelo. "Foundations of the American Image of the Pacific." *Asia/Pacific as Space of Cultural Production*. Eds. Wilson, Rob and Arif Dirlik. Durham: Duke UP, 1995. 17–29. Print.

Levine, Philippa. "States of Undress: Nakedness and the Colonial Imagination." *Victorian Studies* 50.2 (2008): 189–219. Print.

Limón, José Eduardo. *American Encounters: Greater Mexico, the United States and the Erotics of Culture*. Boston: Beacon Press, 1998. Print.

Lott, Eric. *Love and Theft: Blackface Minstrelsy and the American Working Class*. New York: Oxford University Press, 1993. Print.

Lowe, Lisa. *Critical Terrains: French and British Orientalism*. 1991. Ithaca, NY: Cornell University Press, 1994. Print.

Lyons, Paul. "Opening Accounts in the South Seas: Poe's Pym and American Pacific Orientalism." *ESQ: A Journal of the American Renaissance* 42.4 (1996): 291–326. Print.

Mbembe, Achille. *On the Postcolony*. Berkeley: University of California Press, 2001. Print.

McClintock, Anne. *Imperial Leather: Race, Gender and Sexuality in the Colonial Conquest*. New York: Routledge, 1995. Print.

McCoy, Alfred W. *Policing America's Empire: The United States, the Philippines, and the Rise of the Surveillance State*. Madison: University of Wisconsin Press, 2009. Print.

Mengay, Donald H. "Arabian Rites: T.E. Lawrence's 'Seven Pillars of Wisdom' and the Erotics of Empire." *Genre* 27 Winter (1994): 395–416. Print.

Mignolo, Walter. "(Post)Occidentalism, (Post)Coloniality, and (Post) Subaltern Rationality." *The Pre-Occupation of Postcolonial Studies* Eds. Afzal-Khan, Fawzia and Kalpana Seshadri-Crooks. Durham: Duke University Press, 2000. 86–118. Print.

Mitchell, W. J. T. *What Do Pictures Want? The Lives and Loves of Images*. Chicago: University of Chicago Press, 2005. Print.

Nash, Gary B. "The Hidden History of Mestizo America." *Journal of American History* 82.3 (1995): 941–64. Print.

Rodriguez, Dylan. *Suspended Apocalypse: White Supremacy, Genocide and the Filipino Condition*. Minneapolis: University of Minnesota Press, 2009. Print.

Rowe, John Carlos. *Literary Culture and U.S. Imperialism: From the Revolution to World War II*. New York: Oxford University Press, 2000. Print.

Rydell, Robert W. *All the World's a Fair: Visions of Empire at American International Expositions, 1876–1916*. Chicago: University of Chicago Press, 1984. Print.

Said, Edward W. *Culture and Imperialism*. New York: Vintage, 1993. Print.

Said, Edward W. *Orientalism*. New York: Vintage, 1978. Print.

Sandoval-Sánchez, Alberto. "Politicizing Abjection: In the Manner of a Prologue for the Articulation of AIDS Latino Queer Identities." *American Literary History* 17.3 (2005): 542–49. Print.

Scott, Darieck. *Extravagant Abjection: Blackness, Power, and Sexuality in the African American Literary Imagination*. New York: New York University Press, 2010. Print.

See, Sarita Echavez. *The Decolonized Eye: Filipino American Art and Performance*. Minneapolis: University of Minnesota Press, 2009. Print.

Sharpley-Whiting, T. Denean. *Sexualized Savages, Primal Fears and Primitive Narratives in French*. Durham: Duke University Press, 1999. Print.

Shimakawa, Karen. *National Abjection: The Asian American Body Onstage*. Durham: Duke University Press, 2002. Print.

Smith, Andrea. *Conquest: Sexual Violence and American Indian Genocide*. Cambridge, MA: South End Press, 2005. Print.

Smith, Shawn Michelle. *American Archives: Gender, Race, and Class in Visual Culture*. Princeton, NJ: Princeton University Press, 1999. Print.

Smith, Sherry L. *Reimagining Indians: Native Americans through Anglo Eyes, 1880–1940.* New York: Oxford University Press, 2000. Print.

Spurr, David. *The Rhetoric of Empire: Colonial Journalism, Travel Writing, and Imperial Administration.* Durham: Duke University Press, 1993. Print.

Stoler, Ann Laura. *Carnal Knowledge and Imperial Power: Race and the Intimate in Colonial Rule.* Berkeley: University of California Press, 2002. Print.

Stoler, Ann Laura, ed. *Haunted by Empire: Geographies of Intimacy in North American History.* Durham: Duke University Press, 2006. Print.

Stoler, Ann Laura. "Making Empire Respectable: The Politics of Race and Sexual Morality in Twentieth-Century Colonial Cultures." *Dangerous Liaisons: Gender, Nation and Postcolonial Perspectives.* Eds. McClintock, Anne, Aamir Mufti and Ella Shohat. Minneapolis: University of Minnesota Press, 1997. Print.

Tilton, Robert S. *Pocahontas: The Evolution of an American Narrative.* Cambridge: Cambridge University Press, 1994. Print.

Tiongson, Antonio T., Edgardo V. Gutierrez, and Ricardo V. Gutierrez, eds. *Positively No Filipinos Allowed: Building Communities and Discourse.* Philadelphia: Temple University Press, 2006. Print.

Turner, Frederick Jackson. *The Frontier in American History.* 1920. New York: Henry Holt, 1947. Print.

Twain, Mark. *Mark Twain's Weapons of Satire: Anti-imperialist Writings on the Philippine-American War.* Ed. Zwick, Jim. New York: Syracuse University Press, 1992. Print.

Wallace, Lee. *Sexual Encounters: Pacific Texts, Modern Sexualities.* Ithaca, NY: Cornell University Press, 2003. Print.

Wexler, Laura. *Tender Violence: Domestic Visions in an Age of U.S. Imperialism.* Chapel Hill: University of North Carolina Press, 2000. Print.

White, Hayden. *Tropics of Discourse: Essays in Cultural Criticism.* Baltimore: Johns Hopkins University Press, 1978. Print.

Zwick, Jim. "The Anti-Imperialist League and the Origins of Filipino-American Oppositional Solidarity." *Amerasia Journal* 24.2 (1998): 65–85. Print.

CHAPTER 2

Barrett, Terry. "Photographs and Contexts." *Journal of Aesthetic Education* 19.3 (1985): 51–64. Print.

Best, Jonathan. *A Philippine Album: American Era Photographs, 1900–1930.* Manila: Bookmark, 1998. Print.

Blount, James. *The American Occupation of the Philippines, 1898–1912.* New York: G. P. Putnam's Sons, 1913. Print.

Bonsal, Stephen. "The Philippines: After an Earthquake." *North American Review* 174.544 (1902): 409–21. Print.

Brody, David. *Visualizing American Empire: Orientalism and Imperialism in the Philippines.* Chicago: University of Chicago Press, 2010. Print.

Cassidy, Lieutenant Colonel Robert M. "Winning the War of the Flea: Lessons from Guerrilla Warfare." *Military Review* September–October (2004): 41–46. Print.

Chaudhary, Zahid R. *Afterimage of Empire: Photography in Nineteenth Century India.* Minneapolis: University of Minnesota Press, 2012. Print.

Darrah, William C. *The World of Stereographs.* Nashville: Land Yacht Press, 1977. Print.

Dominguez, Virginia R. "When the Enemy Is Unclear: U.S. Censuses and Photographs of Cuba, Puerto Rico, and the Philippines from the Beginning of the 20th Century." *Comparative American Studies* 5.2 (2007): 173–203. Print.

Farrell, John T. "An Abandoned Approach to Philippine History: John R. M. Taylor and the Philippine Insurrection Records." *Catholic Historical Review* 39.4 (1954): 385–407. Print.

Gates, John M. "The Official Historian and the Well-Placed Critic: James A. Leroy's Assessment of John R. M. Taylor's *The Philippine Insurrection against the United States.*" *Public Historian* 7.3 (1985): 57–67. Print.

Goldthwaite, W. M. *The United States of the World.* Chicago: International View Company, 1902. Print.

Gonzalez, Vernadette V. "Military Bases, Royalty Trips, and Imperial Modernities: Gendered and Racialized Labor in the Postcolonial Philippines." *Frontiers* 28.3 (2007): 28–59. Print.

Hart, Donn V. "*The Philippine Insurrection against the United States. A Compilation of Documents with Notes and Introduction by John R. M. Taylor* by Renato Constantino." *Journal of Asian Studies* 33.3 (1974): 503. Print.

Hevia, James L. "The Photography Complex: Exposing the Boxer-Era China (1900–1901), Making Civilization." *Photographies East: The Camera and Its Histories in East and Southeast Asia.* Ed. Morris, Rosalind C. Durham: Duke University Press, 2009. 79–119. Print.

Hoganson, Kristin. *Fighting for American Manhood: How Gender Politics Provoked the Spanish-American and Philippine-American Wars.* New Haven: Yale University Press, 1998. Print.

Holt, Jonathan. "The Subjective Image." *Third Text* 10.37 (1996): 104–6. Print.

Ileto, Reynaldo C. *Knowing America's Colony: A Hundred Years from the Philippine War.* Honolulu: University of Hawai'i at Manoa, 1999. Print.

Kristeva, Julia. *Powers of Horror: An Essay on Abjection.* Trans. Roudiez, Leon S. New York: Columbia University Press, 1982. Print.

Larkin, John A. "The Philippine Insurrection against the United States." *American Historical Review* 81.4 (1976): 945–46. Print.

Le Roy, James. *Philippine Life in Town and Country.* 1973 ed. New York: Oriole Editions, 1905. Print.

Liberty Poems: Inspired by the Crisis of 1898–1900. Boston: James H. West, 1900. Print.

Linfield, Susie. *The Cruel Radiance: Photography and Political Violence.* Chicago: Univerisity of Chicago Press, 2010. Print.

Mbembe, Achille. "Necropolitics." *Public Culture* 15.1 (2003): 11–40. Print.

Mieder, Wolfgang. "The Only Good Indian Is a Dead Indian: History and Meaning of a Proverbial Stereotype." *Journal of American Folklore* 106.419 (1993): 38–60. Print.

Miller, Stuart Creighton. *"Benevolent Assimilation": The American Conquest of the Philippines, 1899–1903*. New Haven: Yale University Press, 1982. Print.

Mitchell, W. J. T. *What Do Pictures Want? The Lives and Loves of Images*. Chicago: University of Chicago Press, 2005. Print.

Mohanram, Radhika. *Imperial White: Race, Diaspora and the British Empire*. Minneapolis: University of Minnesota Press, 2007. Print.

Morris, Rosalind C., ed. *Photographies East: The Camera and Its Histories in East and Southeast Asia*. Durham: Duke University Press, 2009. Print.

Neely, F. Tennyson. *Fighting in the Philippines, Authentic Original Photos*. New York: F. Tennyson Neely, 1899. Print.

Paulet, Anne. "The Only Good Indian Is a Dead Indian: The Use of United States Indian Policy as a Guide for the Conquest and Occupation of the Philippines, 1898–1905." Dissertation. Rutgers University, 1995. Print.

Rafael, Vicente L. "Nationalism, Imagery and the Filipino Intelligentsia in the Nineteenth Century." *Discrepant Histories: Translocal Essays on Filipino Cultures*. Ed. Rafael, Vicente L. Philadelphia: Temple University Press, 1995. 133–58. Print.

Ray, Charles. "Following a War with the Camera." *Royal Magazine* 3.18 (1900): 475–81. Print.

Sekula, Allan. "The Body and the Archive." *The Contest of Meaning: Critical Histories of Photography*. Ed. Bolton, Richard. Cambridge: MIT Press, 1989. 343–88. Print.

Sekula, Allan. "On the Invention of Photographic Meaning." *Artforum* January (1975): 37–45. Print.

Smith, Shawn Michelle. *American Archives: Gender, Race, and Class in Visual Culture*. Princeton, NJ: Princeton University Press, 1999. Print.

Thompson, Lanny. "Representation and Rule in the Imperial Archipelago: Cuba, Puerto Rico, Hawai'i and the Philippines under U.S. Dominion after 1898." *American Studies Asia* 1.1 (2002): 3–39. Print.

Trachtenberg, Alan. "Albums of War: Reading Civil War Photographs." *Representations* 9 (1985): 1–32. Print.

Villard, Oswald Garrison. *Fighting Years: Memoirs of a Liberal Editor*. New York: Harcourt, Brace, 1939.

Vergara Jr., Benito M. *Displaying Filipinos: Photography and Colonialism in Early 20th Century Philippines*. Quezon City: University of the Philippines, 1995. Print.

Waldsmith, John S. *Stereo Views: An Illustrated History and Price Guide*. Radnor, PA: Wallace-Homestead Book Company, 1991. Print.

Welch, Richard E. "American Atrocities in the Philippines: The Indictment and the Response." *Pacific Historical Review* 43.2 (1974): 233–53. Print.

Wexler, Laura. *Tender Violence: Domestic Visions in an Age of U.S. Imperialism*. Chapel Hill: University of North Carolina Press, 2000. Print.

Williams, Walter L. "United States Indian Policy and the Debate over Philippine Annexation: Implications for the Origins of American Imperialism." *Journal of American History* (1980): 810–31. Print.

Williams, William Appleman. *Empire as a Way of Life: An Essay on the Causes and Character of America's Present Predicament along with a Few Thoughts about an Alternative.* Oxford: Oxford University Press, 1980. Print.

Worcester, Dean C. *The Philippines, Past and Present.* 2 vols. New York: Macmillan, 1914. Print.

CHAPTER 3

Almaguer, Tomas. *Racial Fault Lines: The Historical Origins of White Supremacy in California.* Berkeley: University of California Press, 1994. Print.

"American Deserter a Filipino General." *New York Times* October 28, 1900. Print.

Baldoz, Rick. *The Third Asiatic Invasion: Empire and Migration in Filipino America, 1898–1946.* New York: New York University Press, 2011. Print.

Balibar, Etienne. "Racism and Nationalism." *Race, Nation, Class: Ambiguous Identities.* Eds. Balibar, Etienne and Immanuel Wallerstein. London: Verso, 1991. 37–67. Print.

Bederman, Gail. *Manliness and Civilization: A Cultural History of Gender and Race in the United States, 1880–1917.* Chicago: University of Chicago Press, 1995. Print.

Bell Thompson, Era. "Veterans Who Never Came Home." *Ebony* October 1972: 105–15. Print.

Bonsal, Stephen. "The Negro Soldier in War and Peace." *North American Review* 185.616 (1902): 321–27. Print.

Cain, William E. "From Liberalism to Communism: The Political Thought of W.E.B Du Bois." *The Cultures of United States Imperialism.* Eds. Kaplan, Amy and Donald E. Pease. Durham: Duke University Press, 1993. 456–71. Print.

Campomanes, Oscar V. "1898 and the Nature of the New Empire." *Radical History Review* 73 (1999): 130–46. Print.

Carby, Hazel V. "On the Threshold of Woman's Era: Lynching, Empire, and Sexuality in Black Feminist Theory." *Race, Writing and Difference.* Ed. Gates, Henry Louis, Jr. Chicago: University of Chicago Press, 1986. 301–16. Print.

Carby, Hazel V. *Reconstructing Womanhood: The Emergence of the Afro-American Woman Novelist.* New York: Oxford University Press, 1987. Print.

Detweiler, Frederick G. *The Negro Press in the United States.* Chicago: University of Chicago Press, 1922. Print.

Fletcher, Marvin. *The Black Soldier and Officer in the United States Army, 1891–1917.* Columbia: University of Missouri Press, 1974. Print.

Fletcher, Marvin. "The Black Volunteers in the Spanish-American War." *Military Affairs* (1974): 48–53. Print.

Foner, Jack D. *Blacks and the Military in American History: A New Perspective*. New York: Praeger, 1974. Print.

Funston, Brigadier-General Frederick. *Memories of Two Wars: Cuban and Philippine Experiences*. New York: Charles Scribner's Sons, 1911. Print.

Gatewood Jr., Willard B., ed. *"Smoked Yankees" and the Struggle for Empire: Letters from Negro Soldiers, 1898–1902*. Fayetteville: University of Arkansas Press, 1987. Print.

Gilroy, Paul. *The Black Atlantic: Modernity and Double Consciousness*. Cambridge: Harvard University Press, 1993. Print.

Gunning, Sandra. *Race, Rape, and Lynching: The Red Record of American Literature, 1890–1912*. New York: Oxford University Press, 1996. Print.

Holden-Smith, Barbara. "Lynching, Federalism, and the Intersection of Race and Gender in the Progressive Era." *Yale Journal of Law and Feminism* 8.31 (1996): 31–78. Print.

Horseman, Reginald. *Race and Manifest Destiny: The Origins of American Racial Anglo-Saxonism*. Cambridge: Harvard University Press, 1981. Print.

Kaplan, Amy. "Black and Blue on San Juan Hill." *Cultures of United States Imperialism*. Eds. Kaplan, Amy and Donald E. Pease. Durham: Duke University Press, 1993. 219–36. Print.

Katz, William. "Preface." *The Black Press Views American Imperialism (1898–1900)*. Ed. Marks III, George P. New York: Arno Press and the New York Times, 1971. Print.

Kramer, Paul A. "The Pragmatic Empire: U.S. Anthropology and Colonial Politics in the Occupied Philippines, 1898–1916." Dissertation. Princeton University, 1998. Print.

"Lieut. Alstaetter Talks of David Fagin." *New York Times* December 10, 1901. Print.

Litwack, Leon F. *Trouble in Mind: Black Southerners in the Age of Jim Crow*. New York: Vintage Books, 1998. Print.

Lynk, Miles V. *The Black Troopers, or the Daring Heroism of the Negro Soldiers in the Spanish-American War*. Jackson, TN: M.V. Lynk Publishing House, 1899. Print.

Marasigan, Cynthia L. *"Between the Devil and the Deep Sea*: Ambivalence, Violence, and African American Soldiers in the Philippine-American War and Its Aftermath." Dissertation. University of Michigan, 2010. Print.

Marks III, George P. *The Black Press Views American Imperialism (1898–1900)*. New York: Arno Press and the New York Times, 1971. Print.

Mostern, Kenneth. "Three Theories of the Race of W.E.B. Du Bois." *Cultural Critique* Fall (1996): 27–63. Print.

"Negro Deserter Beheaded." *New York Times* December 8, 1901. Print.

Ngozi-Brown, Scot. "African American Soldiers and Filipinos: Racial Imperialism, Jim Crow and Social Relations." *Journal of Negro History* 82.1 (1997): 42–53. Print.

Ngozi-Brown, Scot. "David Fagen." *American National Biography Online*. (2000). Web. March 8, 2013.

"Our Indian Fighters Are There." *Literary Digest* 19.22 (1900): 633–34. Print.

Patterson, Orlando. *Rituals of Blood: Consequences of Slavery in Two American Centuries*. Washington, DC: Civitas, 1998. Print.

"Protest against Manila Censorship." *Literary Digest* 19.5 (1900): 121–23. Print.

Rafael, Vicente L. "White Love: Surveillance and Nationalist Resistance in the U.S. Colonization of the Philippines." *Cultures of the United States Imperialism*. Eds. Kaplan, Amy and Donald E. Pease. Durham: Duke University Press, 1993. 185–218. Print.

Robinson, Michael C., and Frank N. Schubert. "David Fagen: An Afro-American Rebel in the Philippines, 1899–1901." *Pacific Historical Review* 44.1 (1975): 68–83. Print.

Rowe, John Carlos. *Literary Culture and U.S. Imperialism: From the Revolution to World War II*. New York: Oxford University Press, 2000. Print.

San Buenaventura, Steffi. "The Colors of Manifest Destiny: Filipinos and the American Other(s)." *Amerasia Journal* 23.3 (1998): 1–26. Print.

Sandoval-Sánchez, Alberto. "Politicizing Abjection: In the Manner of a Prologue for the Articulation of AIDS Latino Queer Identities." *American Literary History* 17.3 (2005): 542–49. Print.

San Juan Jr., E. "An African American Soldier in the Philippine Revolution: An Homage to David Fagen." *Cultural Logic* (2009): 1–36. Print.

Seraile, William. "Theophilus G. Steward, Intellectual Chaplain, 25th U.S. Colored Infantry." *Nebraska History* 66.272–293 (1985). Print.

Steward, Theophilus Gould. *The Colored Regulars in the United States Army*. 1904 ed. New York: Arno Press and the New York Times, 1969. Print.

Storey, Moorfield, and Julian Codman. *"Marked Severities" in Philippine Warfare: An Analysis of the Law and Facts Bearing on the Action and Utterances of President Roosevelt and Secretary Root*. Boston: Geo. H. Ellis Company, 1902. Print.

Sundquist, Eric J., ed. *The Oxford W.E.B. Du Bois Reader*. New York: Oxford University Press, 1996. Print.

"Three Views of the Philippine Problem." *Literary Digest* 18.1 (1899): 1, 2. Print.

Troy, Rev. William. *Loyalty of the Colored Man to the United States Government, the Late Conflict with Cuba, the Spanish Government and the Philippines, Containing Brief Accounts of the Life of General Antonio Maceo and General Aguinaldo*. Philadelphia: Christian Banner Print, 1900. Print.

Williams, Walter L. "United States Indian Policy and the Debate over Philippine Annexation: Implications for the Origins of American Imperialism." *Journal of American History* (1980): 810–31. Print.

CHAPTER 4

Alzona, Encarnacion. *Julio Nakpil and the Philippine Revolution, with the Autobiography of Gregoria De Jesus*. Rizal: Carmelo and Bauermann, 1964. Print.

Anderson, Warwick. *Colonial Pathologies: American Tropical Medicine, Race and Hygiene in the Philippines*. Durham: Duke University Press, 2006. Print.

Barrows, David P. *A History of the Philippines*. New York: American Book Company, 1905. Print.

Beisner, Robert L. *Twelve against Empire: The Anti-imperialists, 1898–1900*. New York: McGraw-Hill, 1968. Print.

Benjamin, Anna Northend. "Some Filipino Characteristics." *Outlook* (1901): 1003–8. Print.

Benjamin, Walter. *Illuminations*. Ed. Arendt, Hannah. Trans. Zohn, Harry. New York: Schocken, 1955. Print.

Brown, Arthur J. *The New Era in the Philippines*. New York: F. H. Revell, 1903. Print.

Bruno, Thomas A. "The Violent End of Insurgency on Samar 1901–1902." *Army History* 79 Spring (2011): 31–46. Print.

Cannell, Fenella. "Immaterial Culture: 'Idolatry' in the Lowland Philippines." *Spirited Politics: Religion and Public Life in Contemporary Southeast Asia*. Eds. Willford, Andrew C. and Kenneth M. George. Ithaca, NY: Southeast Asia Program Publications, Cornell University, 2005. 159–84. Print.

Carby, Hazel V. "On the Threshold of Woman's Era: Lynching, Empire, and Sexuality in Black Feminist Theory." *Race, Writing and Difference*. Ed. Gates, Henry Louis, Jr. Chicago: University of Chicago Press, 1986. 301–16. Print.

Chinn, Sarah. *Inventing Modern Adolescence: The Children of Immigrants in Turn-of-the-Century America*. Piscataway, NJ: Rutgers University Press, 2008. Print.

Conger, Emily Bronson. *An Ohio Woman in the Philippines*. N.p.: n.p., 1904. Print.

Constantino, Renato, and Letizia R. Constantino. *The Philippines: A Past Revisited*. Manila: Renato Constantino, 1975. Print.

Dauncey, Mrs. Campbell. *An Englishwoman in the Philippines*. New York: E.P. Dutton, 1906. Print.

De Olivares, José. *Our Islands and Their People, as Seen with Camera and Pencil*. St. Louis: N.D. Thompson Publishing Company, 1902. Print.

Funston, Eda Blankart. "A Soldier's Wife in the Philippines." *Cosmopolitan* 29.1 (1900): 65–72. Print.

Gikandi, Simon. *Maps of Englishness: Writing Identity in the Culture of Colonialism*. New York: Columbia University Press, 1996. Print.

Guha, Ranajit. "The Prose of Counter-insurgency." *Selected Subaltern Studies*. Eds. Guha, Ranajit and Gayatri Chakravorty Spivak. New York: Oxford University Press, 1988. 45–84. Print.

Hartman, Saidiya V. *Scenes of Subjection: Terror, Slavery, and Self-Making in Nineteenth-Century America*. New York: Oxford University Press, 1997. Print.

Helmers, Marguerite H., and Tilar J. Mazzeo. "Introduction: Travel and the Body." *Journal of Narrative Theory* 35.3 (2005): 267–76. Print.

Hoganson, Kristin. "As Badly Off as the Filipinos: U.S. Women's Suffragists and the Imperial Issue at the Turn of the Twentieth Century." *Journal of Women's History* 13.2 (2001): 9–33. Print.

Hoganson, Kristin. *Fighting for American Manhood: How Gender Politics Provoked the Spanish-American and Philippine-American Wars*. New Haven: Yale University Press, 1998. Print.

Ileto, Reynaldo C. *Pasyon and Revolution: Popular Movements in the Philippines, 1840–1910*. Manila: Ateneo University Press, 1979. Print.

Kramer, Paul A. *The Blood of Government: Race, Empire, the United States and the Philippines*. Chapel Hill: University of North Carolina Press, 2006. Print.

Kramer, Paul A. "The Water Cure." *New Yorker* February 25, 2008: 38–43. Print.

LeRoy, James A. *Philippine Life in Town and Country*. 1973 ed. New York: Oriole Editions, 1905. Print.

Liberty Poems: Inspired by the Crisis of 1898–1900. Boston: James H. West, 1900. Print.

Martinez, Julia T., and Claire Lowrie. "Transcolonial Influences on Everyday American Imperialism: The Politics of Chinese Domestic Servants in the Philippines." *Pacific Historical Review* 81.4 (2012): 511–36. Print.

McCoy, Alfred W. *Policing America's Empire: The United States, the Philippines, and the Rise of the Surveillance State*. Madison: University of Wisconsin Press, 2009. Print.

"Miscellany." *Time Magazine* April 29, 1929. Print.

Murphy, Erin L. "Women's Anti-imperialism, 'the White Man's Burden,' and the Philippine-American War: Theorizing Masculinist Ambivalence in Protest." *Gender & Society* 23.2 (2009): 244–70. Print.

Newman, Louise Michele *White Women's Rights: The Racial Origins of Feminism in the United States*. Oxford: Oxford University Press, 1999. Print.

Pante, Michael D. "Peripheral Pockets of Paradise: Perceptions of Helath and Geography in Early Twentieth-Century Manila and Its Environs." *Philippine Studies* 59.2 (2011): 187–212. Print.

Pratt, Mary Louise. *Imperial Eyes: Travel Writing and Transculturation*. London: Routledge, 1992. Print.

"Protest against Manila Censorship." *Literary Digest* 19.5 (1900): 121–23. Print.

Rafael, Vicente L. "Colonial Domesticity: White Women and United States Rule in the Philippines." *American Literature* 67.4 (1995): 639–66. Print.

Rafael, Vicente L. *White Love and Other Events in Filipino History*. Durham: Duke University Press, 2000. Print.

Roma-Sianturi, Dinah. "At Home in the Cordillera Wilds: Colonial Domesticity in the Letters of Maud Huntley Jenks, 1901–1903." *Asia-Pacific Social Science Review* 7.1 (2008): 59–74. Print.

Roma-Sianturi, Dinah. "Not Just an Ordinary Tourist: American Women's Travel Writings on the Philippines, 1900s to 1930s." Unpublished. Print.

Roma-Sianturi, Dinah. "Pedagogic Invasion: The Thomasites in Occupied Philippines." *Kritika Kultura* 12 (2009): 5–26. Print.

Schuyler, Montgomery. "The Philippines: A Bright Woman's Book about the American Occupation." Book review. *New York Times* August 25, 1906. Print.

Spurr, David. *The Rhetoric of Empire: Colonial Journalism, Travel Writing, and Imperial Administration*. Durham: Duke University Press, 1993. Print.

Stevenson, Catherine Barnes. *Victorian Women Travel Writers in Africa*. Boston: Twayne, 1982. Print.

Storey, Moorfield, and Julian Codman. *"Marked Severities" in Philippine Warfare: An Analysis of the Law and Facts Bearing on the Action and Utterances of President Roosevelt and Secretary Root*. Boston: Geo. H. Ellis Company, 1902. Print.

Swift, Morrison Isaac. *Imperialism and Liberty*. Los Angeles: Ronbroke Press, 1899. Print.

Tiongson, Nicanor G. *The Women of Malolos*. Quezon City, Philippines: Ateneo de Manila University Press, 2004. Print.

U.S. Congress, 57th. "Charges of Cruelty, Etc. To the Natives of the Philippine Islands." War Department, 1902. 1–57. Print.

"Vagabonding at Fifty." Advertisement. *New York Times* April 7, 1929: BR 7. Print.

Wilson, Helen Calista. "In the Caucasus, Where Two Ages Meet." *New York Times* July 13, 1930: 15, 23. Print.

Wilson, Helen Calista. "A Massachusetts Woman in the Philippines." Boston: [Fiske Warren], 1903. Print.

Worcester, Dean C. "Notes on Some Primitive Tribes." *National Geographic Magazine* June 1898: 284–304. Print.

Worcester, Dean C. *The Philippine Islands and Their People*. New York : Macmillan, 1898. Print.

Zwick, Jim. "The Anti-Imperialist League and the Origins of Filipino-American Oppositional Solidarity." *Amerasia Journal* 24.2 (1998): 65–85. Print.

CONCLUSION

Arnold, James R. *Jungle of Snakes: A Century of Counterinsurgency Warfare from the Philippines to Iraq*. New York: Bloomsbury, 2010. Print.

Bagley, Will. "Philippines Lesson: The Peace Was More Lethal Than the War." *Salt Lake Tribune* April 27, 2003. Sec. Final: B2. Print.

Bankoff, Greg. "A Tale of Two Wars: The Other Story of America's Role in the Philippines." *Foreign Affairs* 81.6 (2002): 179–81. Print.

Benson, Lee. "Philippine Insurrection Rings Familiar." *Deseret Morning News* October 24, 2005. Print.

Birtle, Andrew J. "Persuasion and Coercion in Counterinsurgency Warfare." *Military Review* 88.4 (2008): 45–53. Print.

Brody, Jennifer De Vere. *Impossible Purities: Blackness, Femininity and Victorian Culture*. Durham: Duke University Press, 1998. Print.

Bruno, Thomas A. "The Violent End of Insurgency on Samar 1901–1902." *Army History* 79 Spring (2011): 31–46. Print.

Byler, Charles. "Pacifying the Moros: American Military Government in the Southern Philippines, 1899–1913." *Military Review* May–June (2005): 41–45. Print.

Cano, Gloria. "Filipino Press between Two Empires: *El Renacimiento*, a Newspaper with Too Much *Alma Filipina*." *Southeast Asian Studies* 49.395–430 (2011). Print.

Carby, Hazel. "A Strange and Bitter Crop: The Spectacle of Torture." *openDemocracy* (2004): 1–4. Print.

Cassidy, Lieutenant Colonel Robert M. "Winning the War of the Flea: Lessons from Guerrilla Warfare." *Military Review* September–October (2004): 41–46. Print.

Castellanos, M. Bianet. *Photography and the Philippines.* Ed. Sinopoli, Carla M. and Lars Fogelin. 1998. *Imperial Imaginings: The Dean C. Worcester Photographic Collection of the Philippines, 1890–1913.* Web.

Chow, Rey. *The Age of the World Target: Self-Referentiality in War, Theory and Comparative Work.* Durham: Duke University Press, 2006. Print.

Coursey, Oscar William. *The Woman with a Stone Heart: A Romance of the Philippine War.* Mitchell, South Dakota: The Educator Supply Company, 1914. Print.

Crean, Colonel Peter D. "The Chief's Corner." *Army History* 79 Spring (2011): 3, 60. Print.

Deady, Timothy K. "Lessons from a Successful Counterinsurgency: The Philippines, 1899–1902." *Parameters: U.S. Army War College Quarterly* 35.1 (2005): 53–68. Print.

Delmendo, Sharon. *The Star-Entangled Banner: One Hundred Years of America in the Philippines.* Quezon City: University of the Philippines Press, 2005. Print.

Denger, Mark J. "Californians and the Military: Major-General Henry Ware Lawton, U.S. Volunteers." *The California Military Museum: Preserving California's Military Heritage.* Web.

Diokno, Ed. "Building an Empire Is Much Harder Than It Looks; the Philippines of 100 Years Ago Can Be a Lesson for the United States in Dealing with Iraq Today." *Contra Costa Times* May 25, 2003. Sec. Opinion: P06. Print.

Dumindin, Arnaldo. "Dec. 19, 1899: General Henry Lawton Dies at San Mateo." *Philippine-American War, 1899–1902.* 2006. Web.

Farrell, John Aloysius. "History Could Have Helped Us in Iraq." *Denver Post* May 7, 2006. Sec. Perspective: E-03. Print.

Fogelin, Lars. *Dean C. Worcester, Race and the Philippines. Imperial Imaginings: The Dean C. Worcester Photographic Collection of the Philippines, 1890–1913.* Eds. Sinopoli, Carla M. and Lars Fogelin. CD. Ann Arbor: University of Michigan, Museum of Anthropology, 1998. Print.

Guha, Ranajit. "The Prose of Counter-insurgency." *Selected Subaltern Studies.* Eds. Guha, Ranajit and Gayatri Chakravorty Spivak. New York: Oxford University Press, 1988. 45–84. Print.

"Have We Learned Nothing?" *Akron Beacon Journal (Ohio)* February 22, 2004. Sec. Editorial: B3. Print.

Hebard, Andrew. "Romantic Sovereignty: Popular Romances and the American Imperial State in the Philippines." *American Quarterly* 57.3 (2006): 805–30. Print.

Henderson, Schuyler W. "Disregarding the Suffering of Others: Narrative, Comedy and Torture." *Literature and Medicine* 24.2 (2005): 181–208. Print.

Hersh, Seymour M. "Torture at Abu Ghraib." *New Yorker* May 10, 2004: 42–47. Print.

Hutcheson, Ron. "In Philipines, Bush Vows to Root Out Terror." *Philadelphia Inquirer* October 19, 2003. Print.

Ileto, Reynaldo C. "Philippine Wars and the Politics of Memory." *Positions: East Asia Cultures Critique* 13 (2005): 215–34. Print.

Isaac, Allan Punzalan. *American Tropics: Articulating Filipino America*. Minneapolis: University of Minnesota Press, 2006. Print.

Kaplan, Amy. "Romancing the Empire: The Embodiment of American Masculinity in the Popular Historical Novel of the 1890s." *American Literary History* 24 Winter (1990): 659–90. Print.

Leepson, Marc. "The Philippine War." *Military History* November (2007): 60–67. Print.

Levins, Harry. "War Redux." *St. Louis Post-Dispatch* July 18, 2004. Sec. Newswatch: B01. Print.

Linfield, Susie. *The Cruel Radiance: Photography and Political Violence*. Chicago: University of Chicago Press, 2010. Print.

Linn, Brian McAlister. *The U.S. Army Counterinsurgency in the Philippine War, 1899–1902*. Chapel Hill: University of North Carolina Press, 1989. Print.

McClintock, Anne. "Paranoid Empire: Specters from Guantanamo and Abu Ghraib." *Small Axe: A Caribbean Journal of Criticism* 28 (2009): 50–74. Print.

National Historical Commission of the Philippines. "Reyes, Fidel A." (2008). Web.

Puar, Jasbir. *Terrorist Assemblages: Homonationalism in Queer Times*. Durham: Duke University Press, 2007. Print.

Putnam, Israel. *Daniel Everton, Volunteer-Regular: A Romance of the Philippines*. New York and London: Funk and Wagnalls Company, 1902. Print.

Ramsey III, Robert D. "A Masterpiece of Counterguerrilla Warfare: Brigadier General J. Franklin Bell in the Philippines 1901–1902." Washington, DC: Combat Studies Institute Press, 2007. Print.

Ramsey III, Robert D. *Savage Wars of Peace: Case Studies of Pacification in the Philippines, 1900–1902*. Washington, DC: Combat Studies Institute Press, 2007. Print.

Reyes, Fidel A. "Birds of Prey." *Filipino Nationalism: 1872–1970*. Ed. Agoncillo, Teodoro A. Quezon City, Manila: R. P. Garcia Publishing Company, 1974. 251–54. Print.

Rice, Mark. "His Name Was Don Francisco Muro: Reconstructing an Image of American Imperialism." *American Quarterly* 62.1 (2010): 49–76. Print.

Rowe, John Carlos. *Literary Culture and U.S. Imperialism: From the Revolution to World War II*. New York: Oxford University Press, 2000. Print.

Sharpley-Whiting, T. Denean. *Sexualized Savages, Primal Fears and Primitive Narratives in French*. Durham: Duke University Press, 1999. Print.

Sinopoli, Carla M. *Dean Worcester and the Philippines*. Ed. Sinopoli, Carla M. and Lars Fogelin. 1998. *Imperial Imaginings: The Dean C. Worcester Photographic Collection of the Philippines, 1890–1913*. Web.

Smith, Geoffrey D., ed. *American Fiction 1901–1925: A Bibliography*. 1997. Web.

Storey, Moorfield, and Julian Codman. *"Marked Severities" in Philippine Warfare: An Analysis of the Law and Facts Bearing on the Action and Utterances of President Roosevelt and Secretary Root*. Boston: Geo. H. Ellis Company, 1902. Print.

Streeby, Shelley. *American Sensations: Class, Empire, and the Production of Popular Culture*. Berkeley: University of California Press, 2002. Print.

Streeter, Caroline A. "Was Your Mama Mulatto? Notes toward a Theory of Racialized Sexuality in Gayl Jones's *Corregidora* and Julie Dash's *Daughters of the Dust.*" *Callaloo* 27.3 (2004): 768–87. Print.

U.S. Congress, 57th. "Charges of Cruelty, Etc. To the Natives of the Philippine Islands." War Department, 1902. 1–57. Print.

Index